T0049161

SHRIMP TO WHALE

RAMON PACHECO PARDO

# Shrimp to Whale

*South Korea from the*
*Forgotten War to K-Pop*

# OXFORD
## UNIVERSITY PRESS

Oxford University Press is a department of the
University of Oxford. It furthers the University's objective
of excellence in research, scholarship, and education
by publishing worldwide.

Oxford   New York

Auckland   Cape Town   Dar es Salaam   Hong Kong   Karachi
Kuala Lumpur   Madrid   Melbourne   Mexico City   Nairobi
New Delhi   Shanghai   Taipei   Toronto

With offices in

Argentina   Austria   Brazil   Chile   Czech Republic   France   Greece
Guatemala   Hungary   Italy   Japan   Poland   Portugal   Singapore
South Korea   Switzerland   Thailand   Turkey   Ukraine   Vietnam

Oxford is a registered trade mark of Oxford University Press
in the UK and certain other countries.

Published in the United States of America by
Oxford University Press
198 Madison Avenue, New York, NY 10016

Library of Congress Cataloging-in-Publication Data is available
Ramon Pacheco Pardo.
Shrimp to Whale: South Korea from the Forgotten War to K-Pop
ISBN: 9780197764930
Printed in the United Kingdom

# CONTENTS

Map of South Korea

# LIST OF ILLUSTRATIONS

1. Gyeongbokgung, originally built in 1395, was the main royal palace of the Joseon Dynasty, and continues to sit at the centre of Seoul. Source: Joshua Davenport / Alamy Stock Photo.

2. Koreans celebrate in the streets of Seoul during Korean National Liberation Day, 15 August 1945. Source: US Army, Army.mil.

3. Ceremony of inauguration of the Republic of Korea, 15 August 1948, the day South Korea was established. Source: 경향 신문사 (*Kyunghyang Shinmun* newspaper), public domain, via Wikimedia Commons.

4. Korean refugees crossing the thirty-eighth parallel dividing the two Koreas during the Korean War, 8 December 1950. Source: Archive Image / Alamy Stock Photo.

5. Korean War orphans in front of a US M-26 tank, June 1951. One of the most famous pictures of the war. Source: Flickr (https://www.flickr.com/photos/13476480@N07/32233275137), CC BY 2.0., attributed to www.rarehistoricalphotos.com.

6. Korean War armistice signing, 27 July 1953. Source: US Department of Defense (F. Kazukaitis, US Navy), public domain, via Wikimedia Commons.

# LIST OF ILLUSTRATIONS

# PREFACE

South Korea has the most extraordinary of histories. Located in the eastern corner of the Eurasian landmass, the country has experienced the pain of division, the devastation of war, the hunger that comes with poverty, the exhilaration of rapid economic growth, the joy of democratization and the excitement of recognition as a cool cultural superpower in the span of only seven decades. What took other countries hundreds of years to attain, South Korea has achieved in only seventy. South Koreans of a certain age have witnessed the transformation of a country that has never been as well known and discussed as it is as of 2023.

But few outside South Korea actually know the history of the country. The Korean War? Labelled the Forgotten War. Sandwiched between the end of World War II, the start of the Cold War and the Vietnam War, it is a conflict that remains underexplored outside of South Korea itself. Park Chung-hee? Love him or loathe him, he was arguably one of the key figures of the second half of the twentieth century in Asia and beyond. But he remains almost unknown outside his home country. South Korea's democratization in the 1980s? A remarkable demonstration of people power. Yet, coming right after the democratization of Southern Europe and parts of Latin America and right before the end of the Cold War, not many know about its details. And what about South Korea becoming a fully developed economy by the 1990s? Sure, Hyundai, LG and Samsung are household names. But their role and the role of South Korean workers in propelling their country's economy is little understood.

In fact, North Korea is more talked about than South Korea. It is the only communist dictatorship in history to have been passed on from grandfather to son and then to grandson. It conducts nuclear and long-range missile tests. It abuses the human rights of its own population. It launches tirade after tirade against South Korea, the United States, Japan and any other country it feels offended by. From time to time, it even threatens to destroy them. North Korea indeed makes for a compelling news story, in a way that few other countries do.

And yet, South Korea is the most interesting of the two Koreas. Over fifty-one million people inhabit the southern half of the Korean Peninsula. Its economy is the fourth biggest in Asia and tenth in the world by GDP, powered by electronics, cars, telecommunications, ships and steel. It is a key foreign policy and security actor in East Asia, with a strong, decades-old alliance with the US coupled with burgeoning relations across the region. South Korea is home to the sixth largest music market in the world and second in Asia. It is also the only Asian country with a BTS and a Blackpink: the biggest boyband and girlband in the world as of 2023. South Korea is the sixth largest film market in the world and fourth in Asia as well. It is also the only country in the world to have produced *Parasite*: the first-ever movie not in English to have won the Best Picture Oscar in the history of the awards. The 'average South Korean' is 43.7 years old, has a life expectancy of 83.2 years, earns US$41,960 adjusted for purchasing power parity and lives in a household of 2.2 people.

In recent years, the world has begun to notice South Korea. Millions of fans across the world adore K-Pop, South Korean dramas and the country's movies. Food lovers know their different types of kimchi. Techies admire South Korean home service robots, flat screen TVs and foldable smart phones. Economists and policy-makers study how South Korea went from poor to rich in the span of a mere thirty years. Political scientists discuss how the country has built one of the strongest democracies in the world in only three decades. Health professionals wonder why the South Korean response to COVID-19 was one of the best in the world. And while fewer than five million tourists visited South Korea in 2003, the year after the country co-hosted the football World Cup, over seventeen and a half million went in 2019—the year before the COVID-19 pandemic hit the world.

I first went to South Korea in 2003. Not as a tourist, but to live there as a student. I remember landing in Incheon airport, going through passport control, picking up my luggage and taking the bus that would drive me to Imun-dong, the neighbourhood in Seoul where I was to live for the next year. Gazing out of the window as my bus crossed from Yeongjong Island to the mainland, I marvelled at the beauty of the sea bathing the Korean Peninsula to the west. It was a hot and humid day in late July. And I could not wait to see my new home.

The bus then arrived in Seoul. And it blew me away. It was colourful, lively, exciting. Full of people up and down the streets. Full of life. It reminded me of Spain, the country where I was born and grew up. And indeed, South Koreans sometimes think of themselves as the Italians of Asia. They both live on a peninsula. They like to sing and dance. They like—or rather, love—to eat and drink. They are passionate. Family and friends mean the world to them. Well, they say that Spain and Italy are similar. In my view, so are Koreans and Spanish. Plus, South Korea and Spain both suffered a devastating war between brothers and sisters, went through a dictatorship that coincided with a period of economic development, transitioned to democracy and became rich countries. In fact, it was the similarities between the histories of the two places that first made me want to experience life in South Korea.

# PREFACE

Over the following year, I fell in love with the country. Busan, Daejeon, the DMZ, Gyeongju, Incheon, Seorak Mountain. Each place had a unique history to tell. Each of them looked beautiful to me in their own way. *Bibimbap, jjajangmyeon, kimchi-jjigae, samgyeopsal, sundubu jjigae, tteokbokki.* Plus the *banchan* or side dishes that come with every meal. Amazing, delicious food, cooked slightly differently in each restaurant. And of course the people. For ultimately it is the people who make a country. And South Korea is a blessed country in this respect.

Ever since living in South Korea for the first time, I have been lucky enough to spend most of my life in it, working on it or thinking about it. I had the chance to live in South Korea for a second time, as a PhD student on this occasion. I have been fortunate enough to visit more times than I can remember, often for weeks when not months at a time. Whether to give a lecture, participate in a conference or simply enjoy a holiday, my heart always accelerates as soon as I see one of those buses taking people from and to the airport. And I am lucky enough to have a job—actually, two jobs—allowing me to research, teach, discuss and organize all types of events about the country. Indeed, I am giving the finishing touches to this book in a hanok a ten-minute walk from Gyeongbokgung. For me, a dream come true.

It only remains for me to thank the people who have made this book possible. Michael Dwyer at Hurst embraced this project from the moment I proposed it to him. Also at Hurst, Lara Weisweiller-Wu, Alice Clarke, Kathleen May and Mei Jayne Yew provided excellent advice and help throughout the editing process. Kang Nagyeong provided me with invaluable research assistance. All of them made the book much better. Two anonymous reviewers also provided valuable comments on the manuscript. Any remaining errors are mine. Over the years, countless friends, colleagues, acquaintances and students inside and outside South Korea have helped me understand the country better. There are way too many to list. But I am sure that they know who they are. I also need to thank my parents Ramon and Maria Luisa as well as my sister Marisa. When I first told them I was thinking about spending a year in South Korea, I received nothing but their support. I still suspect that this was so they could have me show them around the country when they went to visit! Finally, there is no way that I would have written this book without the encouragement and love of my two guiding lights: my wife Mina and my daughter Hannah. Sorry for the countless nights I spent on my writing. This is the result of your patience. I hope that all of them enjoy this book. And I hope that readers do too. As for me, I certainly loved writing about a country that I love myself.

Ramon Pacheco Pardo
London and Seoul
May 2023

# PROLOGUE

## BRIEF HISTORY OF KOREA

*The birth of Korea*

A bear gave birth to Korea. Or so the legend goes. The year was 2333 BCE. Hwanin (the 'Lord of Heaven') had a son. His name was Hwanung. But Hwanung abhorred living in heaven. He yearned to live in his own kingdom down on earth, among green valleys and brown mountains. His father gave him permission, and Hwanung and some 3,000 followers descended into the Korean Peninsula. There they established the peninsula's first civilization. Attracted to Hwanung's kingdom, a bear and a tiger prayed to become human. Hwanung heard their prayers and offered them a challenge. They would become human if they could live in a cave for 100 days with only twenty cloves of garlic and a bundle of mugwort. The tiger failed, but the bear did not and was transformed into a woman. She would be known as Ungnyeo (bear-woman).[1]

Ungnyeo soon became melancholic. She started to pray for a child. Moved by her prayers, Hwanung transformed himself into a man, married her, and nine months later a son was born. His name was Dangun Wanggeom, or simply Dangun.[2] In 2333 BCE, Dangun established Gojoseon. Originally known as Joseon, its name was eventually changed to Gojoseon (Old Joseon) to distinguish it from the Joseon dynasty that would eventually go on to rule Korea for over 500 years. Old Joseon, or the 'Land of the Morning Calm'—the moniker by which Korea is still known at the time of writing.[3] And while this story is a legend influenced by a shamanism autochthonous to Korea, there is archaeological evidence that hominids inhabited the Korean Peninsula as early as 200,000 BCE and that modern humans arrived some 30–40,000 years ago.[4] Plus, thousands of years later both South and North Korea celebrate Gaecheonjeol (National Foundation Day) on 3 October to commemorate Korea's foundation in 2333 BCE.

Over the centuries, several proto-states emerged in the region comprising the Korean Peninsula and north-east China all the way to the Liao River. There is evidence from Chinese texts that several of these proto-states in the northern half of the Korean Peninsula and north-east China formed a confederation under Gojoseon around the seventh century BCE. This confederation was dissolved following its defeat to China's Han Empire in 108 BCE.[5] From then on followed a period of turmoil, with the Han conquerors unable to pacify the region or create a unified state. Several successor tribal states occupied different parts of the fallen Gojoseon, seeking to conquer one another to expand their territory.

From 57 BCE, these states consolidated into three different kingdoms. The Three Kingdoms period would comprise Goguryeo, Silla and Baekje, and last until 668. The origins of Goguryeo can be traced back to 37 BCE. At its height, Goguryeo occupied most of the Korean Peninsula, most of Manchuria and parts of modern Far East Russia. Founded in 57 BCE, Silla, meanwhile, occupied part of the southern half of the Korean Peninsula, mainly to its east. To its west, Baekje, founded in 18 BCE, shared this southern half as well. Also to the south was Gaya, a group of city states that formed a confederacy in 42–562 before being taken over by Silla.[6]

Even though the three states fought one another, they shared several common characteristics that revealed a degree of modern statehood. These included a centralized military, essential for their frequent wars of expansion. In addition, they had an organized training system focused on both academic and military skills. The three kingdoms shared a strong hereditary monarchy supported by a powerful aristocracy. They also developed a fairly sophisticated culture, including the compilation of their own history as a way to preserve their legacy and show their power.[7] With China divided due to domestic quarrels, the three kingdoms had the time and space to develop politically, economically and culturally.

In the seventh century, Silla would emerge victorious from the quarrels between the three kingdoms. Allied with China's Tang dynasty, Silla defeated Baekje in 660 and Goguryeo in 668. This would be the first time that most of the Korean Peninsula was ruled under a unified state, a crucial turning point in Korean history. The run-up to this unification of most of the Korean Peninsula was also significant because from the fifth century Goguryeo simplified its name to Goryeo.[8] Centuries later, this would be the name from which 'Korea' would derive. In short, the contours of modern Korea were laid out during this period.

So commenced the Northern and Southern States era. In the southern part, the Later (Unified) Silla period lasted from 668 to 935. The Silla kingdom ruled over what at the time of writing constitutes South Korea plus all the way to the south of Pyongyang. For over 200 years, Silla's rulers brought relative peace and prosperity to their kingdom. Later Silla centralized power in the monarch, a strong military and a well-trained bureaucracy. The aristocracy that had started to emerge during the Three Kingdoms period grew rich, thanks to the end to war between the three of them. Men and women were treated relatively equally, and several queens ruled the kingdom.

Furthermore, Later Silla expanded trade links with China and Japan. China, in particular, had a strong influence in Later Silla since many of its aristocrats undertook trips there to deepen their knowledge of Confucianism—which was displacing shamanism as the main belief system among elites. Aristocrats also benefitted from very limited social mobility. Peasants could not expect to join the ranks of the well-to-do. More often than not, one's birth family determined one's future.[9]

Later Silla can be considered the birthdate of modern Korean culture. In particular, Gyeongju, its capital, became a cultural hotspot. To this day, it remains one of South Korea's most beautiful cities. (In my opinion, best enjoyed in winter and covered by snow.) Influenced by Buddhism and Confucianism, Later Silla developed a distinct style. Wolji Pond was constructed in 674. Bulguksa Temple was rebuilt in 751–74. The Bell of King Seongdeok was cast in 771.[10] They were all magnificent constructions fit for the royal court; they are all South Korean national treasures. In 751, the oldest surviving woodblock print in the world, the Pure Light Dharani Sutra, was printed in Later Silla.[11] Printing flourished in the kingdom, influencing both China and Japan.

In the northern part, Goguryeo refugees founded Balhae (sometimes also spelled Parhae) in 698. The kingdom governed much of Goguryeo's former territory until 926: part of the northern part of the Korean Peninsula plus a large chunk of Manchuria and modern Far East Russia. In other words, Balhae can be considered a successor state to Goguryeo. Balhae rulers certainly did, and they used the name Goryeo in their diplomatic documents.[12] Located next to Tang China, Balhae had thriving trade relations with its neighbours. Similarly to Later Silla, Balhae was dominated by the monarch and the aristocracy. Unlike the kingdom to its south, however, the society of Goguryeo experienced divisions. Indeed, society was split between the newly arrived

Goguryeo population and the Mohe people who were treated as secondary citizens. Domestic weakness was an important reason why Balhae ultimately folded.[13]

Peace would eventually break down in Later Silla as well. With growing internal divisions, Baekje and Goguryeo split from Later Silla. Later Baekje was established in 892. Later Goguryeo (also known as Taebong) followed suit in 901.[14] Thus started the Later Three Kingdoms period, with the rulers of the three of them fighting for control of the Korean Peninsula. Balhae, meanwhile, fell to the Liao dynasty formed by the nomadic Khitan (also spelled Qidan) tribes.[15]

In 918, Wang Geon established Goryeo to replace Later Goguryeo. Wang Geon—also known as King Taejo—came from a merchant family tracing its roots to Goguryeo. A fine military commander, he was crowned as king by high-ranked generals opposed to the existing monarch. Upon his crowning, he established Gaegyeong—modern Kaesong—as Goryeo's capital, located towards the middle of the Korean Peninsula. For Wang Geon led the Goryeo army, buoyed by refugees from Balhae, to victory over Later Baekje and Later Silla by 936. The Korean Peninsula was thus unified under a single ruler, with Goryeo also expanding to the north to take over part of Balhae's former territory. Wang Geon's own title as a king attests to this, for Taejo translates as 'Great Founder' (of Korea).[16]

Goryeo (also spelled Koryo) would survive until 1392. Seeking to lay the groundwork for a distinct kingdom that would outlast him, Wang Geon issued the Ten Injunctions in 943. Arguably, this was the first document to lay down a distinct Korean identity. The injunctions established that Goryeo had its own cultural identity, emphasized the role of Buddhism, geomancy and, in the area of statecraft, Confucianism, and warned of the 'barbarians' north of Goryeo.[17] In particular, the injunctions explicitly indicated that Goryeo was different from China due to its geographical location and the character of its people. Thus, Goryeo should distance itself from China as a model. Wang Geon did not want Goryeo to be absorbed by China or simply become an appendix of its much larger neighbour. In a constant throughout Korean history, Wang Geon stressed that Goryeo could only survive as an independent polity if it focused on what made it distinct. Plus, he considered China to be unsophisticated. This line of thought about foreigners would sometimes resurface in Korean history.

Buddhism, therefore, became central to Goryeo's life, and it continues to be one of the main religions in South Korea at the time of writing. Buddhism provided a belief system to both aristocrats and commoners, even if shamanism continued to have its appeal and influence. It also formed a symbiotic relationship with the state, leading to the proliferation of Buddhist monasteries across the country. Buddhist monks held political influence and they used it to advance their interests.[18] They also helped advance Korean culture to new levels. In 1011, Buddhist monks took woodblock printing to new heights when they started work on a 6,000-chapter *Tripitaka Koreana* carved over 80,000 woodblocks that would end up being completed in 1087.[19] A thirteenth-century version can still be admired in Haeinsa temple in South Gyeongsang Province.

Around 1234, Goryeo went on to pioneer the more resilient and flexible moveable metal type. The first books printed using this new method were actually copies of the Confucian work *Sang-jong-ye-mun* (Goryeo readings for Buddhist ceremonies). This reinforced the point that Buddhism and political power went hand-in-hand.[20] Even though that work disappeared, the oldest surviving book printed with metal type also belongs to Goryeo. This is the *Jikji* (Selected teachings of Buddhist sages and Zen masters), an anthology of Buddhist scriptures printed in 1377.[21]

The economic and military relations of the Goryeo era show its ambivalent position towards its neighbours. Informed by Confucian ideas, Goryeo institutionalized regular tribute missions to its biggest neighbour to the west—Imperial China. Meanwhile, precious metals, books, cloth, silk, food and animals were traded with Imperial China and other nearby countries such as Liao-Khitan and Japan. But Khitan also attempted to invade Goryeo three times between 993 and 1018.[22] Goryeo then became a vassal state of the Mongol Empire in 1270–1356, after the Mongols had taken over Imperial China following several invasion attempts dating back to 1231.[23] It was only after the Mongol Empire started to crumble that the surviving members of the Goryeo dynasty were able to expel them from their country. While doing so, they had to repel attacks from Japanese pirates to the east.[24] The lesson for Goryeo—or Korea—was clear: it was independent, but it may well end up being a 'shrimp among whales'. For as the Korean saying goes, 'when whales fight, the shrimp's back is broken'.

## Joseon dynasty

The year was 1388. General Yi Seonggye had an explicit mission: to invade China, now under Ming rule. But the war hero, who had helped expel the Mongols and withstand Japanese pirates' attacks, had a different idea in mind: to overthrow the Goryeo monarch who had sent him on a mission he believed was foolish. Upon reaching Wihwa Island on the Amrok River (Yalu River), he turned back towards Gaegyeong. With the support of large numbers of military leaders and soldiers, a number of aristocrats and a good part of the general population who were also opposed to the attempt to invade China, he quickly defeated the king's forces and installed a puppet monarch. Eventually, Yi Seonggye exiled the ruling royal family.[25]

In 1392, Yi Seonggye officially took power himself. Yi established the Joseon dynasty and became Taejo of Joseon.[26] It was the beginning of the longest period in Korean history, for the Joseon dynasty would only end in 1910. This 519-year period of history left an imprint across the country that is still felt in contemporary South Korea. Starting with its capital city. In 1394, the new king moved the capital to Hanyang, officially known as Hanseong—none other than modern Seoul. The new capital was easier to defend compared to Gaegyeong, for it was a fortified city towards the middle of the Korean Peninsula. Hanyang was also a commercial and transportation hub, given its location just north of the Han River from where one could navigate towards the west and then China. And the new capital also had good *feng shui*, thanks to its location surrounded by four mountains protecting it from heavy winds.[27] Tracing its roots to 18 BCE as the capital of Baekje, Hanyang quickly became Joseon's main political, economic and cultural centre. Seoul, a name first used in the late nineteenth century, still holds that position over six centuries later.

Confucian scholars had supported King Taejo's coup. They wanted their principles to dominate all aspects of life, displacing Buddhism. They were successful, and as the centuries went by Joseon arguably became the most Confucian country in the world. Neo-Confucianism thus quickly became state ideology during the Early Joseon period. As a result, the administration was strictly and hierarchically divided into two main levels: the Uijeongbu (State Council) and its associated ministries, and the provincial governments sub-divided into counties and districts. In addition, access to government positions was based on a civil service examination that required deep knowledge of Confucian texts.[28] In practice, this restricted access to these posts to the country's elite literati.

These elites, known as *yangban*, went on to dominate the political, cultural and economic life of Korea throughout the Joseon period. (Many Korean families trace their roots back to these early *yangban*.) Below them were the *yangmin*—or commoners—and the *cheonmin*—or base people. And at the very bottom were the *nobi*, slaves that could be bought and sold.[29] These four groups could trace their roots to the Goryeo era. Ideas inherent to Confucianism served to consolidate their division into strict hierarchies during the centuries of Joseon rule.

Culture and scholarship were also dominated by Neo-Confucianism. Anyone in South Korea can attest to this by looking into their own pocket. The KRW1,000 and 5,000 notes have the portraits of two of the most prominent Confucian scholars on their obverse: Yi Hwang and Yi I, respectively. Both of them embodied the Confucian ideal of the scholar versed in philosophy, calligraphy or poetry, but also involved in politics and improving the lives of those sitting below them in a hierarchical society.

For the Neo-Confucianism permeating Joseon's life demanded that the king or ruler be obeyed by their subjects. But, crucially, Neo-Confucian ideas also asked that the ruler set the moral compass for their subjects and provide for them. And no one personified this idea better than Sejong the Great. Ruling from 1418 until his death in 1450, the fourth king of the Joseon dynasty implemented reforms aimed at improving the lives of his subjects through fairer taxation and then-revolutionary ideas such as maternity and paternity leave. He also promoted the study of science and technology to help farmers plan their crops better.[30]

Above all, Sejong the Great created Hangeul, Korea's native alphabet still in use in the modern Koreas. Promulgated in 1446, Hangeul was specifically designed to improve literacy among the general population.[31] Even to the untrained eye, Hangeul looks simpler than the traditional Chinese characters in use in Korea until then. Originally composed of twenty-eight letters—at the time of writing only twenty-four—Hangeul is often considered by (South) Koreans as their country's greatest accomplishment. Even though official documents and the higher classes continued to use Chinese characters for centuries, the king's new alphabet would eventually become dominant. As befits his status, Sejong the Great is bestowed with two of modern South Korea's greatest honours: his portrait graces the KRW10,000 note, the most commonly used, and a statue of him lies in front of Gyeongbokgung (Gyeongbok Palace). Built in 1395, this is the place that served as the main royal residence and seat of government through the Joseon dynasty. As of 2023, the palace and the statue of Sejong the Great in front of it continue to dominate the landscape of central Seoul.

Yet Neo-Confucian ideals also had a darker side for half of Joseon's population. Women were discriminated against, since Neo-Confucianism establishes that the wife must obey the husband and that it is the husband who must provide for the family. Furthermore, the first-born son was prioritized in terms of inheritance and family rituals.[32] The position of women was therefore downgraded compared to previous eras. Shin Saimdang exemplifies this. She was a writer and artist of great renown.[33] In fact, in 2009 she became the first woman to appear on a South Korean banknote when her portrait was included on the KRW50,000 note. But she was included in the note not only for her artistic merit but also because she embodied the idea of the ideal mother—Shin Saimdang's son was none other than Yi I. And she is known as a 'benevolent mother and good wife'.[34] For women, giving birth to a male heir that could carry the family's name became their main purpose in life. Arguably, the problems derived from this interpretation of women's role in society still afflict South Korea at the time of writing.

Early Joseon's foreign relations were also informed by Neo-Confucianism. Joseon rulers continued to send tributary missions to Ming China, the elder brother that in return offered its protection to its younger sibling. Trade with Japan, meanwhile, was circumscribed to Tsushima Island in the Korea Strait between both countries. For the most part, trade continued to include similar products to those making their way throughout North East Asia during the Goryeo era.[35]

Foreign relations were also marked by peace and stability throughout the fourteenth to sixteenth centuries. But the situation changed dramatically towards the end of the sixteenth century. Toyotomi Hideyoshi had unified Japan in 1590. He then turned his sights to the country's west with a plan to conquer Joseon and China. The Imjin War is the name given to the period between 1592 and 1598 during which Japan attempted two invasions of Joseon. The first attempt came in 1592–3. Admiral Yi Sunsin was able to repel the Japanese navy during a battle off Joseon's southern coast. Japan then launched a second invasion attempt in 1597–8. Yi again came to the rescue of Joseon, strategizing a second victory against the invading forces. Yi was killed in battle during this second invasion.[36] At the time of writing, he is immortalized with a statue 250 metres apart from Sejong the Great's in front of Gyeongbokgung.

The Late Joseon period is considered to have started following from the Imjin War. Shortly after, Joseon had to fend off a new invasion attempt. On this occasion, it came from the country's west. The Manchus were seeking to overthrow the Ming dynasty. However, Joseon was ambivalent towards recognizing the new dynasty. The Manchus thus launched two invasions in 1627 and 1636–7. On both occasions, the Manchu forces reached all the way to Hanyang. After occupying the capital during the second invasion, Joseon acquiesced to recognize Manchu rule over China and started to send tributary missions. By 1644, the Manchus finally overthrew the Mings and inaugurated the Qing dynasty that would rule China until 1911.[37] In terms of foreign relations, the 'shrimp'

Joseon would be under the 'protection' of China until the late nineteenth century. This had profound domestic consequences.

Korea remained relatively peaceful from the mid-seventeenth to the mid-nineteenth century, leading to a cultural renaissance. This is best exemplified by the first mention of 'Arirang' in 1756. Korea's best-known folk song had originated in Jeongseon county hundreds of years before.[38] With hundreds if not thousands of variations as anyone travelling across (South) Korea can attest, it had no predetermined lyrics. But all versions spoke about love and sorrow. The love of reaching your partner. The sorrow of losing them. A Korean take on a universal theme. A theme that thanks to the relative peacefulness of the Late Joseon dynasty was now in written form. A theme that survives to this day, since 'Arirang' remains the unofficial national anthem of both Koreas.

But in the midst of a period of peace and quiet, two major changes took place. To begin with, a new merchant class began to emerge. Local markets popped up throughout the country, and astute traders accumulated wealth previously unimaginable to Joseon commoners. In addition, factionalism took hold in the Uijeongbu and ministries. Officials divided themselves into Easterners and Westerners, with Easterners then dividing themselves into Northerners and Southerners. Further divisions took place among the Westerners.[39] Factionalism would never disappear from Joseon politics.[40]

These changes anticipated even bigger ones during the second half of the nineteenth century. In 1860, aristocrat and scholar Choe Je-u launched the Donghak (Eastern Learning) movement calling for the equality of all people and in opposition to Western influence. In 1862 and influenced by this movement, peasants revolted across southern Korea. They were dissatisfied with a tax policy that put a heavy burden on them while government officials, the *yangban*, and the new merchant class enjoyed a much better quality of life. There had been peasant revolts before, including the Hong Gyeong-nae rebellion of 1811–12. But the 1862 revolt spearheaded the expansion of Donghak and a broader movement among the peasantry, resulting in sporadic uprisings.[41] And in 1894, the Gabo reform resulted in sweeping changes. These included an end to the class system, the abolition of slavery, a meritocratic selection process for government posts without discrimination, an end to merchant monopolies and the use of Hangeul instead of Chinese characters in all official documents.[42] Confucianism was starting to crumble as Joseon's organizing ideology.

Domestic upheaval was exacerbated by sweeping changes in Joseon's neighbourhood. In 1866, the US ship *General Sherman* arrived in Pyongyang to force a trade agreement. Joseon was not interested. *General Sherman*'s crew members apprehended Joseon government officials. Fighting ensued, and all crew members were killed.[43] In this way, the age of imperialism arrived in Joseon. Its neighbour to the west, China, had resisted Westernization and sought to close down its borders. It was still forced to open up several ports through unequal treaties, the first one dating back to 1842. But the Chinese imperial family believed that the country's millennia-old history would help it prevail against the 'barbarians' from Europe and the United States.[44] In contrast, Joseon's neighbour to the east, Japan, reacted by following the West's example. In 1853, the first US warship had arrived at Tokyo Bay. Japan had been forced to sign its first unequal treaty only one year later. But by 1868 the country was on the path to Westernization, absorbing European and US thinking, technologies and even clothing following the Meiji Restoration.[45]

Within Joseon, there were divisions over which path to follow. In 1876, however, Japan imposed the Ganghwa Treaty on the country. This was an unequal treaty much like those the Western powers had forced upon China and Japan. Joseon had no option but to open some ports to Japanese merchants and to grant them extraterritoriality.[46] Over the following years, Western powers also signed unequal treaties with Joseon. The world as Joseon had known it was disintegrating. Following the First Sino-Japanese War of 1894–5, Japan became the dominant force in North East Asia and Joseon's tributary status with China finally came to an end. The world was changing around Joseon, and its rulers did not know how to react. It seemed that Japan had chosen the right path by 'copying' the Western powers. This intrigued many in Joseon who wondered whether their country should follow the same path.

This was the time when Joseon was starting to become better known in the West. Diplomats, merchants and missionaries were arriving in the country. Meanwhile, vivid portrayals of the country were attracting even more attention. Teacher and missionary William Elliot Griffis wrote the successful *Corea: The Hermit Nation* in 1882. The title referred to Joseon's isolationist policy compared to Japan, but the book itself was generally positive about the country and sought to show its uniqueness compared to its neighbours.[47] And in 1885, businessman Percival Lowell wrote the also successful and generally positive portrayal *Choson: The Land of the Morning Calm*. The title described the 'peaceful splendour' of the morning hours in Joseon and made this moniker well known in the West.[48]

With Joseon subject to unequal treaties and drawing ever more attention from external powers, both Koreans and the royal family decided to take Joseon's destiny into their own hands, especially after the assassination of Queen Min by Japanese agents in October 1895. Married to King Gojong, the queen was seen as the strongest advocate for Korean independence from Japanese influence.[49] Her death only redoubled Korean efforts to remain an independent country. In 1896, the newspaper *Tongnip Sinmun* (The Independent)—the first-ever newspaper published in

Hangeul—and the Independence Club were launched. They advocated for independence from foreign influence, Korean patriotism and, crucially, the socio-economic development of the country.[50] Koreans increasingly realized that their country's survival as an independent nation required all-out efforts to modernize it. This was a clear rejection of the path that China had set itself upon.

The royal family followed suit shortly after. In October 1897, King Gojong became emperor as he proclaimed the DaeHan Jeguk (Great Han Empire).[51] The symbolism was clear. Korea was an equal to China and all other nations; it was not subordinated to its neighbour to the west or the expansionist power to its east. Certainly, proclamation of the empire was also an attempt by the royal family to retain power. Some voices within the independence movement were demanding a democratic and anti-corruption drive. Seo Jae-pil, one of its key leaders, had lived in the United States for over a decade.[52] It was not a stretch for the royal family and their loyalists to think that he and others might harbour republican ideas, even if there was no evidence of this. Indeed, the Independence Club would be closed in 1898.

Crucially, Emperor Gojong understood that he needed to cater to the needs of the new empire's subjects if he was to retain power. Thus, the king launched the Gwangmu Reform. The traditional class system was abolished, at least legally. An incipient land reform process was also launched to expand ownership and modify taxation. Education and healthcare were expanded and modernized to support Korea's industrialization. Seoul and the rest of the country were transformed. Trams arrived in the Korean capital in 1899. That same year, Korea inaugurated its first railway line connecting Seoul and Incheon.[53] Korea was striving to become an independent, modern country. If Japan was able to compete with Western countries by learning from their ways of thinking and technology, so could Korea.

Japan, however, had other plans. In 1904–5, the Russian and Japanese empires fought over their territorial ambitions in Korea and Manchuria. The Japanese army decisively defeated its Russian opponents while dispatching thousands of troops to Korea. The 1905 Taft–Katsura Memorandum between Japan and the United States and the subsequent Treaty of Portsmouth between Japan and Russia that formally ended their war sealed Korea's fate. Under these agreements, the United States and Russia, respectively, recognized that Korea was part of Japan's sphere of influence.[54] By extension, the international community did too. Korea was not consulted on these terms. And to add insult to injury, US President Theodore Roosevelt was awarded the Nobel Peace Prize for brokering the deal.[55] As if Koreans had to be reminded of a shrimp's place in the whales' world.

In November 1905, Japan and Korea signed the Eulsa Treaty (Protectorate Treaty). The treaty established Korea as a Japanese protectorate. Drafted by the Japanese government, the treaty established that Japan had control over Korea's foreign policy and trade. The Korean government initially refused to sign the treaty. But Japan's military presence in Seoul and across Korea forced its hand. After the agreement was signed, Korea continued to resist it. Righteous Armies (*Uibyeong*) were formed across the country to fight against the Japanese invaders. But they were overpowered by the Japanese army.[56] Meanwhile, Emperor Gojong sent emissaries to The Hague Peace Conference in 1907 to denounce the treaty. Delegates at the conference refused entry to the Korean delegation.[57] Korea was taking matters into its own hands, but the world was not listening. Japan reacted by forcing Emperor Gojong to abdicate, forcibly implementing a treaty that effectively put the administration of Korean domestic affairs into Japanese hands and disbanding the Korean army. Sunjong replaced his father as Korean emperor. He would be the last Joseon ruler in the history of Korea. In August 1910, Japan and

Korea signed an annexation treaty. Sunjong was forced to abdicate and demoted to king under the Imperial House of Japan, ending 519 years of the Joseon rule.[58] Korea had become a Japanese colony.

All these changes had a profound effect on a Korean population that was gaining more freedoms while seeing its leaders unable to withstand changes imposed on the country by foreign powers. *Minjok* emerged as a powerful unifying force, with the concept being used publicly from around 1900. This concept defined a separate Korean identity that presented Koreans as distinct from other ethnic groups and nations, with a single bloodline and history dating all the way back to Dangun in 2333 BCE.[59] In short, *minjok* presented Koreans as unique. It would be a powerful force in the first half of the twentieth century.

## *Japan's colonization of Korea*

Korea's colonial period was a transformational era that would have a deep impact on South Korea. Japan ruled Korea for thirty-five years, from 1910 to 1945. During this period, Korean language and culture were repressed, the Korean economy was put to the service of Japanese imperial ambitions and, ultimately, most Koreans became second-class citizens in their own country.[60] There was also a systematic attempt to eradicate Korean history by burning some 200,000 historical volumes while shipping over 40,000 cultural relics and ancient manuscripts to Japan.[61] The Japanese government appointed a governor-general who ruled over the Korean colony.[62] He reported directly to the emperor. He spent most of his time in Keijo, the new name that Japan gave to Seoul.

In the first decade of the colonial period, Japan established the structures that would be used to consolidate its rule. Above all, the colonial government carried out an eight-year cadastral survey in 1910–18. The survey laid the groundwork for a new land and real estate registration system, with the colonial government itself becoming the largest landowner. Many Korean landowners lost their property rights and became tenants, often serving newly arrived Japanese landowners.[63] By the 1930s, around half of Korean land belonged to Japanese landowners—including most of the highest-quality land.[64] The agricultural sector was overhauled to serve the Japanese economy, and over half of the country's rice and other crops were exported to Korea's colonial master.

Most Koreans were certainly unhappy, and many resisted Japan's occupation, spurred by *minjok*. In fact, it was the Japanese occupation that had really driven a distinct Korean nationalism based on the uniqueness of the country vis-à-vis the colonial master.[65] On 1 March 1919, this discontent was laid bare. South Koreans know that day as marking the birth of the Sam-il (March 1st) Movement. A group of activists including intellectuals and students read a Declaration of Independence in Insadong, within walking distance of Gyeongbokgung, where the residence of the governor-general was based.[66] As of 2023, a copy of the declaration is displayed in Tapgol Park, the original location right next to Insadong where the activists wanted to read it. Aghast at the ongoing discrimination against Koreans, suspicious about the real reason behind (former) Emperor Gojong's death two months earlier and inspired by US President Woodrow Wilson's Fourteen Points speech calling for the self-determination of colonies, those making the declaration called for an end to Japanese occupation. Even though thousands of Koreans across the country had been involved in independence activities since 1910, the Sam-il Movement was the first to serve as a catalyst for mass demonstrations. '*Mansei!*', protestors shouted: 'Long Live Korean Independence!' They were met with thousands of killings and tens of thousands of arrests by the Japanese police forces and the military.[67]

A few weeks later, on 11 April, a group of independence activists established the Korean Provisional Government in Shanghai. Recognized by a small number of countries, the government established the Republic of Korea in exile. Its first president was Rhee Syngman.[68] Rhee would go on to become the first president of South Korea—or the Republic of Korea—upon its establishment in 1948. However, the provisional government did not have a monopoly over Koreans' resistance to Japan. In 1925, a Korean Communist Party was secretly launched in Seoul.[69] In the following year, a group of university and school students in Seoul launched the June 10th Independence Movement. Following from Sunjong's funeral—the former emperor had been living in virtual imprisonment in Changdeok Palace—the students started several demonstrations calling for Korean independence.[70] The Japanese police and army quelled this and other demonstrations. But in November 1929, students in Gwangju started a new pro-independence movement after they refused to sing the Japanese national anthem. Protests spread across Korea until March 1930, when the Japanese army again stopped the movement.[71] And yet other groups both inside and outside of Korea also fought against Japan.

Symbols of Korea's resistance to Japanese occupation also began to emerge, further reinforcing *minjok*. Some of them were brave individuals who paid the ultimate price. Among them, Ryu Gwan-sun stands out. She joined the Sam-il Movement as a sixteen-year-old and led an uprising in her home province of South Chungcheong. She was arrested by the Japanese police, asked to admit her 'crimes' and provide the names of other independence fighters in exchange for a lighter sentence. After refusing to do so, she was tortured and beaten incessantly for months before dying from the wounds inflicted by her captors.[72] But Ryu resisted, and her name went down in history. She was an independence heroine. She became a martyr.

Some other symbols belonged to everyday life. Two novelties that had only recently reached Korea were cases in point: movies and competitive sports. In 1926, the silent movie *Arirang* was released. Named after Korea's most famous folk song, the movie was an allegory of Japanese occupation and came to be considered a nationalist masterpiece.[73] One decade after its release, Sohn Kee-chung won the gold medal for the marathon at the Berlin 1936 Olympics. He symbolized a different type of resistance, arguably more direct. During the medal ceremony, he clutched a young oak tree he had received for his victory in front of his chest. He was covering the Japanese flag adorning his kit. He lowered his head, refusing to acknowledge the Japanese national anthem. In the interviews he gave in Berlin, Sohn stressed that Korea was a separate country.[74] Once the games were over, he had to go back to his occupied land and would have to wait fifty-two years for an independent (South) Korea to have its moment of glory in an Olympic stadium. But in 1936, he was already a hero to most Koreans.

On the other side of the coin, there were also Koreans who decided to collaborate with the new colonial authorities. The *chinilpa*, as they came to be known in the post-colonial period, took government roles, joined the colonial police force and the Japanese military, prospered in their business ventures thanks to their connections to the colonial government or simply spread the narrative that Japan was helping to modernize Korea. In time, Yi Wan-yong came to symbolize the figure of the Japanese collaborator. One of the founders of the Independence Club, he later became a collaborator as Japan started to occupy Korea from 1905. He then became the prime minister who signed the 1910 annexation treaty.[75]

Beyond these divisions, Korean society continued to change during the colonial period. Confucianism continued to dominate people's belief systems, but Christianity started to gain a foothold. It had first arrived in the seventeenth century, but it would be during the 1910s and 1920s that significant numbers of Koreans started to convert. They were attracted to this new religion by the role that they saw the (Christian) United States playing in opposition to Japan. US missionaries had also been opening modern hospitals and schools from the late nineteenth century, further boosting the appeal of Christianity.[76] Meanwhile, patriarchal restrictions on women informed by Confucian beliefs started to loosen—particularly in bigger cities. The magazine *Sin Yeoseong* (New Woman) was launched in 1925 to cater to women who were gaining new freedoms.[77] And a popular culture started to emerge as the governor-general legalized Hangeul publications and communication after the Sam-il Movement. In 1920, *Chosun Ilbo* and *Dong-a Ilbo*—(South) Korea's two oldest surviving newspapers—were published for the first time, radio broadcasts were launched in 1927 and throughout the decade different types of literature started to flourish.[78]

During the 1930s, Japanese imperial ambitions took a new turn. Japan had sought to develop roads and railroads across Korea and, from the 1930s, to build some industries—mainly in what would later become North Korea—to support the Japanese economy but also to prepare for potential war in Manchuria and across East Asia. In late 1931, Japan launched an invasion of Manchuria, which it easily conquered in a matter of months.[79] It was the first taste of a new wave of Japanese imperialism in the region, which had brutal consequences for Korea and its population.

In 1938, Japan promulgated the National General Mobilization Law as preparations for World War II were underway. Over five million Koreans were conscripted as forced labour, with over half a million being sent to Japan, where they mainly worked in factories and mines. Tens of thousands died, exhausted as their labour served to fuel Japan's military ambitions.[80] Meanwhile, tens—if not hundreds—of thousands of Korean women were forced into sexual slavery. Euphemistically referred to as 'comfort women', these women—many of them teenage girls—were sent to 'comfort stations' across the expanding Japanese Empire, to be raped by dozens of soldiers daily.[81] And to erase Korea's identity while symbolizing the country's centrality to Japan's war efforts, the *Soshikaimei* order was passed in 1939 that required Koreans to register under and use Japanese names. Two years later, Korean-language study was eliminated from the school curriculum altogether.[82]

On 15 August 1945, Korean history took its greatest turn of the modern era. Jubilant crowds took to the streets. One of the most famous pictures of the day shows newly released independence activists raising their hands in celebration, in front of a tram in Seoul. That day, South Korea became independent again. Japanese Emperor Hirohito had announced the surrender of Japan that same day, putting an end to World War II.[83] Known as National Liberation Day, the date marked the end of a humiliating experience. Buoyed by what promised to be a new beginning for their country, thousands of soldiers and intellectuals who had been fighting for Korea's liberation inside the country itself, in Manchuria, across China and elsewhere around the world started to descend into Seoul. They had high hopes for their country's future.

### Post-liberation divisions

North and South Korea were not a Korean creation. A few days before Japan surrendered and Korea regained its independence, US army staffers Dean Rusk—who would go on to serve as US secretary of state—and Charles Bonesteel sat down in a quiet room in Washington, DC. They had clear instructions from their country's Department of War: to find a place to divide the Korean Peninsula into two, to ensure that the Soviet Union—which was heading into Korea as part of its offensive against

Japan—would not occupy the whole of the country. They settled on the thirty-eighth parallel in order to keep Seoul in the south.[84] Their proposal was accepted by their superiors. The Soviet Union also agreed to it. Korea's millennia-old history as a unified country was about to come to an end.

Soviet troops had already entered the Korean Peninsula as Hirohito was getting ready to give his historic address announcing Japan's surrender. They would swiftly occupy the northern half of the Korean Peninsula once Japan declared the war was over. US troops would arrive in the southern part shortly after, mainly from Okinawa to begin with. A few weeks later, Washington established the United States Army Military Government in Korea (USAMGIK).[85] Korea was not a priority for either of the emerging superpowers. But neither of them wanted the other to control the whole country, as the early stages of the Cold War were already on the horizon. In December, the United States and the Soviet Union decided to establish a five-year trusteeship for Korea. Koreans themselves were aghast. They wanted independence immediately.[86] But under the trusteeship, the country was only scheduled to regain its full independence at a later date.

Throughout this time, Koreans were busy trying to rebuild their country. Only two days after Korea's liberation, the Committee for the Preparation of Korean Independence (CPKI) was formed. By September, the Korean People's Republic (KPR) started to replace the CPKI. Organized in multiple people's committees, the KPR initially promised to be an inclusive government despite its name—which suggested communist sympathies. In fact, right-wing leader in exile Rhee Syngman was selected as the KPR's leader upon his arrival back in Korea.[87] And many committees in the south—but by no means all of them—were nationalist and leaned conservative rather than communist. Nonetheless, the United States made these committees illegal in

23

the south by December. The committees would be disbanded in the north shortly thereafter.[88]

Up until 1948, only one thing seemed to unite all Koreans: their wish for immediate independence, which explains opposition to the trusteeship almost as soon as the announcement reached the country. But huge domestic divisions, further fuelled by the United States and the Soviet Union, inexorably pushed Korea towards partition. In the north, Kim Il-sung and other communist leaders also newly arrived in the Korean Peninsula established the North Korean Provisional People's Committee, nationalized industries, passed legal reform, started an incipient cult of personality with the establishment of Kim Il-sung University and founded the Korean People's Army.[89] In the south, Rhee and Kim Ku, another returnee, jostled for power. Leftist activists were imprisoned when not killed, strikes and uprisings were brutally quelled and Rhee and other leaders openly discussed the creation of a separate government for the land below the thirty-eighth parallel.[90]

UN-backed attempts to hold elections across the whole country were unsuccessful. A meeting convened in April 1948 in Pyongyang between representatives from the north and the south ended in failure. Southern representatives either refused to attend or left the meeting alarmed. Kim Ku, who did attend, returned to the south convinced that the north could easily take over the south with the help of Soviet troops if it so wished.[91] That same month, the residents of Jeju Island staged the '4.3 Uprising' (also known as the Jeju Uprising). They were tired of their leaders' failure to settle their differences and were opposed to the upcoming elections, scheduled to be held solely in the south. They were met with brutal repression, mainly by the south Korean army.[92] The views of ordinary Koreans were silenced. The division of their country was about to be confirmed.

1

# INDEPENDENCE, WAR AND POVERTY
## 1948–60

*Birth of a republic*

It should have been one of the happiest days in Korean history. Instead, it was a bittersweet date. On 10 May 1948, Koreans living below the thirty-eighth parallel were able to vote for their leaders for the first time in Korean history.[1] They were to elect their representatives for the National Assembly. No Korean had previously had the chance to experience the power of choosing their preferred government. And southern Koreans made the most of it. Over 95 per cent of eligible voters turned out to vote in the UN-sponsored elections.[2] A small number of the 13,000 polling places registered violence. Thirty-eight people were killed on the day of the vote. Inevitably, there were multiple accusations of vote-rigging up and down the country.[3] But the election was considered relatively successful for a country marred by thirty-five years of occupation and three years of almost uninterrupted violence.

Yet the election laid bare an uncomfortable truth. Korea was on the verge of de facto division between its northern and southern halves. The election should have been held across the whole country. However, Kim Il-sung refused to allow the UN to run the elections in the northern half of the Korean Peninsula. He was backed by the Soviet Union, whose forces helped make sure that no UN election monitor could step above the thirty-eighth parallel.[4] As a result, Koreans in the northern half were not able to cast their ballot. The legislative National Assembly set up after the election had unoccupied seats for the northern representatives to take once a vote was held in north Korea.[5] They were to remain empty.

The election showed that Korea remained at the mercy of whales. Elections in the southern part only took place because the United States guaranteed that they would happen. But many south Koreans were unhappy with their country's dependence on foreign powers. Independence leaders Kim Ku and Kim Kyu-sik led a group of prominent politicians who refused to participate in the election.[6] They correctly assumed that this would make it very difficult for the two Koreas to unify. They wanted the Soviet Union and the United States to leave their occupation zones and allow Koreans to rule themselves. They shared the concerns of their fellow citizens in Jeju Island and elsewhere across the country, who opposed foreign occupation.

Ultimately, however, elections were held. Rhee Syngman's National Association for the Rapid Realization of Korean Independence won the election, claiming just over 26 per cent of the vote and fifty-five out of 200 seats in the National Assembly.[7] Rhee quickly became the most influential figure in the new National Assembly. A devout Protestant equipped with a PhD from Princeton University, Rhee had been the Korean independence movement's most prominent figure in the United States. He had been living there almost uninterruptedly since 1904. He had represented the Provisional Government of the Republic of Korea in several international meetings, including the San Francisco Conference that approved the UN Charter. He had also been the president of the Provisional Government between 1919 and 1925. Rhee had met several US presidents and countless American and European political and military leaders.[8] Arguably, he was the only Korean independence figure widely known in the West. He was Washington's preferred choice to lead south Korea; perhaps the only one.

Rhee immediately pressed for the creation of a separate state in the south. On 17 July, the National Assembly promulgated the first Constitution of the Republic of Korea.[9] This marked a new first in Korean history: constitutionalism had arrived in the country, if only in its southern half. But in the whirlwind of events that took over the country post-independence, this landmark moment went by with barely a shrug of most people's shoulders. Much more consequential was the 20 July presidential election, in which members of the National Assembly voted to elect Rhee as south Korea's new president. Rhee received 180 out of the 196 votes cast.[10] His grip over the National Assembly and south Korea at large was becoming evident. Shortly after, he became the first president of a new country.

Barely discussed, the constitution included a crucial clause that would put an end to centuries of Korean history. The clause transferred land to farmers. In 1945, around 70 per cent of southern Korean farmers remained tenants. They paid rent of up to 60 per cent of their crop.[11] The *yangban* still possessed most of the land and dominated political, cultural and, obviously, economic life in the countryside. That is, the lives of well over three-quarters of southern Koreans. The 1948 constitution paved the way for the Land Reform Law of 1950, which radically changed this state of affairs.[12] This would become the most popular measure enacted by the South Korean government. But in 1948, south Koreans did not know this. And many disliked the direction their half of the country was taking.

On 15 August 1948, the Republic of Korea was founded. A picture of the occasion shows a massive Taegukgi, the flag first adopted by the Joseon dynasty in 1883. The flag hangs in front of the National Assembly. Dressed in a plain *hanbok*, Rhee stands in front of the flag. Next to him is General Douglas MacArthur, Supreme Commander of the Allied Forces in (occupied) Japan. This was the last day of USAMGIK, Washington's military government in south Korea. Rhee and MacArthur look at the huge crowds gathering in front of them. These are the new citizens of the Republic of Korea. It is official: South Korea is now an independent country, separate from the north. But the crowds do not cheer and laugh, as they did exactly three years earlier when Japanese Emperor Hirohito had announced the surrender of Japan and Korea had regained its independence. They witness history, yes. But they do not celebrate it.

South Korea was thus born out of pain, rather than joy. Well over half of South Koreans, now with a capital S, had never experienced self-rule. But now that it had come, they started to realize that they may end up being the masters of only one half of the Korean Peninsula. Indeed, North Korea would be founded less than a month later. On 9 September, Kim Il-sung would become the first Supreme Leader of North Korea.[13] Another independence hero, he would go on to rule North Korea until his death in 1994. He would attempt to re-unify Korea by force less than two years later. But South Koreans do not this know yet. All they know, or dream of, is that their country will soon be one again.

The country was also born with huge domestic divisions over its future. Conservative and nationalist, the Rhee government introduced a National Security Law to punish anti-national activities in September. Three months later, the government passed the law.[14] In this way, Seoul could suppress communism, any activity that could be construed as pro-North Korean and more generally any type of opposition to the government. It was becoming clear that Rhee was no democrat at heart. With the acquiescence of the United States—more interested in halting the spread of communism than promoting democracy—authoritarianism slowly started to creep into the new country.

Left-leaning South Koreans, many of them sympathetic to communist ideas and supported by the North, fought back. Jeju Island's '4.3 Uprising' had not been quelled. Demonstrations now broke out across the country. Repression by police forces and soldiers ensued. The rebels did not back down. As a case in point, the Yeosu–Suncheon rebellion erupted in October. Up to 2,000 left-leaning soldiers stationed in Yeosu, Suncheon and other towns nearby in the South Jeolla Province launched an uprising. They refused to be sent to Jeju Island to participate in the repression of their fellow South Koreans. The Republic of Korea Armed Forces—formed in August 1948—moved in. The South Korean army had suppressed the rebellion by early November and executed those suspected of leading or supporting the uprising. Civilians were not spared.[15] Tensions, however, continued throughout 1949. In a particularly grim incident, the police rounded up and executed 300 villagers in a single day in Bukchon, a town on Jeju Island.[16] This was one of many cases of violence against civilians throughout this period.

Violence and repression did not put an end to domestic left–right divisions, which to this date mar South Korean politics. An undeclared guerrilla war lasting almost until the outbreak of the Korean War continued. It even survived the first few months of the war in some pockets of the country. Unrest was particularly violent in the southern provinces, in a pattern that would repeat itself throughout South Korean history. But the Rhee government was close to being firmly in control of the country by mid-1949. So much so that the last remaining US forces withdrew from South Korea in late June.[17] US politicians wanted out of the Korean Peninsula, and fast. Their country's forces, however, would be back one year later.

## The Koreas at war

There was a sense of anticipation at the National Press Club, a ten-minute walk from the White House. US Secretary of State Dean Acheson was to deliver a speech to discuss 'the relations between the peoples of the United States and the peoples of Asia'. Delivered on 12 January 1950, the speech established an American defence perimeter in Asia to guard against the advance of communism.[18] The Korean Peninsula did not make the cut. One week later, US Congress voted against a US$60 million aid bill for South Korea.[19] Washington's message was clear.

Slightly over 11,000 kilometres away, the speech and vote were met with dismay. In Seoul, the Rhee government was making plans to take over the north. By force if necessary. Domestic violence was mostly under control. Left-leaning guerrillas continued their fight against the government. But the South Korean army was on its way to achieving almost full control of the situation, which it did by the spring. By then, up to 30,000 political prisoners were in jail. Some 305,000 were enrolled in the Bodo (National Guidance) League, a re-education movement.[20] Rhee had control over the National Assembly. Kim Ku, who could have spearheaded an opposition movement, had been assassinated the year before.[21] Kim Kyu-sik, another potential opposition leader, had retired from politics. Considering the connections he still maintained in Washington, Rhee could have expected support from the US government in his plans to take over the north. Acheson and US Congress had put an end to such hopes.

And then war broke out. On 25 June 1950, at dawn, the (North) Korean People's Army launched an attack across the thirty-eighth parallel. Just like Rhee, Kim Il-sung wanted to be the leader that reunified Korea. And he did not hesitate to strike the South as soon as he felt his army was ready. Under-equipped and exhausted from almost two years of inter-Korean border skirmishes, South Korean troops were no match for their opponents from the north. In fact, North Korean soldiers had been training and fighting along with their Chinese counterparts in 1948–9, during the last two years of the Chinese civil war. The North Korean military was also well equipped. The Soviet Union had provided tanks, artillery and other material assistance that the United States had denied to South Korea. Within two days, North Korean forces had reached Seoul.[22] The Rhee government had to flee further south.

The early seeds of what ended up becoming a brutal three-year conflict were planted on the same day of the North Korean surprise attack. With the Soviet Union boycotting the UN Security Council, the council was able to pass a resolution condemning North Korea's move.[23] Two days later, it authorized member states to provide military assistance to South Korea.[24] The United States wasted no time, and its B-29 bombers launched a strike on Pyongyang on 29 June. Two days later, the first American troops landed in South Korea.[25] Up to fifteen other countries would end up sending soldiers as well. US President Harry Truman had determined that the Soviet Union was unlikely to send its troops to the Korean Peninsula even if the United States did, so there was no threat of the Korean War leading to direct hostilities between the two superpowers.[26] The need to protect Japan from the potential threat of a communist, unified Korea, the early stages of the Cold War and the threat that China posed to Taiwan (then Formosa) were crucial factors behind Washington's decision to intervene in the Korean War. In short, South Korea was saved not for its own sake—or at least not only. It was saved because of great power politics. A shrimp among whales, indeed.

Notwithstanding US intervention, the North Korean troops continued to march south. Tens of thousands of communist sympathizers scattered across mountains and villages joined them. Countless South Korean soldiers defected to the northern army or simply refused to fight for a government they did not believe in. Often portrayed as a 'simple' confrontation between North and South, the reality was more nuanced. Many would flee North Korea during the war because they feared life under a communist regime. But also, many in South Korea joined the advancing troops from the north because Kim Il-sung offered them more hope than Rhee. In a matter of weeks, South Korea was essentially reduced to the Busan (then Pusan) Perimeter.[27] In their retreat, the South Korean army rounded up and killed thousands of real and alleged communist sympathizers. North Korean troops matched or surpassed their brutality, killing scores of local politicians, businesspeople and anybody who could vaguely be considered anti-communist.[28] After decades of fighting Japanese oppression, Koreans were now fighting each other almost as viciously. In quite a few cases, they were settling long-standing family or neighbour feuds. In many cases, ideology had little to do with it.

Stretching roughly 240 kilometres from the Korea Strait to the East Sea (Sea of Japan), the Busan Perimeter was the area were South Korean and UN forces were to make their final stand until the United States and other countries sent more reinforcements. On 4 August, the Battle of the Busan Perimeter began. Two weeks later, the Rhee government was forced to move inside the perimeter. The joint South Korean and UN army was holding strong. UN forces—above all the United States—were sending bombers, battleships and tanks. But an offensive by the North Korean army along the Nakdong River threatened to break the South Korean and UN defensive lines.[29] North Korean soldiers no longer had a material advantage. But they certainly had—or seemed to have—a moral strength that their enemies lacked.

In Incheon, a port city 27 kilometres to the west of Seoul, the tide of the war changed. As of 2023, a bronze statue depicts three US marines in front of a column. Another one shows six other marines climbing up a seawall. Nearby, there is another statue, of General Douglas MacArthur in his World War II uniform. Standing 3 metres tall, the statue honours the man who led the Incheon (then Inchon) landing. On the morning of 15 September, over 70,000 troops began to land on three different beaches. Five days later, the UN forces had won the Battle of Incheon. They started to march towards Seoul, which they recaptured within two weeks.[30] The North Korean forces fighting at the Busan Perimeter were cut off from their supplies. They started a hasty retreat north. Many defected to the advancing South Korean army. They, too, did not believe in their government or its ideas. So if the South was going to win the war, they might as well be on the right side of history.

For it seemed that Korea would indeed reunify under a nominally democratic government. By mid-October, South Korean and UN forces had reached the border region separating the Korean Peninsula from China. The UN had established a Commission for the Unification and Rehabilitation of Korea, with the mandate to establish an independent democratic government for a unified Korea. Truman had been right. The Soviet Union was providing guns and tanks to North Korea. A handful of disguised Soviet pilots were flying MiG-15s in air battles. But Joseph Stalin had no appetite for a full-blown war with the United States for the sake of North Korea. Kim Il-sung and other North Korean leaders were isolated. MacArthur had requested the Korean People's Army's surrender. It had perhaps 25,000 troops left. Combined, South Korean and UN forces were fifteen times larger.[31] Rhee could afford himself a smile. His long-term goal to lead an independent Korea was within his grasp.

But this was not to happen. On 25 October, Chinese soldiers who had secretly crossed the Amrok River launched an offensive. Under the guise of the People's Volunteer Army, hundreds of thousands of Chinese soldiers eventually battled the South Korean and UN forces. Where Stalin hesitated, Mao Zedong did not. Mao had agreed to support North Korea's war effort back in May, when Kim Il-sung had paid him a visit.[32] This had looked unnecessary in the early stages of the war, when North Korean forces were making their way towards the south of the Korean Peninsula. But now the situation had changed. Chinese intervention resulted in a retreat by South Korean and UN troops. By the spring of 1951, the battle lines were stabilized around the thirty-eighth parallel.[33] The artificial line that Rusk and Bonesteel had drawn now separated the two sides at war. That is where they remained until the end of the war, and it is the line that continues to separate the two Koreas at the time of writing, more than seventy years later.

But the war lasted for two more years. In one of its most famous pictures, a young girl is seen carrying her small brother on her back. She is no more than seven or eight years old; he must be no more than three or four. She is wearing traditional Korean clothes. She stands in front of an M-26 tank, one of dozens of medium tanks deployed by the US army during the war. The date is June 1951. They are refugees. The worst of the fighting is over. But millions of South Koreans have been displaced by the war, including countless children who will never see their parents again. The girl and the boy look at the camera. They do not understand what is going on. This was the feeling that many South and North Koreans had throughout 1952–3. Fighting continued, despite peace negotiations and even though it was clear that no side could defeat the other. Mass killings of civilians were also commonplace, as were summary executions of prisoners of war (POWs).[34]

In the middle of this carnage, South Korea had the time to hold its second-ever presidential election. Following the May 1950 National Assembly vote, Rhee could only count on the support of a quarter of the legislature's members. Thus, he forced a constitutional amendment that would make the president directly elected by voters. In August 1952, South Korea held its second presidential election. Rhee won easily, obtaining almost 75 per cent of the vote on an 88 per cent turnout.[35] He was buoyed by the war. There was no credible opposition. In fact, US government officials were disparaging of the South Korean president given their many policy differences.[36] But no one could replace him. Rhee had given a master class in politics. It would not be his last.

Rhee clang to the hope that the South could still win the war, with US support. North Korea, China and the United States were engaged in negotiations to cease hostilities. On the US side, the government just wanted to end the war and bring its soldiers back home. But if US soldiers left the Korean Peninsula, would they come back if North Korea launched another war, especially if Kim Il-sung had the support of Chinese troops? Rhee had his doubts. So he boycotted the talks to put an end to the war. On 18 June 1953, the South Korean president ordered the release of some 25,000 North Korean anti-communist POWs imprisoned in the South under UN custody.[37] US President Dwight D. Eisenhower was livid. This was against the explicit wishes of the UN and could scupper end of war talks, which included discussions about the repatriation of POWs. But the move worked. The Eisenhower administration agreed to a mutual defence treaty with the South once the fighting had formally ended, as well as economic aid.[38] US troops would remain in the country.

The fighting finally came to an end on 27 July 1953, with an armistice signed by North Korea, China and the United States on behalf of the UN. South Korea refused to sign. Rhee still did not want to give up on his hope of reunifying Korea, whether peacefully or by force.[39] But most South Koreans greeted the news with relief. Over one and a half million civilians were killed during the war; this was over 5 per cent of the Koreas' combined pre-war population. Around 217,000 South Korean soldiers lost their lives, along with an estimated 36,568 Americans, up to 406,000 North Korean troops, some 600,000 Chinese and an estimated 3,063 UN forces from other nationalities.[40] On top of the human horror, the Korean Peninsula lay in ruins after three years of combat.

Thus ended the so-called Forgotten War. Sandwiched between World War II and the Vietnam War and with coverage censored, the conflict is little known to most Americans. In South Korea, of course, the war left a vivid memory that persists to this day. Long known as 'Six-Two-Five' (*Yu-gi-o*) due to the date when it began, the war gave way to over three decades of authoritarianism and anti-communism as the underpinning forces driving successive South Korean administrations. Anti-Americanism also emerged as a strong force among many South Koreans, especially those on the left wing of the political spectrum. They blamed the United States for having divided Korea and they resented the atrocities committed by some American soldiers during the war. But above all, South Koreans wanted economic prosperity after decades of colonization first and war afterwards. The Rhee government, however, failed on this account.

### 'A country poorer than sub-Saharan Africa'

It is difficult to exaggerate how poor South Korea was following the Korean War. Official numbers tell us that GDP per capita was estimated at US$67 dollars in 1953.[41] Seventy-eight per cent of Koreans were illiterate by the end of Japanese colonization in 1945,[42] and the figure could hardly have improved since then considering the recurrent violence. Not only that, but the limited industry left behind by the former colonial power lay mostly in North Korea. It was difficult to find any country in the world poorer and with worse prospects than South Korea. In 1953, South Korea was poorer than sub-Saharan Africa, then the poorest region in the world. And the little country on the eastern corner of Asia did not have the natural resources that, some thought, promised a better future for the African continent. South Korea was a 'hopeless case', as many an economist and pundit put it at the time.

Notwithstanding the country's post-war poverty, the period of relative peace and stability following the armistice resulted in a baby boom.[43] And there was a clear preference for boys, which was only partially explained by Confucian ideas about who the head of a family should be. South Korea remained a largely agrarian society, with around 75 per cent of the population living in rural areas. And thanks to the land reform implemented from 1950 onwards—even as war had ravaged the Korean Peninsula—1.6 million farmers owned land for the first time.[44] But they owned little, if any, modern farming equipment. There was a need for physical strength. In this context, there was discrimination against girls.

The baby boom came as South Korea had several pressing social issues to address. To start with, it was difficult to find a South Korean who had not seen a relative killed or gone missing during the war. Countless South Koreans went searching for their lost relatives. If they had been killed, Confucian burial practices demanded an elaborate ritual lasting several days and involving generations of the extended family when not a whole village. Japanese colonial authorities had sought to put an end to this practice through a 1912 decree.[45] Over forty years later, however, the practice survived. Many South Korean families wished to follow Korea's ancestral burial rite not only to honour their loved ones but also to bring closure to a tumultuous time and start anew.

For many South Koreans, their pain came from not knowing the fate of their missing relatives. Was your wife still alive in North Korea, unable to cross south before the inter-Korean border was closed for good? Was your husband in a hospital, affected by memory loss as a result of a wound received in battle? And what about your younger brother or sister? Had you left them behind when evacuating Seoul or some other city, and were they now unable to find their way home? An unknown number of South Koreans had to ask themselves these questions once the war was over. Decades later, there are South Koreans still going to their graves with no answers.

The war had also left tens of thousands of orphans around the country. Thousands were sent to orphanages and hospices, but many were left to roam the streets. With Confucian ideas about the importance of blood ties still widespread, orphans created a 'problem' because adoption did not come naturally to many South Koreans—even those who could have afforded to feed extra mouths.[46] Similarly, many 'GI babies' with a South Korean mother and a US or other UN soldier as a father also ended up in orphanages. GI babies continued to be born even after the war, as US soldiers moved into South Korea to protect the country against a possible North Korean invasion. With few economic prospects, many women resorted to prostitution to make a living. And US soldiers had readily available cash. More GI babies were born.[47] Mixed race in a country where ethnicity-based *minjok* still informed Koreanness, and with often untraceable fathers who had returned home anyway, they were abandoned in the hope that someone would adopt them.

Very soon, a 'solution' came up that helped to partially address this issue: international adoption. Starting from 1954 and often moved by greater awareness about GI babies and the plight of South Korean orphans more generally, American families first and Australian, Canadian and European families afterwards began to adopt orphaned South Korean children. To an extent, this exacerbated the problem of separated families, since little children were sometimes sent overseas for adoption without their families knowing.[48] But the thinking was that for many adoptees their future was probably brighter from an economic point of view, without consideration for their future psychological wellbeing.

### Rhee Syngman's authoritarian government

It is in this context that Rhee Syngman implemented an ever-more authoritarian government system. Rhee sought to justify and strengthen his government following principles that would not have looked out of place during the Joseon dynasty and the period of Japanese colonial rule: the leader as the basis of moral authority and a militaristic approach. His government was based on the idea that the leader—Rhee himself—knew what was good for 'his' people—the South Korean population—together with repression and zero tolerance towards dissent. This was of course a far cry from the democratic ideals of the people choosing their leader and this leader serving the people. As a result, Rhee's government quickly moved away from democratic principles and became authoritarian.[49] This was topped by regular clashes with the United States, which had signed a Mutual Defence Treaty in October 1953 but whose politicians and policy-makers generally disliked Rhee.[50]

In May 1954, South Korea held its first National Assembly elections since the war. The elections gave Rhee's Liberal Party a majority of seats in parliament. Six months later, a two-thirds majority in the National Assembly abolished the two-term presidential limit set out in the constitution, allowing Rhee to run for a third term. He went on to win the May 1956 presidential election with 70 per cent of the vote.[51] A huge majority. But the victory margin was lower than in the 1948 and 1952 elections. And to the surprise of probably even himself, Democratic Party candidate Chang Myon narrowly defeated his Liberal Party opponent to win the vice-presidential election also held in May. Buoyed by a growing number of urban voters, Chang's election showed that the Rhee government could not be guaranteed the people's vote despite widespread vote rigging and voter manipulation. Indeed, the Liberal Party's share of the vote in urban centres was steadily declining while its share of the rural vote—more easily controlled by the government—remained almost unchanged.[52]

The Rhee government upped its violence in response to the emergence of a viable opposition. Cho Bong-am, the former independence activist who had run against Rhee in the 1956 election as an independent, was arrested in 1958 on charges of being a communist sympathizer—illegal under South Korea's National Security Law—and executed in 1959. His sentence would be overturned posthumously in 2011.[53] Chang, meanwhile, was shot shortly after his election as vice-president in 1956. He survived the assassination attempt, but there were suspicions that the shooter was linked to the Liberal Party.[54] Protests by university students and other groups opposed to the Rhee regime, meanwhile, were often met with violent crackdowns by the police.

Notwithstanding the ongoing repression, a viable left-wing opposition did emerge during the 1950s. Before the 1956 election, the Democratic Party was able to bring together the left-wing parties and movements opposed to the Rhee government.[55] This was the first of a long line of South Korean left-wing or liberal parties opposing right-wing or conservative parties. This division into two main blocs continues as of 2023. And even though the Democratic Party was not able to defeat Rhee, its emergence sowed the seeds of the eventual end of his presidency.

In terms of economic development, the Rhee government did little to implement viable policies to promote long-term growth. With corruption endemic and necessary to maintain power, Rhee turned his eyes towards the United States, and he successfully negotiated huge aid packages with South Korea's new ally. Between 1954 and 1960, when Rhee left office, South Korea received US$3.6 billion in grants and loans.[56] This was arguably Rhee's greatest achievement in the years after the war. In addition, in January 1958 the United States introduced nuclear weapons into South Korea. It was a commitment to its long-term presence to protect the country—but Seoul negotiated a payment from Washington in return. With the South Korean economy also propped up by the presence of US troops stationed in South Korea to prevent a new invasion by North Korea, the country became dependent on US largesse. Following from a huge withdrawal after the Korean War, the number of US troops in South Korea stabilized around 50,000 for the remainder of the Rhee presidency.[57] This further reduced the incentive for the South Korean leader to implement a proper economic plan.

But Rhee did understand that education was key if resource-poor South Korea was to escape poverty. With only 22 per cent of South Koreans able to read and write by the time the colonial period ended in 1945, South Korea's literacy rate was extremely low. Rhee pushed for universal primary education enrolment to address this issue. By 1960, the male illiteracy rate had been reduced to slightly above 15 per cent, a rate that women would reach six years later. Meanwhile, primary education enrolment levels were on their way to reach 90 per cent by the early 1960s.[58] This fixation with making universal education a cornerstone of

South Korea's future would continue for decades and still defines the country in the twenty-first century.

Education could help South Korea in the long-run. But for Rhee, it came at the expense of his political career. The Daegu Democracy Movement of February 1960, spearheaded by high school students to protest against Rhee's authoritarianism, signalled that better education could come with democratic ideals.[59] Rhee did win the March presidential vote unopposed after his opponent died a few weeks before the election.[60] In the vice-presidential election, however, Chang lost to Liberal Party candidate Lee Ki-poong, who obtained an unfathomable 79 per cent of the vote.[61] This led to student and labour protests to denounce the results of the rigged election. The April 19 Revolution—as it was later labelled—started in Masan, a port city in the southeastern corner of the country. With a 30 per cent urbanization rate in 1960, protests rapidly spread to Seoul and other cities across South Korea. A picture of Masan-based student Kim Ju-yul's head, disfigured by the grenade that killed him, galvanized protesters. This time, police violence was having the opposite effect of previous attempts to quell unrest. In late April 1960, Rhee was forced to resign. A month later, he went into exile in Hawaii. US President Eisenhower had encouraged Rhee to leave the country, and a jet belonging to the CIA actually flew Rhee covertly to US territory.[62] He would never be able to go back to South Korea; his body would be returned to the country in 1965, shortly after his death.

*South Korea's first democracy*

South Korea's first-ever democracy lasted all of thirteen months. The Second Republic was established in April 1960, as Rhee had effectively lost his grip on the country and was about to resign. In July, South Korean voters elected a new parliament. Its members then elected a different president for the first time: Yun Posun.[63] A former independence activist, he had been one of the founders of the Democratic Party. But South Koreans wanted to prevent the excesses of the Rhee government. Therefore, the Second Republic had established a parliamentary system. And indeed, the president was the head of state, while the prime minister was the head of government. Chang Myon was selected as the prime minister by parliament.[64] This way, he fulfilled his long-term dream of becoming the leader of his country.

The Chang government launched an ambitious plan to establish a real democracy. The new government ceased the political persecution of opponents and ended curbs to freedom of speech. As a result, demonstrations became commonplace. Different groups including workers and university students were enjoying their newfound freedom. This came as the government launched a new law to crack down on corruption: the Special Law for Dealing with Illicit Wealth Accumulation. Government officials, police officers, army officers and others who had benefitted from the corrupt practices of the Rhee government were put under investigation.[65] Ordinary South Koreans could feel that those at least partly responsible for their previous plight were now paying a price for their actions. For many in South Korea, this was the first time that the promises that the end of Japanese colonization had brought were within their grasp.

But even though South Koreans were regaining their freedom, most remained poor. Chang thus called for a 'Miracle on the Han River' in his New Year's address of 1961. The river running through Seoul had a centuries-old mystique, which it still maintains at the time of writing. It symbolized the promise that South Korea would one day be rich. So the Chang government announced South Korea's first-ever five-year economic plan.[66] In contrast to the Rhee government, the new ruling coalition seemed to have a blueprint to help develop the South Korean economy. Focusing on the modernization of the agricultural sector and the development of light industries such as textiles, shoes and food, the plan emphasized the area where South Korea had a comparative advantage: labour. Given the country's high fertility rate and with increasing numbers of South Koreans reaching working age,[67] the Chang government saw the future of South Korea in employing masses of people to produce goods cheaply. And the government also gave more power to bureaucrats with technical expertise to manage the economy.[68] These ideas stuck even after Chang was removed from power and the Second Republic itself was dissolved.

For the freedoms granted during the Second Republic laid the groundwork for its own end. Several generals in the South Korean army who were dissatisfied with the country's poor economic performance during the Rhee government were already plotting a coup to take power for themselves. They looked enviously across the East Sea, with their gaze reaching Korea's former colonial master. The Japanese economy was enjoying an economic boom, leading to a quick recovery from the ashes of the country's defeat in World War II. Many South Korean generals and other military officers had served in the Imperial Japanese Army, and several secretly admired their neighbour's militarist ethos.[69] Under the Chang government, the South Korean economy continued to be afflicted by high inflation and unemployment. Crime started to increase. Military leaders might have held their noses and accepted this for a short while. But the government also placed thousands of military officers under investigation for suppression of democracy or corruption. And in early May 1961, students launched demonstrations to demand immediate reunification with North Korea. Enough was enough. On 16 May, Park Chung-hee led a successful military coup and removed the Chang government from power.[70]

South Korea's first-ever experiment with democracy was over. It would be the last time that South Koreans would live in a truly democratic country until 1988. However, many of the groups that had tasted freedom would not forget it. For two decades, students would lead the resistance to the Park Chung-hee regime that followed the coup. Workers would often join. And Christians—especially Catholics—would also fight against the Park government.[71] After all, Chang Myon was a Catholic himself, and his faith had informed his opposition to the Rhee government. The Second Republic, therefore, was short-lived, but its spirit lived on. Indeed, to this day South Korea's constitution commits the state to uphold 'the democratic ideals of the April 19th Uprising of 1960 against injustice'.[72]

# 2

# THE PARK CHUNG-HEE ERA
## 1961–79

*Park Chung-hee's coup*

Some coups are bloody affairs. Others take place almost quietly, as if the legitimate government had not been removed from power. The '5.16 Revolution' (16 May Revolution), as it was called, belonged to this second category. Almost no shots were fired. Military vehicles did not have to occupy the streets for long. No political leader was assassinated. At dawn, South Koreans woke up in a democracy being overthrown by a coup. At dusk, they went to bed in the early stages of an authoritarian regime. Most South Koreans woke up poor and went to bed equally poor. The Chang Myon government had failed to bring about an immediate improvement in the economic conditions of ordinary South Koreans. With their empty stomachs, few of them thought about standing up for the democracy that was about to disappear. It was not worth fighting for, especially since the United States tacitly accepted the coup. In fact, the first demonstrations that Seoul witnessed were in support of the military uprising. Three days after the coup, Chang Myon and his cabinet resigned.[1] This was a lesson that the leader behind the coup took to heart: he had to make South Koreans wealthier, or else.

The leader was none other than Park Chung-hee, arguably the most important and consequential figure in the history of twentieth-century South Korea. Clad in his military uniform and often wearing sunglasses, surrounded by the military leaders and ordinary soldiers who supported his coup, Park cut a figure that many South Koreans liked. He was in command. Self-assured. This was in contrast to the civilian government that—many South Koreans felt—had lost its grip on the country. As Park told his fellow mutineers on the morning of the coup:

> We have been waiting for the civilian government to bring back order to the country. The Prime Minister and the Ministers, however, are mired in corruption, leading the country to the verge of collapse. We shall rise up against the government to save the country. We can accomplish our goals without bloodshed. Let us join in this Revolutionary Army to save the country.[2]

A dictator trying to justify himself? Without doubt. An assessment of the situation in 1961 that many South Koreans shared? Also true. Some, perhaps most, may not have agreed with the solution—a coup—but most thought that South Korea needed to change direction. They were tired of instability. Their country had been beset by violence and corruption for over a decade, and not even the end of the Korean War had helped improve their lives. Park brought the promise of a better future.

Park himself knew what poverty was. He was born into a *yangban* family, but his parents were poor. And they lived in Gumi, a small town far away from the lights and excitement of Seoul or Busan. Korea was still occupied by Japan. So Park did what many ambitious young Korean men did. He joined the Imperial Japanese Army. Park had expressed his admiration for Japan's rapid modernization. Joining its army came naturally to him, and he fought with the Japanese forces during World War II. Once the war was over and Korea regained its independence, Park laid low. He enrolled in the newly established Korea Military Academy and prepared to move up the military ranks. But Park had joined the Workers' Party of South Korea. A communist sympathizer in a country whose leaders abhorred communism, he was arrested and sentenced to death. His life spared at the urging of South Korean military leaders, Park fought in the Korean War and then continued his rapid rise. In 1958, he was promoted to major general.[3] He had become one of the most powerful men in the Korean army. By the time of the 1961 coup, he was also a charismatic leader who commanded his soldiers' respect.

Park took little time in consolidating power. Within a month and a half of the coup, he had become the chairman of the Supreme Council for National Reconstruction—the provisional military government that replaced the Second Republic.[4] Park then promoted himself to full general in November 1961. He also helped establish the Korean Central Intelligence Agency (KCIA). The inspiration behind this body was obvious. But this was not a 'Korean CIA'. Throughout Park's time in power and later Chun Doo-hwan's presidency, the KCIA became the most feared organization in all of South Korea. It engaged in arrests, torture, kidnappings and, on occasion, assassinations. Anyone suspected of being pro-communist, pro-North Korean or simply anti-government could fall prey to the KCIA.[5] Its reign of terror would only come to an end in 1988, after South Korea became a democracy. Its early actions were but a presage of the Park government's moves towards authoritarianism and militarism.

But at least in the early stages of his time in power, Park craved legitimacy. Yun Posun remained as president as a way to legitimize the coup. He would only resign in March 1962, when he sought to distance himself from the growing authoritarianism encroaching on South Korean politics. Park thus also became acting president.[6] By then, Park had already announced his January 1962 five-year plan to kick-start economic growth. Much like that launched by the Chang government two years before, Park's plan focused on textiles and light industry as the key engines to launch South Korea on the path towards economic development.[7] Furthermore, Park also introduced a number of policies to claim the spirit of the April Revolution that had ultimately led to the downfall of Rhee. They included writing off the debt of impoverished peasants, supporting SMEs and the arrests of criminals who had supported Rhee's corrupt government.[8] Park had decided that development would be the basis of his government and hoped-for popularity, not 'old-fashioned' Confucian ideas about the role of the leader and his subjects.

Under pressure from the John F. Kennedy administration in the United States and aware that there was growing domestic concern at his accumulation of power, Park then announced an election to be held in October 1963. Despite his support for certain authoritarian regimes and violent anti-communist revolts, the newly elected Kennedy presented democracy promotion as a way for the United States to 'win' the Cold War by example rather than through force. As Park's authoritarian rule sat uncomfortably with this purported policy, the Kennedy administration pressed for a return to democratic and civilian rule.[9] Meanwhile, an increasing number of South Koreans had buyer's remorse about Park. The economic situation was not improving. They could not vote for their president. And whereas violence had decreased, this had come as a result of growing repression.[10] In 1963, South Korea was hardly in a better position than at the time of the 1961 coup.

*Authoritarianism during the Third Republic*

South Korea finally held a presidential election in October 1963. Park was forced to step down from the military to run for the civilian presidency, which suggested that he might have been willing to shed militarism from public life. Park then ran a fairly clean campaign, with Yun—the previous president—as his main opponent. Indeed, measured by the standards of previous South Korean elections, this one was a hotly contested affair. There was little voter suppression, and all candidates had a fair chance to make their pitches to South Korean voters. As a result, Park's victory was far from certain. The civilian opposition had coalesced around Yun to avoid splitting the 'civilian' vote. As the day of the vote approached, it looked like a wise decision. When viewed from Seoul, it seemed as if Yun would prevail. But with 46.6 per cent of the vote against his opponent's 45.1 per cent, Park narrowly won the election. Yun indeed won comfortably in Seoul and carried the four richer northern regions. Park, in contrast, prevailed in the five southern, more agrarian provinces plus Jeju Island.[11] The country was split. Park had yet to convince urban workers and students that he was the right man for the job.

Now a democratically elected president, Park moved quickly to shore up his power base. In November, his Democratic Republican Party received a third of the vote in the legislative election. This result translated into over 60 per cent of the seats in the National Assembly, which allowed the Park government to establish the Third Republic in December.[12] Park could now claim that South Korea had returned to civilian government. It was sufficient to please the United States, now that Lyndon B. Johnson had become the new US president following the assassination of Kennedy in November.

But Park soon started to make authoritarian moves. His government put anti-communism at the heart of domestic politics. In fact, anti-communism was tied to *minjok*. Koreans were a single ethnic group, but true (South) Koreans were anti-communist. Thus the leaders of North Korea could not be truly Korean and those who supported their ideas were at the very least suspect. From the president's perspective, South Korea was under threat both from a possible North Korean invasion and from communist sympathizers inside the country.[13] And he was the 'saviour' of South Korea preventing its downfall to communists from the North and from within.

In this context, the KCIA grew more powerful, with the government looking the other way when not encouraging its illegal arrests, kidnappings and other actions. The police and the military took an outsized role in civilian life and were frequently deployed to quell dissent. The Park government used violence and threatened martial law whenever it felt demonstrations might be getting out of hand.[14] Many South Koreans simply went along as their country became more authoritarian whether out of support for Park or simply from exhaustion following years of division and rancour.

There were other South Koreans, however, who chose to resist. The main opposition figures were Yun, Kim Young-sam and Kim Dae-jung, together with Kim Jong-pil; the last three came to be known as the 'Three Kims'. Kim Young-sam had entered politics after the Korean War. He became a prominent critic of Rhee first and Park afterwards. Hailing from Geoje Island in the south-eastern corner of the Korean Peninsula, Kim Young-sam held a degree in philosophy from Seoul National University, which marked him as an intellectual opposed to the crippling authoritarianism of South Korean politics.[15] Kim Dae-jung, meanwhile, had also entered politics in the 1950s and had won a seat in the National Assembly both in 1961 and 1963.

Charismatic and a skilled orator, he came to be known for his power base in Jeolla Province—where he was born—located in the south-western tip of the Korean Peninsula. His pointed criticism of the Park regime made him a clear target.[16] After Yun lost the 1967 election against Park, these two Kims became the main thorn in the sides of South Korean dictators throughout the 1970s and 1980s. As for Kim Jong-pil, he embodied a more moderate face of the Park regime. Married to Park's niece, Kim took part in his May 1961 coup, founded the KCIA and served as his prime minister in 1971–5.[17] But he would eventually help the two other Kims become presidents in the 1990s. He never had the top job himself, but he dominated South Korean politics for decades.

University students, religious groups and workers were the three main groups resisting the growing authoritarianism of the Park regime. They all had reasons for their opposition to the Park government. Students demanded the restoration of a full democracy. They had not forgotten the promises of the 1960–1 period. And, for the most part, they had not voted for Park anyway. Religious groups, meanwhile, objected to Park's authoritarianism on moral grounds. Catholic and Buddhist leaders, in particular, held this view. As for workers, they gained a sense of class consciousness as they powered South Korea's economic growth in return for meagre wages.[18] For back in the 1960s and 1970s, South Koreans were the cheap labour making the shoes, shirts, toys or electronics that US consumers craved.

Students, in particular, led mass demonstrations against the Park government in 1964. The reason? In February, the Park government had announced its intention to normalize diplomatic relations with none other than the former colonial master—Japan. Chang had entertained the same idea, but he had run out of time to move ahead. In the case of Park, his position seemed safe and his party had control of the National Assembly. In the eyes of the opposition, he had the tools to move ahead with normalization. Thus, students began a hunger strike in March. In June, over 10,000 of them took to the streets of Seoul. The government responded by declaring martial law on 3 June. The police arrested over 1,000 students, politicians and other opponents of normalization.[19] But they were ultimately proved right: Park had the power to implement a decision that most South Koreans opposed. In June 1965, the National Assembly approved the Treaty on Basic Relations between Japan and the Republic of Korea. The treaty, however, did not settle individual claims for compensation. In the eyes of many South Koreans, Japan and their own authoritarian government had simply ignored the suffering of South Koreans enslaved during the colonial period.[20] This position would eventually be endorsed by the United Nations decades after the treaty was signed.[21] But Park had won. There would be no other significant demonstrations over this issue.

This period was also marked by another controversial decision that showed Park's ability, and willingness, to press ahead with his preferred policies. In 1964, the government announced the deployment of the South Korean army in support of US troops fighting in the Vietnam War. Participation in the war, of course, fitted perfectly well with Park's anti-communism. But Rhee had already put forward the idea to deploy South Korean troops in Vietnam in the 1950s. And once again, it was Park who was able to implement a policy where previous governments had failed. In February 1965, the first South Korean soldiers set foot in South Vietnam. The country's military would remain in the South East Asian country until 1973.[22] In the process, Park was projecting an image as someone who could carry his policies through.

As if to make up for these controversial decisions, Park commissioned a statue of one of the greatest Koreans of them all in the most iconic place in modern South Korea. In March 1967, Park commissioned Seoul National University professor Kim

Se-jung to produce a statue of Admiral Yi Sun-sin, to be placed at the intersection between a road leading to Gyeongbokgung—the palace where Joseon emperors sat—and another road leading to Insadong and Tapgol Park, where South Korea's declaration of independence was read. The 6.3-metre tall statue, sitting on a 16.8-metre pedestal, was unveiled thirteen months later, in April 1968.[23] The statue remains in place to this day. For Yi transcended and continues to transcend ideological divisions. With the statue in place, Park hoped that no one could still call him pro-Japanese.

Earlier, the May 1967 election had pitted Park against Yun as his main opponent for a second time. On this occasion, Park prevailed with over 51 per cent of the vote against Yun's 40.9 per cent. This time, Park carried the five eastern provinces of the country plus Jeju Island. Yun, meanwhile, won in Seoul—albeit with a smaller majority—plus the four provinces in the western part of South Korea.[24] One month later, Park's party renewed its majority in the National Assembly. Growing domestic repression had undoubtedly helped Park retain power. But Park was also becoming more popular thanks to economic growth and greater domestic stability.

Park's popularity and authoritarianism grew from January 1968. That month, a commando unit composed of thirty-one North Koreans was intercepted within 100 metres of the Blue House, then the official residence of the South Korean president. Disguised as soldiers and civilians, they had a single goal in mind: to kill Park, along with any other senior government officials they might encounter. The South Korean police and military defeated the assassination plot with all but one of the North Korean commandoes killed or committing suicide.[25] Park had survived. His aura only increased.

To the surprise of almost no one, Park decided that he wanted to stay in power beyond his constitutionally mandated two-term limit. To the surprise of exactly no one, the opposition rejected and denounced this possibility. And also to the surprise of exactly the same number of people, the Democratic Republican Party stream-rolled the constitutional amendment allowing Park to run for a third time. A referendum held in October 1969 confirmed the decision by the National Assembly. Two-thirds of South Korean voters approved the constitutional change. The government certainly interfered in the referendum. But Park cleverly made the referendum a vote of confidence on his leadership, threatening to resign if the amendment was not approved. And many South Koreans preferred his increasingly authoritarian but certainly effective leadership style to the chaos that could come, were Park to resign. The opposition nevertheless labelled the amendment a 'second coup'.[26] It prepared to try to defeat Park at the next presidential election.

In April 1971, Park faced Kim Dae-jung. The young Kim—still in his forties—was among a new generation of opposition politicians who had successfully manoeuvred to take control of the party over the older generation represented by Yun. The general expectation among the South Korean public was that Park would win easily. He was popular, repression was commonplace, the economy was growing and Kim had to contend with his young age—which did not sit well among the many South Koreans still influenced by Confucian ideas. Park won, but his victory margin was lower than it had been in 1967: he received slightly over 53 per cent of votes against Kim's 45.2 per cent.[27] And Kim carried Seoul easily. Park realized that he could not be assured of winning future elections, particularly as more South Koreans moved to cities and entertained ideas of post-authoritarian politics. The solution was obvious. His authoritarian regime would soon become a full-fledged dictatorship.

## *Miracle on the Han River*

*Seonjinguk.* Advanced nation. *Hujinguk.* Backward country. Park explained his regime's move away from democracy in fairly simple terms: his goal was to transform the backward South Korea into an advanced nation in which its people could live comfortably. He repeatedly talked about *joguk geundaehwa*: modernization of the motherland.[28] In fact, Park tied *minjok* to developmentalism as well. Race was important. Anti-communism too. And becoming an advanced nation could drive Korean unification under South Korean—that is, non-communist—terms. After all, Korea had been a rich and technologically advanced country during the Joseon dynasty. It was only natural for (South) Korea to become advanced again. *Seonjinguk* would go on to inform South Korean authoritarian rule all the way until the restoration of a full democracy in 1988. Or to justify a dictatorship, for those opposed to Park and his successor. As Park said in his 1964 National Liberation Day address: 'Not only meaningful progress towards democracy but also promotion of national might to overcome communism and to unify the nation ultimately depend upon the success or failure of economic policy.'[29]

Park's push to make South Korea an economically advanced country proved successful. In academic jargon, South Korea underwent what is known as 'compressed development'. In barely two to three decades, the South Korean economy moved through stages of development that took Western countries between 100 and 200 years to complete. A *'pali pali'* ('hurry, hurry') culture developed. South Korea had to develop, and fast. Annual GDP growth averaged over 10 per cent between 1963 and 1979, when Park's rule ended.[30] The agricultural sector as a share of overall output went down, from a whisker above 29 per cent in 1970 to under 21 per cent in 1979. Meanwhile, the share of the industrial sector increased from slightly over 27 per cent to over 35 per cent during that same period.[31] The value of exports increased from a paltry US$157 million in 1963 to almost US$16 billion in 1979—over 100 times more.[32] Not bad for a country dismissed as a hopeless case by the World Bank in 1963 due to 'the intractable nature of Korea's basic economic weakness'.[33]

For South Koreans, the pace of change was simply astonishing. A South Korean born in 1920 would probably have lived in dire poverty in the countryside. This person's house would probably have been little more than four walls and a roof, with no running water or inside toilet. This person would have worked the land owned by a *yangban*, hopefully scraping enough food to get by. Or worse. This person could have been made a slave and sent to a factory in Japan or a sex facility in Manchuria. By 1979 and before turning fifty, this same South Korean could have become a middle-class worker and would live in a fairly modern apartment equipped with a TV, a radio set and a fridge. And a nice toilet. From the apartment's window, this person would see the factories popping up almost daily in Seoul, Busan, Daegu or Daejeon. They would be working a reasonably well-paid job in a factory or an office, spending the week's day off watching a movie or listening to the latest ballad. And if this person had done well enough, a holiday to Jeju Island awaited.

And the very visible hand of the government was everywhere to be seen for this average South Korean. Shortly after his coup, Park had set up an Economic Planning Board to formulate and coordinate economic policy. Park was its head. In fact, he made all the major economic decisions. Key ministers would attend, led by the minister of trade and industry in charge of industrial policy. Throughout the 1960s and most of the 1970s, it would have been difficult to distinguish the economic plans of the two Koreas. Industrialization was king. The minister of finance in charge of managing state-owned banks was another key minister in attendance. For credit was extended by these banks, which meant that the government controlled the allocation of funding across the economy.[34] Populated by some of the brightest South Korean minds, the Economic Planning Board dominated South Korea's economic life during the Park years.

The *chaebol* became the other dominant force in the South Korean economy during Park's rule. Literally meaning 'wealth clan', *chaebol* are large industrial conglomerates dominated by a single family. Their origins can be traced back to small firms set up by entrepreneurial Koreans in the period between the late stages of Japan's colonial rule and the aftermath of the Korean War. Samsung was founded in 1938, Hanjin in 1945, Hyundai and LG—the latter established as Lucky Chemical Industrial— in 1947 and SK in 1953. *Chaebol* generally started as businesses far removed from those they would later become better known for. Famously, Samsung started as a grocery trading firm with some manufacturing of flour and textiles on the side.[35] But *chaebol* quickly expanded, becoming highly diversified conglomerates with complex ownership structures.

Park and the *chaebol* were a match made in heaven. Park wanted to exercise control over the South Korean economy, with domestic firms driving growth. The *chaebol* had business acumen and harboured the same dream of a South Korean economy dominated by domestic firms. If possible, of course, by themselves. The Park government offered selected *chaebol* licences and cheap credit while shielding them from competition, mainly through an economic environment hostile to would-be foreign competitors.[36] *Chaebol* chairmen such as Hyundai's Chung Ju-yung, LG's Koo In-hwoi and his son Koo Ja-kyung, Samsung's Lee Byung-chul and SK's Chey Jong-hyon became household names. They found themselves advising the Economic Planning Board. There were some frictions, certainly, since Park's micromanagement of the economy included setting economic goals that the *chaebol* had to achieve.[37] And sometimes there were more than frictions. Park could threaten to imprison *chaebol* leaders who refused to comply with his demands, often under corruption charges. *Chaebol* leaders could thus either work with the Park government—or lose everything they had worked to build and end up in a cell.[38] Park and the *chaebol* consequently ended up in a symbiotic relationship. What was good for one of them was good for the other. And for the South Korean economy. For young, ambitious university graduates from the country's top universities, there was only one dream: to join a *chaebol* and enjoy the riches and status that a job in any of them promised.

Equipped with total control over economic policy and acquiescent *chaebol*, Park set his *seonjinguk* plan in motion. In 1967, the same year as his re-election, the government launched its second five-year plan. The plan had a decidedly export-oriented face.[39] South Korea would use its cheap and abundant labour to become a 'factory' for the United States and the rest of the Western world.

That same year, the government opened the Guro Industrial Complex. Located south of the Han River that gave its name to South Korea's economic miracle, this was the first complex of its kind in the country.[40] Men and, increasingly, women were cramped in massive rooms producing clothes, shoes and other cheap products. In 2000, it would be rebranded as Guro Digital Complex, a testament to the astonishing transformation that this area in south-west Seoul came to symbolize. It is a place that anyone interested in the economic history of South Korea ought to visit. Back in 1967, the government also selected Korea Tungsten to form a joint venture to run a steel mill in Pohang, a seaport city towards the country's south-east. One year later, Pohang Iron and Steel was founded.[41] Known as POSCO at the time of writing, the firm was tasked with ensuring South Korea would become self-sufficient in steel production. South Korea should be a factory for American and European consumers, yes. But it should also become less reliant on foreign materials.

The Guro Industrial Complex and POSCO came to exemplify the 'miracle on the Han River'. But the Park government dreamt big. For now, it was an economic shrimp. But one day, South Korea would be an economic whale able to compete head-to-head with the United States, Japan and Western Europe. To achieve this aim, the government invested heavily in education. By 1979, enrolment in secondary education had reached 79 per cent of the population,[42] and over 30 per cent of young South Koreans were attending university.[43] The Park government preferred university students to focus on engineering and other technical subjects. So it launched KAIST in 1971,[44] South Korea's answer to MIT and as of 2023 a place to visit to understand the future of the South Korean economy. The government also started to develop a universal healthcare system. Inspired by the Western European model, Park wanted healthy workers to help South Korea escape poverty. In 1977, he launched a compulsory health insurance system for workers in private firms. Government employees were added in 1979.[45] Meanwhile, Hyundai and other *chaebol* were building the roads, railways, airports and seaports required to power the economy. In 1974, line 1 of the Seoul subway was opened.[46] The capital's commuters had to get to work more quickly. Plus—as governments across the world know—a subway station near someone's home can help to shore up the support of the local population.

But for all the talk of economic nationalism, South Korea also benefitted from its links with the outside world. Above all, the United States provided large amounts of aid and investment. It is estimated that up to US$8.3 billion in aid flowed to South Korea during the Park years.[47] US firms provided much-needed hard currency, technology transfers and technical expertise. The US government also gave South Korean exporters preferential access to the country's market. And participation in the Vietnam War gave a further boost to US aid and its favourable treatment of

South Korea, with South Korean firms becoming preferred suppliers of military provisions to US troops fighting in the South East Asian country.[48] Park was both anti-communist and laser-focused on economic development. The Vietnam War helped both. Finally, US soldiers stationed in South Korea continued to be major spenders. Successive US governments were encouraged to support South Korea due to Park's staunch anti-communism and the country's geopolitical importance.

The economic compensation Japan provided to South Korea following the normalization of diplomatic relations in 1965 also helped support economic growth. Japan provided US$500 million in reparation payments and US$300 million in commercial loans following the agreement. The Park government used this money to boost the coffers of state-owned banks lending to the *chaebol*, to support new industries—particularly POSCO—and to upgrade the country's infrastructure. Some Japanese *keiretsu*—firm networks allied with each other—also started to outsource part of their production to their neighbouring country. Japanese experts also offered some technical assistance as South Korea sought to develop its steel, petrochemical and machinery industries.[49] The United States encouraged this cooperation as a way to start to heal relations between its two allies.

The South Korean economy also received a boost from remittances sent by South Korean emigrants. The government encouraged the country's best students to study in the United States. Many of them stayed there. They were joined by scores of South Korean families dreaming of a better life once the Johnson government passed the Immigration and Nationality Act of 1965, which eliminated de facto discrimination against Asians in US immigration policy.[50] By 1979, hundreds of thousands of South Koreans had moved to the United States.[51] In addition, up to 20,000 South Koreans moved to West Germany. Experiencing labour shortages, the West German government particularly encouraged the migration of South Korean mine workers and nurses.[52] Other European countries, some countries in the Middle East, such as Saudi Arabia, and Japan also became preferred destinations for South Korean emigrants. It is impossible to calculate the value of the remittances that they sent back home, but it is undeniable that they helped to boost the South Korean economy from the 1960s onwards.

*The dark side of economic development*

There were downsides to Park's push for all-out economic development. Jeon Tae-il is commemorated in the 1995 movie *A Single Spark*. In 1996, a street in central Seoul was named after him. His 2001 posthumous biography became a best-seller. One can visit his memorial hall or a statue of him, both in central Seoul. On 13 November 2020, his family received a state medal posthumously awarded to Jeon. By then, his mother, Lee So-sun, had also been well known for decades in her own right. His younger sister, Jeon Soon-ok, had served in the National Assembly.[53] Jeon Tae-il is a name that few outside South Korea know. Yet it is a name that every South Korean worker celebrates.

Jeon was a labour activist who, on 13 November 1970 and at the age of twenty-two, burned himself to death. He did so in protest against the conditions he and his fellow sewing workers—over 90 per cent of them young girls—had to endure, and the conditions that most South Korean workers had to suffer in their factories at the time. His last words were, 'do not let my death be in vain!'[54] And in vain it was not. Jeon was credited with sparking South Korea's labour movement. He was certainly not the only person behind it: his own mother, for example, spent her life pushing for better conditions for South Korean workers. But Jeon's ultimate sacrifice spurred a process to improve the conditions of workers up and down the country. In the year that Jeon died, the average pay for sewing workers for a sixteen-hour shift was around KRW100 per day, or less than US$1.[55] Many workers had perhaps two or three days off per month. It was only from the 1970s and, especially, the 1980s onwards that salaries started to improve for most South Korean workers. By then, Jeon's self-sacrifice and the efforts of countless South Korean workers had resulted in the creation of over 2,500 independent trade unions.

Lee Hyo-jae exemplified the solution to another problem exacerbated by the focus on economic growth: sexism. Women were joining the workforce in droves. And they were not only working in factories. Careers such as journalism or academia started to see a small but growing influx of women. 'Office ladies' were becoming commonplace, almost invariably working the secretarial jobs that men shunned. But more often than not, women had to leave their careers once they had children or even as soon as they got married. 'Yakult *ajummas*' became ubiquitous, pulling carts of this fermented drink around cities and towns. 'Insurance *ajummas*' went door to door selling life, home and other types of insurance. *Ajummas*—married or middle-aged women—working from home in all sorts of odd jobs from sewing to assembling carboard boxes were also common.[56] These were considered acceptable jobs for *ajummas*, as opposed to a professional career.

Sexism was exacerbated by Confucian-infused ideas and their interplay with the new reality of the South Korean economy. Under the *hoju* system—introduced in 1953 and based on Confucian thought—a man was legally considered a household's head. Upon his death, the first-born son rather than the wife became the head. Women, therefore, technically joined their husband's family upon marriage, leading to discrimination in inheritance, access to bank accounts and all sorts of economic matters.[57] *Hoju* could also be used as one of the justifications to pay women less for the same type of job. After all—the thinking went—women would only work until they found a husband who would take care of them. Until then, the father or older brother would do the same. Many men thought that girls were an economic burden. Even though abortion was technically illegal under a 1953 law and then only allowed under special circumstances from 1973 onwards, abortion of female foetuses became an open secret.[58] After all, the Park government was launching campaign after campaign to reduce the fertility rate. For the most part, political leaders and society at large looked the other way when it came to abortion.

Which takes us to Lee, who became the most recognizable figure of the women's rights movement in South Korea and a symbol for many people around the country. In 1958, she founded the Department of Sociology at Ewha Womans University, arguably home to South Korea's most beautiful university campus and the university that did the most to educate women during the years of dictatorship. It was here that Lee would eventually launch South Korea's first women's studies course in 1977. At university, she went on to educate many future women leaders. But Lee was more than an educator. Much more. Lee was an activist. Even better: a very effective one. She led campaigns to abolish the *hoju* system and related patriarchal laws and practices. She led campaigns to obtain equal pay and the same retirement age for women.[59] And not only did she press for women's rights on the streets but her thoughts became canon for future generations of South Korean feminist leaders. Lee was certainly not the only one who fought for equality between women and men. But no one did more than her to fight against sexism during the Park era, a fight she then carried on throughout the Chun Doo-hwan years.

Corruption was yet another issue affecting the South Korean economy. In 1960, the *New York Times* carried the following headline: 'Seoul Unit Set Up to Bar Aid Abuse'. The article went

65

on to detail how the post-April Revolution government wanted to stamp out the corruption attributed to the Rhee government.[60] In 1979, the *New York Times'* obituary of Park started with the line: 'His enemies called him a corrupt and ruthless dictator'.[61] This pointed to an issue that opponents of Park's government liked to highlight: Park and his family, government officials and the *chaebol*-owning families formed a close-knit elite. And the Park family and his government officials received payments in exchange for awarding contracts or looking the other way when required.[62] This was not necessarily surprising. But it was problematic.

One last problem was the growing urban–rural divide. South Korea was essentially becoming two separate countries, with rich industrialized cities on the one hand and poorer rural villages on the other. To address this issue, Park launched the Saemaul Undong (New Village Movement) in April 1970. Based on a community spirit, the movement promoted cooperation among village inhabitants by providing them with materials free of charge for them to build whatever they considered necessary. The movement was very successful in improving agricultural production, income and village life more generally.[63] Most notably, housing improved dramatically across the countryside. Many South Koreans living in rural villages were enjoying modern housing for the first time in the history of their clans. So it came as no surprise that the countryside became a stronghold of support for Park. As of 2023, someone travelling around South Korea can see modern buildings and infrastructure dotted around the villages of the country. Jobs, however, are scarce compared to big cities. The Saemaul Undong movement helped to start the former. Economic development during the Park years paved the way for the latter. The urban–rural divide did not disappear.

*Dreams of reunification*

Park understood that reunification with North Korea would eliminate any lingering questions about his legitimacy. Even more: reunification would cement his place in Korean history. As a staunch anti-communist, Park dreamt of Korean reunification under South Korean terms. He had made this clear in his first New Year's address as the new South Korean president, in 1964.[64] But he was fully aware that the realities of the division and the broader geopolitical context of the Cold War meant that an invasion of North Korea was not an option. Even if Park had wanted to launch a full-scale attack on South Korea's northern neighbour, the United States would have sought to stop it out of fear of a bigger conflict also involving China and the Soviet Union.

The South Korean president, therefore, set out to smooth relations with Kim Il-sung. The North Korean leader, however, had a different idea in mind. Prevented by China and the Soviet Union from launching a new invasion, he set out to undermine South Korea from across the DMZ and across the globe. Between 1968 and 1971, North Korean soldiers provoked incidents along the DMZ, commandoes from the communist country tried to infiltrate their capitalist neighbour multiple times and agents hijacked a South Korean plane.[65] Kim seemed to have a cunning plan in mind. With the United States embroiled in the Vietnam War, proxy wars, anti-communist coups and other activities across the world, raising tensions across the DMZ could make Johnson rethink Washington's commitment to the protection of South Korea, particularly since the Park regime sometimes retaliated against North Korea without consultation. The plan did not work. But it put a temporary end to Park's plans to improve inter-Korean relations.

And then history took a monumental turn. In February 1972, US President Richard Nixon stepped down from his plane. He was taking a monumental step. He had travelled to Beijing to meet with Chinese Communist Party Chairman Mao Zedong. The meeting between the two leaders capped 'the week that changed the world', in Nixon's own words.[66] For once, this was not an exaggeration. The Chinese leader agreed not to attempt to invade Taiwan to reunify China under Beijing's model. In return, China replaced Taiwan in the United Nations and other multilateral fora. The visit opened the door for China and Japan to normalize diplomatic relations only seven months after Nixon's visit. And in 1979, Washington and Beijing would finally establish diplomatic relations as well.[67]

Park and Kim Il-sung were astonished. The two Koreas grasped the opportunity in front of them with both hands. On 4 July 1972, they issued the North–South Joint Communiqué. This was the first document signed by both Koreas since their country was divided. It established three principles for reunification: independence, peace and national unity. The two Koreas were done with being a shrimp among whales. Above all, reunification would be the result of an independent process without foreign interference. The Koreas were also done with violence. Reunification would be achieved through peaceful means. And unity between the peoples of the two Koreas should precede and transcend ideological differences.[68] The joint communiqué also included some practical measures to guarantee its implementation. The Taedong River Centre in Pyongyang hosted official inter-Korean Red Cross talks between late August and early September. After twenty-five preliminary meetings dating back to August 1971, they were holding actual discussions to reunite separated families.[69] South Koreans were expectant. Could they be witnessing the first steps towards making Korea one again?

The answer came very quickly. The niceties of the joint communiqué were not soon to be repeated. A few more rounds of Red Cross talks proved inconclusive. Soon South Korea would

take a decidedly more authoritarian turn. US–China normalization talks stalled, due to the Watergate scandal involving Nixon
first and the death of Mao and subsequent instability in China
afterwards. Thus, developments in South Korea and in the
broader geopolitical context affected the mood around inter-
Korean relations. Kim then sent new infiltrators to South Korea.
South Korean soldiers discovered three infiltration tunnels dug
under the DMZ. The third one was big enough to allow up to
30,000 soldiers, accompanied by light artillery, to infiltrate South
Korea every hour.[70] Between 1973 and 1976, North Korea conducted a campaign of provocations around five strategically
important islands in the West Sea (Yellow Sea), which were
under the military control of the UN Command.[71] Park's dream
of reunification remained that, a dream.

*The Yushin Constitution years*

A self-coup is uncommon. But then, Park was not a leader of the
common type. Despite high rates of economic growth and an
expanding middle class, resistance to Park's rule had been growing. Opposition politicians had proved their popularity in the
1971 election. Many students and workers continued to oppose
the regime. Religious groups also became more vocal, particularly
Catholics and Buddhists. Writers and intellectuals also found
ways to criticize the regime despite high levels of censorship.
And South Koreans living in the country's south-west joined the
growing chorus criticizing the Park regime, since they felt that
Seoul and the south-east were receiving favourable treatment
from the government. After all, Park lived in the capital and
hailed from Gumi. The general perception was that those two
regions were treated favourably.

Park was also concerned about the alliance with the United
States. Nixon was implementing a less stridently anti-communist

policy. Aside from his rapprochement with China, it was becoming clear that the new US president wanted to pull out of the Vietnam War. With Park basing his rule on anti-communism, there was a real threat that the United States might at some point consider South Korea dispensable. These concerns only grew in 1971, when Nixon announced his decision to withdraw 20,000 troops from South Korea.[72] This might not have been a shock, for Nixon had already been insisting that South Korea should take more responsibility for its own security for a couple of years. But Park did not welcome the announcement. Following the withdrawal, some 40,000 US troops would remain on South Korean soil.[73] For all his success on the economic front, the impression was that Park was losing his grip on relations with the United States.

It was in this context that Park declared martial law, dissolved the National Assembly and suspended the constitution in October 1972. This was the 'Yushin' (Restoration) that promised to revitalize South Korea. Opposition politicians, the South Korean population, the US government and even most pro-government National Assembly members were unaware that a self-coup was coming. But restoration could only come with a new regime. Park thus commissioned a National Council to come up with a new constitution. In November, the Yushin Constitution was approved with over 92 per cent of the vote on a turnout of almost the same figure—91.9 per cent.[74] If these numbers sound far-fetched, it is because they were. The vote was marred by accusations of fraud. But the country remained under martial law. Therefore, protests against the new constitution and the result of the referendum were subdued. In a matter of months, South Koreans had gone from the dream of reunification to the reality of living under a dictatorship.

For the Yushin Constitution established a full-blown dictatorial regime. This was not a democratic regime imbued with authoritarianism and repression. The authoritarianism and the repression continued. But the regime was not democratic anymore. Among the changes introduced by the new constitution, three stood out. To begin with, presidential term limits were abolished. Park could run for president for as long as he wanted. In addition, the direct election of the president was also eliminated. A National Council for Reunification controlled by Park would elect the president. Finally, the president appointed a third of the members of the National Assembly.[75] This guaranteed that he would have a majority. Not that it mattered much, since the new constitution effectively guaranteed that Park also had the right to rule by decree and de facto institutionalized restrictions akin to the permanent application of martial law.

In December, the electoral college elected Park—the only candidate—and the Fourth Republic began.[76] Repression reached new heights. The KCIA acted with impunity. Its tentacles now even reached beyond South Korea. Opposition leader Kim Dae-jung had been in exile since 1971, following a suspected assassination attempt. In August 1973, Kim was kidnapped in a Tokyo hotel. As a boat was carrying him away from Japan, his captors attached a weight to his wrists. A devout Catholic, Kim was saying his last prayers.[77] Suddenly, a Japanese aircraft flew over the boat: probably a reconnaissance plane. Back in South Korea, US Ambassador Philip Habib and his Japanese counterpart Ushiroku Torao had interceded to spare Kim's life. He was spared.[78] But others were not so lucky. Not only the KCIA but the police and the military also engaged in kidnapping, torture and executions. The courts also found it easy to condemn alleged opponents of the Park regime to death.

On 15 August 1974, Park's dictatorial instincts became even more personal. The president was giving a speech to celebrate National Liberation Day. The National Theatre of Korea was packed to the rafters, full of Park's supporters. Or almost full. Mun Se-gwang, a Zainichi Korean,[79] had made his way to the theatre. With a gun. He took out the gun but injured himself by inadvertently firing it. Having alerted the security services, Mun ran towards the stage as he aimed at Park. He missed the president. But one of the bullets hit his wife, Yuk Young-soo. Yuk was rushed to the hospital. In the meantime, Park continued his speech. The audience in the theatre did not know what to do. Millions watching on KBS—the national TV broadcaster—were astonished. Park finished his speech and left the theatre. By night, he was a widow. Yuk had not survived despite five hours of surgery.[80] His daughter, twenty-two-year-old Park Geun-hye, became the first lady. One day, she would become the first female president of South Korea. But that would be the future. With the assassination of his wife, Park's bedrock was gone. As the president wrote in his diary, Yuk's death brought him great sorrow. It also made him less willing to trust others.[81] Park intensified the crackdown on his opponents, whether real or imaginary.

The KCIA became even bolder, both domestically and overseas. Inside South Korea, the April 1975 People's Revolutionary Party incident was a case in point. In 1974–5, the KCIA arrested over 1,000 left-wing South Koreans allegedly involved in re-establishing this party in support of North Korea. Hundreds were sentenced to prison. Eight were sentenced to death in April 1975 and executed less than twenty hours later.[82] Outside South Korea, the KCIA launched a plot in Washington, DC, to bribe congressmen to influence US policy. Tongsun Park, a well-connected businessman, was accused of distributing the bribes and passing on the messages from the KCIA. Park fled the United States when the bribery scandal became public, first flying to London and afterwards to Seoul. Well known in Washington, DC before the scandal broke due to his extravagant parties, he only returned to the US capital in 1978 for a hearing in which he testified in return for his immunity. Even though only one congressman went to prison, at least ten of them were involved in the scandal.[83] For the KCIA, there were no limits to how bold its actions could be.

## Consolidation of the middle class

The 1970s were witness to another phenomenon new to Korean history: the emergence and consolidation of a mass middle class. For the first time, large numbers of (South) Koreans were making enough money to escape a subsistence economy. They had enough disposable income to spend it on that hobby they always wanted to pick up, buy themselves that nice treat that only one year before seemed unaffordable or take that short holiday they fully deserved. Indeed, mass consumer culture was 'born' in South Korea in the 1970s. Cho Yong-pil made South Koreans dance, asking his brother to 'Come Back to Busan Port'.[84] Youn Yuh-jung transported them to the glory days of the Joseon dynasty from their TVs with her unforgettable portrayal of royal concubine Jang Hui-bin.[85] And Chang Mi-hee made South Koreans dream with her starring role as a sexually liberated young girl in *Winter Woman*.[86] South Koreans were working hard. And when they were not, they wanted to enjoy themselves in the way that Americans did. By the end of the decade, TV ownership was almost universal. And South Koreans packed the clubs from where the next big rock or pop star might emerge.

The middle class continued to expand thanks to ongoing economic growth and the modernization of the South Korean economy. Park did not want the country to forever remain the factory of cheap shirts or trousers for foreigners to buy. That did not befit his *seonjinguk* vision. And his popularity was tied to a version of *minjok* increasingly based on developmentalism. Plus, Park wanted a strong South Korean army. Dependence on the US military for

South Korea's defence did not make for a strong country. Therefore, Park's 1972 and 1977 five-year plans underscored his push to make South Korea a developed nation. The 1972 plan signalled a shift from light to heavy industry. Out with clothes and toys. In with electronics, machinery, petrochemicals and ship-building. The 1977 plan doubled down on these industries.[87]

Park clashed with the World Bank and other foreign experts who believed that the South Korean economy was not ready to compete in more technologically advanced industries. Some of his own advisors also had doubts. To many sceptics of South Korea's ability to compete with more developed countries, the Hyundai Pony became a symbol. The Pony was South Korea's first domestically developed car. Production began in the last month of 1975. Within a few more months, it was being exported to Latin America. It would eventually make its way to Europe and North America. But early models caught fire. Sometimes, the doors would fall off. And the paint looked cheap, because it was.[88] Experts cracked a condescending smile. But Hyundai's Chung knew better. The quality of the Pony improved quickly. Consumers realized this. Sales soared. The Pony had become a cheaper car lasting as long as more expensive American or European alternatives. Chung was vindicated. Park as well. So was South Korea at large.

Economic growth consolidated social changes already over a decade old. Urbanization continued apace. Ambitious South Koreans were moving to Seoul to work at the Guro and other industrial complexes, to Ulsan to build cars for Hyundai, to Pohang to find work at its steel mills and to Geoje to build ships in the shipyard that opened there in 1977. Other South Koreans followed suit to offer the services that those working in factories needed: restaurants, bars, shops and hair salons continued to pop up in the biggest cities and industrial centres. As of 2023, South Korean cities offer a beautiful combination of colourful businesses.

Their modern origins can be traced back to the growth of a mass middle class. This exacerbated the move away from the countryside. The number of South Koreans living in cities reached a new high in 1979.[89] In 1973, the manufacturing sector became bigger than agriculture in terms of economic output.[90] The difference between them has only grown ever since.

Urbanization came with a decreasing fertility rate, heralding a shift away from clans and towards nuclear families. Three generations living together were not uncommon. But more and more households only included parents and children.[91]And as South Koreans moved away from their hometowns, links to cousins, uncles and aunts and other members of one's extended family and clan became weaker. To be sure, families still gathered together to celebrate Chuseok (Harvest Moon Festival) or Seollal (Lunar New Year). But the daily meetings among clan members or the mutual support system more common to the older, rural Korea was becoming a memory of the past for increasing numbers of South Koreans.

And as these dramatic social changes took place, entrepreneurial South Koreans stepped in with new ways to make their lives easier. Emblematic of this change was Lotte Food Industrial Company. Part of the Lotte *chaebol* and founded in 1965, the firm specialized in instant noodles and snacks. Busy South Koreans living in nuclear families did not always have the time to cook. Lotte Food catered to their needs. But it was not the first instant noodle firm. It needed to innovate and come up with the flavours that South Koreans would choose when going over a supermarket aisle containing countless other brands. Shin Choon-ho, the firm's founder, understood this. So he instructed his workers to try out new tastes. Which they did. By the mid-1970s, Lotte Food had a third of the instant noodle market. And in 1978, it changed its name to Nongshim—Farmer's Heart.[92] It was not enough to innovate. To cater to ever-fuzzier customers, firms had to appeal to their feelings.

Yet, the ills associated with fast economic growth did not go away. Exploitation of many workers, the second-class status of many women and corruption continued to be a feature of South Korea's economic landscape throughout the 1970s. Many South Koreans continued to emigrate to find what they believed would be a better life in the United States or Europe.[93] But the repression concomitant to the Yushin years had the effect of reducing domestic instability. Demonstrations were more difficult to organize or they were simply dispersed violently. And many South Koreans, in any case, were busy enjoying their newfound middle-class status. They were not ready to support violence to change a regime that was working for them. The 1978 National Assembly election revealed this division within South Korean society. The opposition New Democratic Party actually won the election with almost 33 per cent of the vote, powered by an expanding middle class concerned about the growing authoritarianism of the Park government. But the ruling Democratic Republican Party came a close second with almost 32 per cent.[94] It then went on to gain a majority of the seats thanks to the president's power to appoint one-third of the seats.

Resistance to the Park regime therefore came from within the same mass culture that the president's economic policies fostered. There was heavy censorship. But human ingenuity triumphed and worked around it, as it often does. *Winter Woman* exemplified this. It made Chang Mi-hee a star as a sexually liberated young girl. But her sexual liberation was a critique of the fate of many young women often hailing from the countryside who were working as prostitutes. In the film, Chang gave her body for free because she could; her character was from a middle-class background. Many South Korean women did not have that luxury. And in the movie, Chang's character became a journalist who found love or at least companionship with a teacher. She covered the work of women working in factories, while he taught the children of poor city workers. Chang's character was therefore not a carefree 'prostitute', as conservative critics would put it. She represented and raised awareness of the underbelly of South Korean society.[95] Many other movies from the 1970s including *Yeong-ja's Heydays*[96] and *Heavenly Homecoming to Stars*[97] also offered a critique of South Korean society and economic model with similar allegories. Watching them decades later, one can start to understand the tensions inherent to a country in the midst of rapid industrialization.

Musicians and writers also became part of the movement to resist Yushin from within the mass culture that had developed throughout the decade. *Minjung-Gayo* or protest songs grew in popularity in the 1970s. Arguably, 'Morning Dew' was the song that gave birth to this protest song movement. Composer Kim Min-ki put together a powerful ballad in 1970, calling on people to resist the South Korean government and Americanization. The latter was linked to the Park regime and Korea's division. The song was banned in 1975, but South Koreans continued to sing it well into the late 1980s.[98] The government could not stop the tide of similar songs. And it could not stop the stream of protest literature that writers were writing. Thanks to the increasing literacy rate, literature became a popular medium to protest against the Park government. And no writer did more to popularize this type of protest than Kim Jiha. His 1970 poem 'Five Bandits' criticized five corrupt bandits representing generals, *chaebol* oligarchs, cabinet ministers, members of the National Assembly and bureaucrats. Kim was arrested and sentenced to death, before his sentence was commuted to life in prison. Kim would eventually be released as a result of domestic and international pressure.[99] His literature was an example to many other writers who used their pens to fight the regime's guns.

Buddhism and Christianity were not part of the mass culture to emerge in the 1970s, as they had deeper roots in Korean society. But they were closely associated with the resistance movement of the 1970s and mixed together with its mass cultural elements. By 1945, only 2 or 3 per cent of Koreans were Christian.[100] But the religion's appeal grew as many South Koreans started to turn their backs on Confucianism, which after all had not helped to prevent colonization by Japan. Kim Jiha, for example, was influenced by his Catholic faith. Many Buddhist monks and Christian priests were known as social justice warriors. In the case of the latter, American and European missionaries moved to South Korea and supported the anti-Park movement. Park, in fact, had promoted Buddhism and Christianity as he sought to root out shamanism and other 'superstitious' practices from South Korean society. The Park government even linked Christianity and modernization. But these religious groups eventually helped to lay the groundwork for the *minjung* movement that would firmly take root in the 1980s.[101] Religious movements enjoyed considerable autonomy from the state, which helped them support and facilitate resistance.[102] Many Buddhist temples and Catholic churches became safe spaces. And figures such as Cardinal Kim Sou-hwan commanded a huge following while asking for democracy. Buddhism and Catholicism may not have been as important as mass culture to South Korean society. But they still played a crucial role.

## A bloody end to Park's rule

Every South Korean then alive remembers where they were when they heard the news. It is 26 October. Friday evening. Many are enjoying the customary work dinner regaled with *soju*—South Korea's preferred spirit drink. Others are taking a rest before their Saturday shift. The luckiest ones are preparing to enjoy the luxury of a two-day weekend. None of them knows that Park had sat down for dinner at 6pm, had been shot twice an hour and a half later and had been pronounced dead at 7.50pm. But soon they will know. An official announcement comes in the early hours of 27 October. The prime minister has been named acting president due to the incapacity of Park. Rumours have started to swirl all across the country. At 8.35am, the public information minister makes the announcement: Park has been killed.[103] Some South Koreans have just woken up. Others are already on their way to work. Yet some others are nursing their headaches after a night of heavy drinking, partying or both. Ask a South Korean who was alive back then. They will tell you what they were doing when they learnt the news. They will tell you that the whole country was in shock. But many will also tell you that the shock came together with a feeling that a violent end to Park's reign was inevitable.

The months leading to the murder were marked by growing criticism and protest against the Park regime and, in return, increasing violence. Protests came from opposition politicians. Kim Young-sam was named as leader of the New Democratic Party in May and decided to take no prisoners. His opening salvo came in July, when he called for Park's resignation and the restoration of democracy in a speech at the National Assembly. Kim followed with his second salvo by giving an interview in the *New York Times* asking the Jimmy Carter government, which had been critical of South Korea's human rights record, to end its support for Park's 'minority dictatorial regime'.[104] The KCIA called Kim to task and asked him to retract his words. Kim refused, so he was arrested and suspended as leader of the New Democratic Party.[105] In October, he was expelled from the National Assembly. So he launched his third salvo by leading all opposition National Assembly members in walking out of parliament.[106]

Protests came from workers as well. In August, Y. H. Trading Company announced that it would close down its wig exporting business. Up to 200 of its workers—all of them young women—took the decision to protest against the closure. Kim opened the headquarters of the New Democratic Party for them to carry out their protest. The protesters made public their demands, and Kim called on the government to negotiate with them. The government refused and instead took the decision to put an end to the protest. The police entered the building to remove the protesters. One of them, Kim Kyung-suk, was killed in the process. Her death and the forceful removal of the protesters triggered new rounds of demonstrations and condemnation of the government's use of violence.[107]

And protests came from students too. In October, students at Pusan National University launched a call to demand the end of the Park regime. Protests spilled over to the streets of Busan, where workers and many others simply fed up with the Yushin system joined in. Some 50,000 demonstrators ended up fighting against the police. Within two days, the government declared martial law in Busan. But demonstrations then erupted at Kyungnam University in Masan, about an hour away from Busan. Some 10,000 demonstrators took to the streets, once again including workers and others opposed to the Park regime. The government imposed a curfew within hours. But the 'Bu-Ma Uprising' was adding more fuel to the anti-Park movement.[108] Protests in other cities across the country then followed suit.

Kim Jae-gyu was sent to investigate the Bu-Ma protests. He was the director of the KCIA, a position he had held for three years and nine months by the time of the demonstrations. Kim had been born in Gumi—where Park also hailed from—and had graduated from the Korea Military Academy the same year as the South Korean president. He became a trusted Park ally after his coup, rising through the ranks all the way to KCIA director. But

Kim was not as hard-line as Park. He had been the one asking Kim Young-sam to retract his words, for the sake of South Korea but also for Kim's own sake.[109] And after visiting the site of the Bu-Ma protests he asked Park to compromise with the opposition, which the president refused to do. In Kim's view, these were not regular student protests. These were the protests of average citizens demanding freedom.[110] Years after Kim Jae-gyu's death, the public would learn that he had been in regular contact with opposition figures and that, quite possibly, he was trying to find a peaceful end to Park's regime.

For Kim died only seven months after his argument with Park. He was hanged. Because he was the man who shot Park twice. During the '10.26 Incident', as the event is known in South Korea, Kim killed Park while he was having dinner at the KCIA headquarters in the Blue House compound. Partly, because he thought that the Park government had become too dictatorial and repressive. Partly, because he was falling out of favour with Park as other, more repressive leaders became more powerful. After Park's assassination, Kim was promptly arrested, placed on trial and sentenced to death.[111] But he is the man who changed South Korean history. It was an intra-regime feud that ultimately led to the end of the Park regime, not a case of the opposition forcing Park's hand or a successful North Korean operation.

Park received a state funeral eight days after his assassination, a first in South Korean history.[112] An estimated two million people lined the streets of Seoul to wave him goodbye.[113] This underscored the fact that many South Koreans were genuinely thankful to Park for having set the foundations for their country to escape poverty and become a prosperous nation. At the same time, there were high expectations that Park's death would allow South Korea to become fully democratic. It was autumn, but there was talk of a 'Seoul Spring'—a nod to the Prague Spring in Czechoslovakia a decade before. Prime Minister Choi Kyu-hah became the acting president upon Park's death, before the National Assembly confirmed him as the new president in December. He promised free elections and a new constitution to replace the by-then detested Yushin Constitution.[114] Most South Koreans had prospered under Park and joined the ranks of the middle class. Yet a large majority of those same middle-class South Koreans, along with students, lower-paid workers and many other groups, wanted democracy. This was the paradoxical legacy of Park's eighteen years in power.

# 3

# ON THE ROAD TO RICHES AND DEMOCRACY
## 1980–87

*A new dictatorship is born*

Ask a South Korean to come up with a list of the most reviled people in the country's history. It is safe to say that the name of Chun Doo-hwan will be close to the top of the list, if not at the very top. Park Chung-hee was dead. Shocking as this was, his assassination had brought the prospect of democracy and freedom to South Korea. The people craved this. Chun did not. Quite the opposite. Chun wanted to replace Park's dictatorship with one of his own. He had been preparing for years. When the time came, he executed his plan perfectly. Barely two months after Park's assassination, Chun was the de facto leader of South Korea. Ten months later, he was the country's new president, ruling over a dictatorial regime that would be in place for seven years.

Chun was born into a large, poor family, while Korea was still a Japanese colony. But then, most Korean families were the same back then. One route to escape poverty was to join the army. So

Chun did. He joined the Korea Military Academy while the Korean War was still ravaging the Korean Peninsula. After the war, Chun went about trying to slowly progress through the army ranks. When Park came to power, Chun showed his support. He thought that South Koreans were not ready for democracy and feared that communist sympathizers could still take over. He held increasingly more powerful positions, moving between the army, KCIA and Park's junta. Chun went on to serve in the Vietnam War. As US ally South Vietnam lost the war to communist North Vietnam, Chun felt vindicated: South Korea needed to avoid falling to communism itself. One year before Park was assassinated, Chun was promoted to brigadier general. By the time Park was killed, he had been promoted once more. Chun was commander of the Security Command.[1] The right post, at the right time.

Thanks to his post in the Security Command, Chun took charge of the investigation of Park's death. His was not much of an investigation. It was the starting shot for Chun's carefully laid out plan to take power. Chung Sung-hwa was the army chief of staff when Park was shot. He imposed martial law and arrested Kim Jae-gyu, Park's assassin. Chung was clearly an obstacle to Chun's plan. So Chun had him arrested on 12 December 1979 and purged many of his followers. This was the '12.12 Military Insurrection', a coup in which some military men got rid of some other military men. Choi Kyu-hah actually continued to be the president.[2] Chun did not even bother to remove him, but following the coup, it was clear that Chun was the de facto leader of the country. And Chung continued to be the biggest threat to his rule. After a quick trial in March 1980, he was sentenced to ten years in prison. The reason? Chung was accused of having provided support to Park's assassination. The evidence? It had taken him too long to arrest Park's murderer. Was this true? In 1981, once he was no longer a threat to Chun, Chung was pardoned and released from prison.[3] Whether he had taken too long to arrest Kim or not, Chung's fate was the result of politics within the military. That much was clear. Chung would eventually have his revenge against Chun. But it would only come after South Korea had become a democracy.

With his main opponent out of the picture, Chun continued to implement his plan. In April, he became the new head of the much-feared and all-powerful KCIA—which he renamed Agency for National Security Planning (ANSP). On 17 May, Chun staged yet another coup for good measure. He extended martial law. Within three days, he ordered the National Assembly to be dissolved.[4] The Three Kims were arrested, for they could rally those opposed to Chun's nascent dictatorship. Kim Dae-jung was even sentenced to death, first commuted to twenty years in prison and then replaced by exile following an intervention by the United States and Pope John Paul II.[5] With all opposition out of the way, Chun felt secure enough to resign from his position in the ANSP and to get himself discharged to the army reserves. In August, Choi Kyu-hah resigned from his post of president. Before the end of the month, Chun had been elected president of South Korea by an electoral college he now fully controlled.[6]

Dictators crave legitimacy. And Chun was no different. So he did what authoritarian leaders tend to do: he called an election he knew he would win. This was an indirect election, of course. In February 1981, the electoral college gathered in a massive gym in downtown Seoul. Over 90 per cent of electors voted for Chun. A few days later, on 3 March 1981, Chun proclaimed the Fifth Republic. The new republic came with its own constitution, to replace the late Park's Yushin. Aware of Park's enduring popularity, Chun decided to eliminate any vestige of his rule. Later in the month, legislative elections were held. With all the main political figures in the opposition barred from running when not in prison, Chun's Democratic Justice Party (DJP) received over 35 per cent of the vote.[7] Not that it mattered much.

The re-established National Assembly continued to have no power. Chun was the new, unopposed ruler of South Korea.

### The Gwangju Uprising

The Gwangju Uprising symbolizes South Koreans' thirst for democracy like no other event. Known as '5.18', the uprising came to represent the democratic spirit already taking over the country between the late 1970s and early 1980s, at least for progressive South Koreans. For the people of South Korea did not passively witness the birth of yet another dictatorship but fought against the seemingly inevitable on the streets of Gwangju, Seoul and many other cities across the country. And even if ordinary South Koreans lost the first battle against the newly installed Chun regime, they would eventually win the war. The spirit of Gwangju never left them.

In the lead-up to the Gwangju Uprising, there was the ongoing Seoul Spring. On 15 May 1980, over 100,000 people demonstrated in the city centre—right next to Seoul City station, the main gateway in and out of the South Korean capital. Aware that their dream of a new democracy was rapidly slipping through their fingers, students and workers held the biggest demonstration to have taken place that year. The government responded by extending martial law two days later. Soldiers were dispatched throughout the country to quell any further demonstrations.[8]

One of the biggest cities in South Korea, Gwangju was the capital of South Jeolla Province. Left-leaning, Jeolla had traditionally been one of the most restless regions in Korean history. (Remember the Yeosu–Suncheon rebellion of 1948, for example.) And Kim Dae-jung originally hailed from the region, where he had his main power base. Kim had been arrested immediately after the extension of martial law. This created an explosive cocktail, which resulted in the Gwangju Uprising.

On 18 May, students began to demonstrate at the gate of Chonnam National University. In line with the instructions laid out in the martial law decree, the university was due to close. The students were directly defying the Chun government. Paratroopers clashed with students, who decided to march towards Geumnan Avenue in central Gwangju. More than 500 people were arrested, both demonstrators and passers-by who happened to be in the vicinity. The day after, more paratroopers arrived. And the first victim was killed. Kim Gyeong-cheol was clubbed to death. This took the demonstrations to another level. It became a full uprising. Students, workers and other citizens gathered in central Gwangju. They did not simply clash with the paratroopers; they battled with them. For days and days. The local MBC radio station and KBS TV station were set on fire. On 21 May, telephone lines were cut. Gwangju could not communicate with the rest of the country. Demonstrators were now in battle with the soldiers struggling to stop the uprising, so they got hold of military trucks, armoured vehicles and weapons. Paratroopers retreated. On 22 May, the army blockaded Gwangju, which was now isolated from the rest of the country. The city's residents formed the Citizens' Settlement Committee and established their own government. The insurrection lasted until 27 May, when tanks and troops took control of Gwangju's city centre.[9]

The human costs of the Gwangju Uprising are disputed. According to the May 18 Memorial Foundation set up after South Korea's democratization, 154 people were killed, seventy-four went missing and 4,141 were wounded. At least twenty-two soldiers and four policemen were killed as well, with over 100 of each wounded.[10] The psychological scars were also very deep. An already unpopular government had turned against its own people. It variously blamed the demonstrations on communist sympathizers, spread the rumour that North Korea may have been ready to enter South Korea and accused Kim Dae-jung of being the instigator behind the uprising. Many conservative South Koreans did not necessarily believe the official version but still thought that the demonstrators were to blame and that there was a North Korea connection. Conservatives would dispute the true cost of events at Gwangju for decades to come.[11] Meanwhile, pro-democracy South Koreans who regularly demonstrated against the government in the 1980s used the Gwangju Uprising as an inspiration but also as a lesson about how to press ahead with their demands.[12] Furthermore, Washington's tacit approval of the deployment of troops to repress the uprising provoked a bout of anti-Americanism. Many pro-democracy activists felt a sense of betrayal and changed their views of the United States: rather than a liberator, it was just another neo-colonial power.[13]

The battle for the narrative about the uprising continued once South Korea democratized. In 1988, the National Assembly officially renamed the events in Gwangju as the Gwangju (People's) Uprising. The May 18 Memorial Foundation was established. In 1997, the government declared 18 May an official memorial day, and in 2002, the first progressive government since democratization elevated the May 18 Gwangju Cemetery to national status.[14] In May 2017, a new progressive government launched an official investigation of the May 1980 events, with a truth commission being launched in May 2020 to try to heal the wounds that still scarred many South Koreans forty years after the uprising.[15] And throughout South Korea's history since its democratization, several books have depicted the events in Gwangju. For example, in 2017 the film *A Taxi Driver* was the second highest-grossing movie in South Korea that year. The movie dramatized the story of taxi driver Kim Sa-bok, who took a German journalist to Gwangju; this journalist was the first to film and broadcast footage of the Gwangju Uprising to the rest of the world.[16]

*Economic development*

The Chun government came to power as South Korea was suffering from its first economic recession since the 1950s. From the mid-1970s, Park had sought to move the South Korean economy up the value-added chain. Out with the cheap toys, shoes and shirts. In with the ships, steel and chemicals, as well as an incipient electronics industry, especially TVs. The plan was sound. But it would take time to bear fruit, as investment in these sectors often does. And the transition came just as Western economies were suffering from the second oil crisis in 1979, years of high inflation throughout the 1970s, rising unemployment and a bout of protectionism. Hardly the best environment for South Korea's export-oriented economy. As a result, the South Korean economy contracted by almost 2 per cent in 1980.[17]

Chun shared Park's goal of making South Korea an advanced nation (*seonjinguk*), leaving behind its past as a backward country (*hujinguk*). But he faced a dilemma. South Korea could no longer rely on the export of cheap goods, since other countries offered even cheaper labour. Yet, the country needed to employ ever larger numbers of working-age people. In Chun's mind, providing jobs would have the added bonus of limiting social unrest and reducing the number of protests against the new government. So, the new president recalled the technocrats behind the rapid economic growth of the Park years in the hope of a second 'economic take-off'.[18] Chun would stake his legitimacy on economic growth, just as Park had done. The question was how he could do this.

The answer lay in market forces. Chun embarked on an economic liberalization policy that loosened the ties between government and the *chaebol*, reduced barriers to imports and investment so that domestic firms either became more competitive or went bust and relaxed the rules regulating the involvement of foreign firms and banks in the South Korean economy.[19] To an extent, liberalization was the logical result of the internationalization of the South Korean economy. Samsung, Hyundai and LG were becoming too international for the government to guide. A growing share of their profits was coming from overseas. Their reliance on credit from state-owned banks was rapidly decreasing. The *chaebol* wanted to be free from state intervention.[20] And a manager dispatched to the US, or a sales manager working in Europe, had a better sense of shifting consumer tastes than a bureaucrat sitting in their office in downtown Seoul. The Chun government understood this.

In addition, South Korea was under international pressure to liberalize. Ronald Reagan had become US president in January 1981. In his inaugural address, he uttered one of his most famous mantras: 'Government is the problem'. This included foreign governments. Throughout the 1980s, the US Department of Treasury, the IMF and the World Bank pushed the 'Washington Consensus' across the developing world. Deregulation, privatization, liberalization. That was the mantra coming out of Washington.[21] The Chun government got the memo and flirted with these ideas. The government did not fully embrace them, but they helped to tilt the balance of its economic policy away from the heavy-handed interventionism associated with the Park years.

This did not mean that the Blue House and the bureaucrats sitting in the Ministries of Trade and Industry or Finance simply allowed the private sector to take over. In 1982, Chun issued South Korea's fifth five-year economic plan. The plan aimed to shift the South Korean economy towards the manufacturing of electronics and semiconductors.[22] The sixth plan, issued in 1986, continued to emphasize these sectors.[23] Bureaucrats working in small cubicles until late at night did not dream up the Galaxy smartphones sitting in hundreds of millions of pockets from Brazil to Germany, or the smart flat screen TVs sitting in countless living rooms from the Philippines to Spain. But those same bureaucrats did dream that South Korean firms would one day come up with the latest gadget that consumers around the world would buy. Decades later, these bureaucrats would be able to crack a smile as they enjoyed their well-deserved government pension.

The Chun government also understood that South Korea could only become a modern economy if its workers were well educated and healthy. Primary education had already become universal by the late 1970s.[24] Secondary education enrolment continued to increase, reaching 98 per cent of all teenagers by 1987.[25] And 44 per cent of high school graduates went on to enrol in a university degree course that same year.[26] In Chun's view, those pesky arts and social science students were a nuisance. But engineering and science majors? They were a blessing. Especially if they were in good health. Chun was the president who truly achieved universal health insurance, adding the self-employed to the compulsory health insurance system launched by Park. In 1989—two years after Chun left office—South Korea achieved universal health coverage.[27]

The South Korean economy changed thanks to this combination of the growing competitiveness of the private sector and government intervention. By the mid-1980s, South Korean firms were churning out hundreds of thousands of PCs, TVs, videotape recorders and semiconductors. Since American and Japanese firms were becoming more reluctant to transfer their lower-end technologies, and Chinese and South East Asian firms were catching up, South Korean firms had to shift their focus towards technology products.[28]

And there were also signs that the South Korean economy was moving towards a more innovative model. South Korea became the second-largest shipbuilding country in the 1980s. Ships built at the Geoje and Ulsan shipyards were starting to become known for their quality and design, and not simply because they were cheaper copies of foreign products.[29] And in 1986 there was a shock that showed where the South Korean economy was heading—the Pony made it to the United States. Renamed the Excel for the American market, it was the first South Korean car ever exported there. And it sold 169,000 units in its first year. If tens of thousands of consumers in the richest and most sophisticated market in the world were willing to shed US$4,995 for a South Korean car,[30] the sky really was the limit for South Korean exporters.

Exporters that now included all sorts of firms. That same year of 1986, instant noodle market leader Nongshim launched Shin Ramyun, a spicy cabbage and beef stew, traditional in South Korea. Nongshim had hit the jackpot. On the back of Shin Ramyun, it would become the undisputed market leader. And the firm would become South Korea's most successful instant noodle exporter,[31] with Shin Ramyun still leading the way at the time of writing. (One can even order a serving when flying in and out of South Korea if taking a South Korean airline.) Shin Choon-ho, the firm's president, correctly predicted that South Korean firms could become internationally competitive even in sectors that the country's politicians and economists did not pay much attention to.

High rates of economic growth once the South Korean economy started to recover from the 1980 recession, however, could not mask two structural problems affecting the interaction between the South Korean economy and society. The first was the imbalance between the rural and urban areas, which only continued to grow. The share of the agricultural sector in South Korea's economic output had plunged to 10 per cent by 1987.[32] South Koreans were leaving small towns and the countryside in droves. Cities were booming.[33] And the government could do nothing to stop it. Chun expanded investment in projects such as roads, railroads and communication lines. The infrastructure continued to improve in the countryside.[34] But South Koreans wanted a piece of the action. And for many, the action was in Seoul, Busan and Daegu.

The other issue was arguably even more fundamental in the context of 1980s South Korea. Economic liberalization, South

Koreans noted, was in sharp contrast to political repression. There is a popular political science theory that tells us that economic liberalization eventually leads to the liberalization of politics as well. Academic theories do not always work in practice. But in the case of South Korea, this one certainly did. South Korean workers clashed with government as they pressed for democracy. The number of labour strikes increased from ninety-eight in 1983 to 276 in 1986.[35] Thousands upon thousands of workers also regularly joined anti-government demonstrations. Together with students, they were the most active group in pressing for political change during Chun's rule.

## A changing society

Economic change did not bring political change during the Chun years. But it certainly brought change to society. Or more accurately, the trends already seen from the 1960s accelerated. Family ties continued to loosen. Clan links continued to weaken, as growing numbers of young South Koreans moved to cities and daily contact with their extended families became a thing of the past. They still met on special occasions, such as Seollal or Chuseok. They could call using the landline phones that became more common during the 1980s. But clan relationships inevitably became more distant. Three-generation households were down to 16 per cent of the total in 1985.[36] And the birth rate plunged. When Chun consolidated power in 1980, the fertility rate still stood at 2.82. Within seven years, it was down to 1.53.[37] This was already below the 2.1 replacement-level rate.

Change was most obvious in the emergence of a growing urban middle class. Professionals in the services sector made up 50 per cent of the total workforce in 1987 for the first time in South Korean history. The manufacturing sector employed 40 per cent of workers that same year.[38] Salaries were not always great, but an ever-growing number of South Koreans could call themselves middle class. They could buy their own apartment. They could afford cars, TV sets and fridges. They could go to a fancy restaurant or splash out on a haircut. They could travel overseas for holidays, as the government began to remove restrictions on foreign trips.

This growing middle class started to change the character of South Korean culture, coinciding with a period of relaxation of the censorship from the Park years. *Deep Blue Night*—South Korea's most popular movie from the Chun period by ticket sales—depicted the travails of an illegal immigrant in California in search of a wife to obtain a green card, break his sham marriage and bring his pregnant wife from South Korea.[39] *Whale Hunting*—the second most popular movie—focused on a disillusioned young man rejected by his crush, who then ends up helping a prostitute reunite with her mother.[40] They were movies that told the stories of people looking for something beyond what their daily lives offered them, a theme that played well with the growing middle class.

Change also came to the music sector. The South Korean ballad had emerged in the 1960s, influenced by blues and American ballads. But it was only in the 1980s that it became mainstream. Ballads spoke to South Korean hearts with stories about love and heartbreak. In 1985, Lee Gwang-jo's 'You're Too Far Away to Get Close To' sold 300,000 copies. And late in the decade, Byun Jinseob debuted and soon after was dubbed 'The Prince of Ballads'.[41] For middle-class South Koreans who could think about dating and marriage in terms of love rather than family arrangements, ballads represented their feelings. Suffering, for them, was about unrequited love. Joy was finding that special person to spend your life with.

The changes underway in South Korean society also brought a novel push for women's rights. For many in South Korea, women continued to be less valuable than men. The wider availability of abortion meant that the sex ratio imbalance at birth crept up from 106.8 boys per girls in 1981—which is natural in biological terms—to 116.5 in 1990, well above what is natural for humans.[42] Also, overseas adoption from South Korea peaked in the mid-1980s.[43] Social mores were changing, especially in the cities. But women who got pregnant out of wedlock had little option but to give away their babies, unless the father agreed to marry them. And when it came to job prospects for married women, the situation for most of them had not improved compared to the Park years. Upon marriage, a woman was expected to leave her job and take care of her husband, children and probably her in-laws as well. This was especially true for women living in cities.[44] Women in cities could take the odd job working from home or in one of the '*ajumma* jobs'. But they could not think about having a career of their own.

It was in this context that a new wave of feminism swept the country. Influenced by the *minjung* movement that emphasized women's rights and with swelling ranks thanks to the growing number of women attending university, feminist movements started to empower women to speak out. The first Women's Conference was held in 1985, demanding better labour rights for women. One year later, Seoul National University student and labour activist Kwon In-sook made history. After being sexually abused at a police station, she became the first South Korean woman to file sexual abuse charges against the government. Her case galvanized South Korean women. A few months later—in 1987—twenty-one women's organizations created the Korean Women's Associations United, which in later years was instrumental in pressing the government to improve women's rights.[45] Growing numbers of women did not want to continue to be second-class citizens in their own country. South Korea's feminist movement also supported causes specific to South Korea, especially calls for an end to Chun's dictatorial regime.

For the changes that society was experiencing were another reason why the Chun government came under criticism. South Koreans were free to choose their job. They could choose their car or TV set. They could choose how they wanted to entertain themselves. Why were they unable to choose their president? For most South Koreans, there was no satisfactory answer to this question. As offices and factories filled up with swelling numbers of middle-class South Koreans, the incongruence of living under a dictatorial regime while enjoying so many other freedoms became too apparent.

### The long-lasting pain of division

On 26 June 1983, KBS started to run a strange TV ad. The national broadcaster had come up with an original idea: four days later, on 30 June and in commemoration of the upcoming thirtieth anniversary of the end of the Korean War, it would air a programme for South Koreans separated during the war to find their long-lost relatives. Producers hoped to air 200 stories; they received 1,000 applications during the first two days alone. The director had planned a one-day special; the programme ran for an astonishing 138 days, only finishing on 14 November. An average of 60,000 people called every day; 100,952 South Koreans applied to join the broadcast and 53,536 of them made it on to the show. Some 10,189 people found their long-lost relatives.[46] Mothers and their sons, brothers and their sisters, grandparents and their grandchildren. TV screens were filled with tears, laughter and joy. Decades spent apart had come to an end for those lucky 10,189 people. *Finding Dispersed Families* was the name of the TV show that made it possible. At the time of writing, parts of the programme can still be viewed online.

The area surrounding KBS' main TV studio filled up with thousands of people looking for their relatives. Walls were plastered with calls for fathers, aunts, cousins and daughters to return to their families. Others shouted and cried for them to reappear. The police had to send dozens of officers to control the crowds. Over twenty TV networks from around the world broadcast live from the area at some point during the programme. 'War-Scattered Korean Kin Find Their Kin at Last', wrote the *New York Times*—a picture of a crying mother held by her adult son illustrating the story.[47] UN Secretary-General Javier Pérez de Cuéllar expressed his deep sympathy.[48] And yet, the success of *Finding Dispersed Families* laid bare South Koreans' pain. Theirs remained a divided country. What is more, theirs remained a country with hundreds of thousands of divided families.

Not that Kim Il-sung seemed to be interested in helping divided families heal their wounds. In fact, the North Korean leader was bent on destabilizing South Korea. Inter-Korean relations had been at a dead end since the talks following the 1972 joint communiqué. Over the years, there had been discussions about resuming bilateral talks or even holding trilateral talks together with the United States.[49] While both countries still formally adhered to the goal of reunification, based on the principles of independence, peace and national unity, there was a difference between this formal adherence and the reality on the ground.

On 9 October 1983, Chun was on an official visit to Myanmar (then known as Burma). His schedule included a visit to the Martyrs' Mausoleum in Yangon (then known as Rangoon). Chun was going to lay a wreath to commemorate Aung San and six other independence heroes. But he did not get to do so. Three agents from the (North) Korean People's Army had secretly entered the country days before. They had planted three bombs on the roof of the mausoleum, to be activated remotely. The agents had a clear goal in mind: to assassinate the South Korean president.[50] We will probably never know why Kim

Il-sung ordered the murder of his South Korean counterpart. But clearly the goodwill of the 1972 joint communiqué was gone.

As fate would have it, Chun delayed his departure from the State Guest House where he was staying. His wife was due to have tea with a group of Burmese women. Due to a scheduling error, the ceremony clashed with Chun's departure from the guest house. Thus, the departure was delayed by a few minutes to make sure that Chun could receive the group of women first. But most of the group departed on time. They arrived at the mausoleum ahead of Chun. And the North Korean agents pressed the trigger. The bombs exploded, killing twenty-one people—including four cabinet ministers—and wounding forty-six others.[51] Chun's motorcade, on its way to the mausoleum, turned back. The president survived, but South Korea was shocked. And enraged. The Yangon bombing had come barely a month after the Soviet Union had shot down a civilian Korean Air Lines plane that had entered Soviet airspace by mistake, killing all 269 passengers and crew on board.[52] Seoul could not strike back against Moscow, but it could against Pyongyang. Arguably, only Reagan's visit to South Korea one month after the Yangon bombing prevented South Korea's retaliation.

Inter-Korean relations, however, took an unexpected and promising turn a few months later that brought hope to those still separated from their families. In August 1984, Chun announced that South Korea stood ready to provide North Korea with goods and technologies to improve the lives of its people. Shortly after, however, Seoul, Gyeonggi Province and Chungcheong Province suffered catastrophic floods that killed almost 200 people and left thousands homeless. Now it was Kim Il-sung who offered aid to South Korea. It was not the first time that North Korea had offered to provide aid since the division of Korea. But it would be the first time that a South Korean government would accept help from its northern neighbour. Throughout September, the Red Cross in the two

Koreas held talks in the truce village of Panmunjom located on the inter-Korean border. For a period of six days, 1,373 North Koreans crossed the border to deliver rice, fabric, medicines and cement.[53] South Koreans were shocked and grateful.

An even bigger shock came in 1985. The goodwill generated by Chun's warm words, North Korea's delivery of aid and the Red Cross talks made the unimaginable happen. On 20 September, 150 South Koreans crossed the DMZ on their way to Pyongyang as the same number of North Koreans travelled the other way to Seoul. Each group included folk-art performers, journalists, support personnel and a very special group: people separated from their families during the Korean War.[54] For four days, South Koreans were glued to their TV sets as Koreans from South and North met their relatives for the first time in over thirty years. Millions of South Koreans had shed tears while watching *Finding Dispersed Families*. They shed them again as they saw the first-ever meeting between Koreans on both sides of the DMZ.

Unfortunately, this would also be the last time separated families got to meet until 2000. The truth of the matter was that the two Koreas were growing apart. In theory, both countries were competing to gain recognition as the legitimate representative of the whole of Korea. In practice, however, by the mid-1980s it had become clear that there was no such competition. In 1974, South Korean GDP per capita had surpassed North Korea's. By 1986, it was twice as big.[55] As the South Korean economy continued to boom, North Korea's stalled. Furthermore, in 1981 Seoul was selected as the host of the 1986 Asian Games and—more importantly—the 1988 Olympic Games. South Korea was about to become only the second country in Asia to host the biggest sports event on earth, following from Tokyo 1964. In terms of international recognition, South Korea was clearly ahead. In fact, North Korea had retracted its bid for Pyongyang to host the 1986 Asian Games once it had become clear that the Seoul bid would win.

As the Asian and Olympic Games approached, Kim Il-sung was furious. He successfully called on communist countries to boycott the 1986 Games. All of them complied, except for China, which was undergoing its opening up process under Deng Xiaoping. A sign that even in the communist camp there was a degree of recognition of South Korea. A few days before the Asian Games, Pyongyang upped its pressure on Seoul. A spy sent by the North Korean government detonated a bomb in Gimpo International Airport—the main gateway into South Korea back then—killing five people.[56] South Korea successfully hosted the games nonetheless.

And South Koreans now had Seoul 1988 to look forward to, a veritable coming out party. This was intolerable to North Korea. So in November 1987, two North Korean agents planted a bomb on a Korean Air flight making the route from Baghdad to Seoul. The device exploded mid-air, killing all 115 passengers and crew on board.[57] This did not deter the South Korean government, which went ahead with its plans to host the Olympic Games. Kim Il-sung was now desperately calling on North Korea's purported communist allies to boycott them. Only Cuba officially did. Throughout the 1980s, even the communist bloc had recognized what many South Koreans already knew: Seoul had 'won' its competition with Pyongyang. Theirs was the most successful country. The pain of Korea's division was at least partially mitigated by this knowledge.

### Clash of legitimacies

Despite South Korea's obvious success when compared to its northern neighbour, economic development was not enough for growing numbers of South Koreans. Society was changing rapidly, led by labour, student, religious and, more recently, feminist movements demanding change. Dwindling numbers of South

Koreans saw North Korea as a real competitor—never mind a threat. And after more than three decades as an independent country, was a communist takeover a real possibility? The Chun government had a problem. The traditional levers of legitimacy that had worked for his predecessors were no longer applicable. South Koreans wanted their country to be an advanced nation, of course. But advanced nations were not only rich—they were also democratic. South Koreans' idea of *seonjinguk* had evolved.

The 1980s were the heyday of the *minjung* movement. Memories of the Gwangju Uprising and the Chun government's violent response stoked an unrelenting push towards freedom and democratization. Many likened their fight against dictatorship with the fight for independence during the years of Japanese colonialism. Kim San (whose real name was Jang Jirak)—a colonial-era revolutionary—became a symbol. His 1941 memoir *Song of Arirang: The Story of a Korean Revolutionary in China* was finally published in Korean in 1984. Kim had left Korea to fight for Korean independence, inspired by the Chinese and Russian revolutions. He also fought for the working class.[58] Here was a true Korean patriot who did not hesitate to fight for the liberalization of his country and people. Reading Kim's memoirs and similar works extolling the virtues of resistance against more powerful opponents became an act of subversion.

The *minjung* movement believed that it was not only foreign powers who had suppressed the South Korean people. Authoritarian governments had as well. This included Chun Doohwan as much as Park Chung-hee, for after all both had good relations with the former colonial power—Japan—and supported the presence of troops on South Korean soil of what many believed was the new colonial master: the United States. But a growing number of South Koreans also blamed Washington for enabling the country's dictators. This included Chun's violent repression of the Gwangju Uprising, for South Korean military units were under the operational control of the US commander of the country's forces in South Korea. The growing anti-American sentiment was symbolized by an arson attack against the Busan American Cultural Service building in March 1982.[59] This was the worst instance of anti-Americanism in South Korea in decades.

The *minjung* movement received a double boost in February 1985. To begin with, Kim Dae-jung returned from exile. Accompanied by thirty-seven supporters from the United States—including former Jimmy Carter administration officials—Kim landed in Gimpo International Airport. The ANSP swiftly apprehended Kim and his wife and took them home, where they would spend months under house arrest.[60] But Kim's return was a glimmer of hope for South Koreans, who believed that strong political leadership was as important as popular resistance in bringing about change to their country.

A second dose of optimism came only a few days after Kim landed in Seoul. South Korea was scheduled to hold its second National Assembly election of the Chun era. Neither Kim Dae-jung, nor Kim Young-sam or Kim Jong-pil were allowed to run. But seeking to give the vote a modicum of legitimacy, Chun had decided to allow hundreds of politicians previously banned from politics to run for the election, and they scrambled to put together a new opposition party. In December 1984, the New Korea and Democratic Party (NKDP) was born. Legalized three weeks before the election and with campaigning severely restricted, the NKDP won 29.2 per cent of the vote in the February legislative election. This was below the 35.2 per cent share of the vote that Chun's DJP received.[61] But opponents of the Chun regime were emboldened by the DJP's declining share of the vote and the NKDP's strong showing a mere three weeks after its official foundation. And a turnout above 84 per cent showed that South Koreans wanted their votes to be heard. Shortly after the election, the ban on the Three Kims engaging in political activities was lifted.[62] This further strengthened the hand of the opposition NKDP.

The Chun government's response to the *minjung* movement and South Korea's general thirst for democracy was more repression. Indeed, its response to the Gwangju Uprising was a taste of what would come throughout the 1980s. Shortly after the uprising, scores of activists and intellectuals were sent to 'purification camps', where they were joined by thousands of 'vagrants'—homeless, disabled, drug dealers and others the regime deemed undesirable. Over 60,000 people passed through these camps between August 1980 and January 1981, enduring harsh, military-like conditions far away from cities for the purpose of 're-education'.[63] Together with the government's failure to account for the events in Gwangju, the camps denied Chun any lasting legitimacy for his regime almost from the beginning.

Throughout the 1980s, the ANSP and the police continued to behave as they had done throughout the Park era. Detention, torture and extrajudicial killings were commonplace. Many prosecutors were also complicit in the repression unleashed by the Chun government, ensuring that opposition politicians, students and activists received harsh sentences essentially banning them from public life. And as the Seoul Olympic Games approached, the Chun government added growing numbers of 'vagrants' to the list of undesirables. Between 1981 and 1986, the number of detainees in thirty-six nationwide facilities jumped from 8,600 to 16,000. Violence against the detainees was common, and hundreds of them died while in one of the facilities.[64] Chun also used the 'North Korea threat' to try to legitimize his rule in the run-up to the Games. In November 1986, the government announced that it would build a 'Peace Dam' to protect Seoul against the threat of North Korea unleashing 20 billion tons of water to flood the South Korean capital.[65] There was never any proof that Kim Il-sung had any such plan, but the announcement did scare South Koreans. If the government had to frighten its own people to remain in power, so be it. Decades later, South Koreans would still bitterly remember how Chun had fooled them. Simply put, the South Korean president had no interest in compromise with those who disagreed with him or those he thought gave a poor image of South Korea. He clung to the hope that economic progress would legitimize his rule.

*The final struggle for democracy*

A picture shows Lee Han-yeol wearing a T-shirt emblazoned with a simple word: *Yonsei*. The name of his university. One of South Korea's top universities in fact. But the young Lee is lying motionless in the arms of a friend. His gaze is lifeless. Blood is pouring out of his head and slowly starting to cover his face. A tear gas grenade has just penetrated his skull. Indeed, a closer look at the picture reveals that Lee and his friend are surrounded by tear gas. Sadly, this will be the last memory for the young boy. He will never regain consciousness again. After twenty-seven days on a life-support system, Lee passes away.[66] This will come as no consolation to his family, but this young, surely bright university student will forever symbolize the final fight of ordinary South Koreans to gain their democracy. Within six months of the picture, the late Lee will have won. His country will have held its first truly free elections in almost thirty years. There will be no turning back. The struggle for democracy will be over.

In 1987, South Koreans forced the hand of the Chun military dictatorship and successfully pressed for their first free elections since the 1960s. Students, workers and religious groups who had been resisting Chun's rule were joined by middle-class office workers and their managers, many of whom were veterans of the student movement themselves—or influenced by it. Branded the 'neck-tie brigade', this group joined the democratization movement in droves in 1987. In the 1990s, this group would be labelled the 386 generation: in their thirties, having studied in university in the 1980s and born in the 1960s.[67]

Back in 1987, these middle-class South Koreans were still the 'neck-tie brigade'. They had a goal: to support and fight for South Korea's transition to democracy. And they had a key reason for their fight, which they shared with the veterans of the labour and student movements. In the view of most South Koreans, Chun had never been their legitimate president. More so following his response to the Gwangju Uprising. But according to the amended South Korean constitution of 1980, Chun could only rule for a non-renewable seven-year term. And the president had promised that he would not seek to amend the constitution to allow him to run again as Park Chung-hee had done. This gave South Koreans hope that the end of Chun's rule would give way to democracy. And indeed, in 1986 the president launched negotiations with the NKDP that—South Koreans hoped—would lead to a peaceful transition to democracy.[68]

As negotiations dragged on, however, it became clear that Chun was not interested in South Korea becoming a real democracy. He had been grooming Roh Tae-woo to become his successor and wanted to make sure that he would become the next president. A former commander who had supported Chun's coup and then served in several cabinet posts, Roh had become the leader of the DJP in 1985. Chun wanted a strong National Assembly, which—he hoped—would provide Roh with the necessary support to become president. In contrast, the opposition supported a strong president voted for by all South Koreans in a direct election. The stand-off led to a split in the NKDP, with Kim Dae-jung and Kim Young-sam becoming critical of their party when it looked like it would seek a compromise with the government. Chun sensed an opportunity. In April 1987, he announced there would be an indirect election to choose his successor.[69] Kim Dae-jung and Kim Young-sam were enraged, so much so that they decided to leave the NKDP and form their own party.[70]

South Koreans were also enraged with Chun's announcement, which came in the context of an avalanche of protests, demonstrations and strikes. Furthermore, policemen had tortured Seoul National University student Park Jong-cheol to death in January. The authorities initially tried to cover up the real cause of Park's death, but a group including a doctor, a prosecutor, a reporter, a pastor and others came together to reveal the truth.[71] Not only was the Chun regime killing South Koreans; it was also trying to cover up what it was doing.

Some 2,600 kilometres away, Filipino dictator Ferdinand Marcos had been doing the same for decades. But in February 1986, he was deposed in the People Power Revolution and the Philippines became a democracy. South Koreans had an example of what the people could achieve in their own backyard. When Chun made his announcement in April, South Koreans only doubled down in their push for democracy. Protests became constant. Strikes as well: there would be 3,749 in 1987 compared to 276 the year before.[72] South Korea became ungovernable. Only the military could restore a modicum of order. The risk, however, was a repeat of the bloodbath of the Gwangju Uprising. Reagan was concerned, and his administration lobbied Chun directly to push for democracy—both publicly and privately.[73] The International Olympic Committee (IOC) was concerned as well, with its president lobbying Chun in person.[74] Seoul was due to host the Olympic Games. Roh was president of the Games preparation committee. Something would have to give.

On 9 June, Lee Han-yeol received the fatal hit to his head. One day later, Roh was nominated as the candidate of the DJP for the presidency. Hundreds of thousands of South Koreans demonstrated across the country. The June Democratic Struggle had started. More and more South Koreans from all walks of life came on to the streets. The number of strikes grew. Chun—and now Roh—were under growing international pressure not to resort to violence. And the police forces were running out of the tear gas that they were using to disperse the demonstrators.[75] South Koreans realized this. Now it was millions of them on the streets, all across the country. Nothing but a full, free democracy would do. This was a struggle. The people had to win.

On 29 June, Roh gave up. Violence had to stop. The people should have their wish. Roh sat down on his chair. In front of him and to his sides, a room filled with members of his cabinet, other politicians and journalists. He was about to deliver one of the most consequential speeches in South Korean history: the Special Declaration for Grand National Harmony and Progress Towards a Great Nation, forever known as the 'June 29 Declaration'. Roh spoke in a monotone voice. There was neither anger nor joy as he told South Koreans what they had been longing for: South Korea would soon become a democracy.[76] Roh's declaration included eight points. The first three?

> 1. The ruling and opposition parties have agreed to a presidential amendment to be made as soon as possible, and there will be a peaceful regime transition in February 1988 following a presidential election under a new constitution.
>
> 2. The presidential election law will be revised to ensure free candidatures and fair competition.
>
> 3. In the name of national reconciliation and unity, Kim Dae-jung and all political prisoners will be granted amnesty.[77]

A picture shows a coffin draped in a South Korean flag. The Taegukgi. A final gesture reserved for heroes. A big portrait of the deceased accompanies the coffin. And a wave of people surrounds it. They are in front of Yonsei University's main gate. They will make their way to Seoul City Hall, where there will be a funeral service. Over a million people will honour the deceased that day, lining the streets of South Korea's capital. It is 9 July. Lee Han-yeol had finally passed away four days earlier, on 5 July.[78] He died a hero. A hero like millions of women and men, young and old, who never gave up. Who forced their government to make a declaration. Who brought democracy to South Korea.

*Democracy at last*

In October 1987, the South Korean constitution was amended for the tenth and—as of 2023—final time. After the National Assembly approved the new bill, over 94 per cent of voters approved it in a referendum.[79] The constitution established a presidential system, with presidents only allowed to run for a single and non-renewable five-year term. The president would be directly elected by the voters.[80] So South Korea would have a strong president, but the president would have to give way to someone new after five years. This should ensure the renewal of South Korean democracy fairly frequently.

The election was scheduled for 16 December. The key contenders had already been informally running their campaigns for months. Maybe for years. But with the constitution approved and South Koreans assured that this time they would be able to vote for their preferred president, the campaign could now start in full swing. Roh was the DJP candidate. He could not run on a promise of continuity with Chun's policies, given that the newly approved constitutional amendment had effectively killed the Fifth Republic. But he did run on a continuity platform, espousing conservative values and focusing on economic growth and social stability. Roh's image had improved thanks to his 29 June declaration and his role as the president of the Olympic

Games preparatory committee. By all accounts, he would be a formidable candidate. But who would be his main opponent in the progressive camp? Kim Young-sam and Kim Dae-jung could not agree. So both of them ran. Kim Jong-pil also joined the presidential race. Thus, the Three Kims contested the election. Predictably, this resulted in the liberal vote splitting into three different camps. Which—along with his own credentials—allowed Roh to win the election.

Roh received almost 37 per cent of the vote. He carried the vote of socially and politically conservative urban voters plus a large share of the rural vote. Kim Young-sam came second in the polls, with 28 per cent of the vote—followed by Kim Dae-jung with 27 per cent. Kim Young-sam carried the vote of a large number of liberal urban voters. Kim Dae-jung, meanwhile, received the support of many workers and more left-leaning progressives—along with his home province of Jeolla. Kim Jong-pil could only manage slightly over 8 per cent.[81] Thanks to his clear victory over his opponents, a voter turnout above 89 per cent and the absence of any major incident on the day of the election, Roh was about to become the first president of South Korea's restored democracy.

By a twist of fate, Samsung founder Lee Byung-chul had died a month before the election. Throughout the Fifth Republic, the *chaebol* had become the dominant actor in the South Korean economy—at the helm of a private sector that was powering high rates of economic growth. Lee Kun-hee, his son, took Samsung's chairmanship eight days after Roh's election. The younger Lee had grand ambitions. He wanted Samsung—already South Korea's biggest conglomerate—to become a world-leader, known for its innovation rather than for copying technologies developed by others.[82] As 1987 drew to a close, South Korea was on the verge of launching a free democracy in need of consolidation, seeking to transform its economy into a world-leading innovator and—let's not forget—preparing to host the Olympic Games.

Not one, not two, but three tall orders. But then, nothing seemed impossible for this country about to turn forty.

# 4

# FREEDOM AND CRISIS
## 1988–97

*Early days as a democracy*

The Sixth Republic was officially inaugurated on 25 February 1988, the day when Roh Tae-woo took office as the sixth South Korean president. There was no going back. The Sixth Republic would eventually become the longest running in South Korean history, still going strong into the 2020s. Roh was aware of the momentous nature of the occasion. And he was also aware that a formal democracy was not enough to satisfy South Koreans. In his inauguration speech, he pledged that the date would launch 'a great era for the ordinary people thanks to democratic reforms and national reconciliation.' Roh also promised that 'the era when freedoms and human rights could be neglected for the sake of economic growth and national security [were] over.'[1] To highlight this point, a general amnesty was announced only days after his inauguration—with 7,000 political prisoners freed from jail.[2] To distance himself from Chun Doo-hwan and his regime,

Roh promised to be an 'ordinary man'. Street sweepers, farmers and factory workers were invited to his inauguration.[3] Roh also took to carrying his own bag. A small gesture, but one that was meant to symbolize that he was not above anyone else.

Roh's critics, however, were quick to dismiss his presidency. They chided Roh as a product of Chun's regime. Yes, he had won the 1987 election. But he had participated in Chun's coup, had been appointed by Chun and had only agreed to start a transition towards a democracy after it had proved impossible to continue a Chun-style dictatorial regime. Plus, many members of the Roh government were old colleagues from the Chun regime. And the government apparatus and bureaucracy of the Chun years—which in many cases dated back to the Park regime—continued to be in place.[4] Critics labelled Roh's presidency the 'Five-Point-Five' Republic[5]—somewhere between Chun's Fifth Republic and the Sixth Republic that in their view had yet to arrive.

And indeed, critics talked—and still talk—about South Korea's 'conservative democratization'. Dictators were gone, South Koreans could vote for their president in free and fair elections and political parties competed against each other to gain power and implement their preferred policies. But there had been no wholesale transformation of the system. No new generations came to power, displacing the old elites that were seemingly as comfortable in a democracy as in a dictatorship as long as they remained in power. Institutions and political parties failed to renew themselves. And groups including young people remained excluded from sharing the spoils of democratized political power.[6]

In this context, strikes and protests continued to be commonplace in South Korea throughout 1988–9.[7] Students wanted reform of the ANSP, police force, judiciary and all other institutions central to the repressive system in place during the Chun years. They also wanted an end to the use—or abuse—of the National Security Law and anti-communist legislation that had been used to imprison thousands of activists over the decades. There were also students demanding unification with North Korea. Workers, meanwhile, shared many of the students' demands for domestic reform. But they also wanted wages to increase substantially. Many felt that the system was rigged against them and believed that cosy government–*chaebol* relations were limiting their gains from South Korea's impressive economic growth. The workers were successful: average wages doubled between 1988 and 1993.[8] Their plight was starting to improve under the new government.

Judges and prosecutors joined in with their own grievances. They wanted the restoration of judicial independence, last seen in South Korea before the Park government.[9] The judiciary had been part of the repressive system in place during the dictatorship years, handing out lengthy sentences to activists and deploying the death penalty fairly regularly. Sometimes, individuals had decided to defy the system. The prosecutor involved in the Park Jong-cheol torture investigation was a case in point. But more often than not, judges and prosecutors had been unwilling or unable to challenge South Korea's dictatorial governments. Realizing that South Korea was changing, they pressed forward with their demands. The Roh government indeed successfully promoted judicial independence.[10] The Sixth Republic brought the promise of genuine change to the judiciary as well.

Whether of his own volition, forced by the people, pressure within his government or a combination of all three, Roh was indeed implementing changes that were making South Korea more democratic and South Koreans freer. The people of the country sensed that change was in the air. In 1989, a few civil society groups organized the first-ever public service to commemorate the Jeju Uprising of 1948–9. Forty-one years after the events that had shocked the island, the locals and other South Koreans from all over the country felt safe to commemorate this tragic event. The police did not intervene. Several weeks of com-memoration and celebrations followed suit, mixing traditional plays, movie screenings, testimony hearings and shamanistic exorcism rituals.[11] Some victims even spoke about their experi-ence in public for the first time. Four decades of suffering in silence were over. The commemoration was a metaphor of the social and political changes underway in South Korea.

Roh's reforms were also the result of a seismic change in the National Assembly. The April 1988 legislative election returned a parliament in which the ruling party did not have an absolute majority for the first time since 1950. A right-wing president and a left-wing National Assembly. For the first time in South Korean history, the president could not count on the unconditional sup-port of the National Assembly. Roh's DJP did come first in the election, winning 34 per cent of the vote. But the opposition, with each one of the Three Kims running for a different party, was able to capture a larger share and a majority of the seats in the National Assembly. Kim Young-sam's Reunification Democratic Party received almost 24 per cent of the vote, Kim Dae-jung's Peace Democratic Party obtained slightly over 19 per cent and Kim Jong-pil's New Democratic Republican Party won over 15 per cent.[12] The opposition was now able to check the govern-ment's legislation and activities, launch investigations related to suspected abuses of power by the Roh government or the actions of the Chun government and present its own legislative agenda. A proactive National Assembly was a novelty brought about by the nascent South Korean democracy.

Roh reacted as politicians in a democracy have to do: by trying to persuade the opposition to support his agenda. On 23 January 1990, a political earthquake shook South Korea. Following a ten-hour meeting, Roh, Kim Young-sam and Kim Jong-pil merged their three parties to form the Democratic Liberal Party (DLP). Concerned by declining economic growth—which almost halved from 12 per cent in 1988 to 'only' slightly over 6 per cent in 1989—criticized by business leaders for his failure to enact economic reforms and frustrated by his inability to pass legislation, Roh wanted a strong conservative party. Kim Young-sam and Kim Jong-pil agreed with this vision.[13] They had the example of the Liberal Democratic Party (LDP) in Japan. The LDP had been in power for over three decades, without inter-ruption. The leaders of different factions took turns to become head of government. If conservative Japanese politicians could do this, why not South Korea? Kim Dae-jung expressed his frustration, calling the merger 'a coup d'état against democ-racy.'[14] And for some, the merger symbolized that the old politi-cal elites who had ushered in a 'conservative democratization' would continue to dominate the country even if it was now a democracy. But the reality was that the DLP commanded two-thirds of the seats in the National Assembly. The merger allowed Roh to move ahead with his reform agenda.

Less noticed but aptly symbolizing the changes and freer atmosphere that were taking hold in the country, Lotte World opened in 1989 in Seoul. It was one of the biggest indoor amusement parks in the world at the time of its launch. It remains a fun day out—or days—well into the twenty-first cen-tury. For many South Koreans wanted to leave behind upheaval, protests and demonstrations. They wanted to enjoy their hard-won salaries—and democracy. Still, there were limits to which the new theme park could represent a break from the past. Construction had actually begun in 1984, during the Chun years. And Lotte was one of South Korea's biggest *chaebol*, established in 1967 and now branching out into amusement parks. In some respects, evolution, not revolution, marked South Korea's transition to democracy.

# SHRIMP TO WHALE

*The Seoul 1988 coming out party*

A sixty-six-year-old man carries the Olympic torch into the Seoul Olympic Stadium, located south of the Han River. It is a sunny and balmy September morning in the South Korean capital. It is clear that the man used to be a professional runner. He enters the stadium, torch in his right hand. The crowd roars. All 100,000 of them. Millions join at home and on the streets, watching from TV sets. Actually, make that tens of millions. The man waves to the crowd. The crowd roars even louder. He takes a few more steps and extends his arm to pass the torch. Throughout this whole sequence, we can clearly see the logo adorning his T-shirt. Right in front of his chest. The Seoul 1988 logo.[15]

For South Koreans, this was poetry in motion. Fifty-two years earlier, this same man had tried to hide the flag in front of his chest, even though he had just won the Olympic marathon. For this man was none other than Sohn Kee-chung. A Korean hero who in 1936 had had no option but to run under the flag of his country's colonial master. Who for years had been fighting for the IOC to recognize his gold medal under his (South) Korean citizenship, albeit to no avail. And who in 1988 symbolized the pride that South Korean people had in their country. A fairly rich, newly democratized country. A country that could look others in the face as an equal. Not as a colony. Not as an economic basket case. Not as a dictatorship. And not as a shrimp.

The importance of the Seoul 1988 Olympic Games for South Korea cannot be overstated. Tokyo 1964 had allowed Japan to show that it had become a modern country that had left its imperialistic past behind. Beijing 2008 would one day allow China to proudly showcase its economic development. Countless countries—in Asia and elsewhere—have used Olympic Games for political purposes. Chun Doo-hwan had sought to do the same when he put forward South Korea's bid to host the Olympic Games in 1981. Seven years later, it was actually the people of South Korea who were beaming with pride.

Seoul 1988 allowed South Korea to show to the rest of world that it was joining the ranks of the developed economies. Thanks in part to the Olympic Games, South Korean trade reached record levels in 1988. Furthermore, there was an IT drive in the run-up to the Olympic Games. And over 30,000 jobs were created to build the Olympic venues and upgrade South Korea's infrastructure.[16] There were still pockets of poverty across South Korea for sure. But this was not the war-ravaged, poor country that the American TV series *M\*A\*S\*H\**—set during the Korean War—had been showing viewers across the world between 1972 and 1983.

The Olympic Games also served to boost South Koreans' pride in traditional Korean culture, which the organizers showcased during the opening ceremony. Koreana—one of the few South Korean bands relatively well known outside the country—mixed Korean and English in their rendition of 'Hand in Hand', the official song of Seoul 1988. And the flag bearers of all the participating countries entered the Olympic stadium ordered according to Hangeul. This was the first encounter with the Korean language for tens of millions of TV viewers watching around the world. The opening ceremony also featured a mass demonstration of taekwondo, the traditional Korean martial art that was a demonstration sport in 1988 and became a full medal sport from the 2000 Olympic Games onwards. Traditional Korean turtle ships, musicians playing the Korean drum, women displaying their colourful *hanboks* ... Korea's traditional culture was introduced to the rest of the world in all its glory.[17] For many TV viewers and visitors alike, this was the first time they had encountered Korean culture.

The Olympic Games also symbolized the acceptance of South Korea by the global community of nations. Even the fact that the IOC had entrusted South Korea to host the Olympic Games was hugely symbolic, for it was an acknowledgement by Olympic committees across the world that they believed that the country was capable of managing the logistics of such a complex event. Seoul 1988 was also a diplomatic victory for South Korea. The United States and its allies had boycotted Moscow 1980. The Soviet Union and its allies responded in kind at Los Angeles 1984. But the Soviet Union, China and almost every other communist country attended the Seoul Olympic Games.[18] And the visiting delegations from China, the Soviet Union and Central and Eastern Europe were able to witness South Korea's economic development compared to their own countries first-hand. The Olympic Games was the final impetus for many political leaders across the communist bloc to decide to establish diplomatic relations with South Korea.[19] As he opened the Olympic Games on that September morning, Roh could afford himself a smile. His country had arrived on the global stage. South Korea was one of the world's whales.

*The South 'defeats' the North*

Shortly before the Seoul 1988 Olympic Games, Roh had stepped on to the stage in Seoul to deliver a crucial speech. The day was 7 July. It was hot and humid in the South Korean capital, as is often the case during the summer. There were some rain showers that day, but rainier days were yet to come. Roh's speech was meant to define the Sixth Republic's foreign policy, particularly its policy towards North Korea. And indeed, the six principles that Roh introduced that day would end up guiding South Korean foreign policy in the decades to come. In his speech, Roh set out the six principles of *Nordpolitik* (Northern Policy)—

South Korea's policy towards North Korea and the communist bloc. The principles included boosting cooperation between the two Koreas; expanding humanitarian and separated family exchanges; establishing inter-Korean trade relations; ending Seoul's opposition to exchanges between its allies and North Korea; foreign policy cooperation between the two Koreas; and increasing trade, cultural and people-to-people exchanges with the communist bloc.[20] Arguably, the '7 July Declaration' became one of Roh's crowning achievements—if not the main one.

*Nordpolitik* was not a new concept per se. Lee Beom-seok, Chun's foreign minister at the time, had introduced it in 1983. But it was Roh who had reintroduced the concept during his election campaign and in his inauguration speech. The ultimate goals presented by Roh in his speech were not particularly innovative. They came down to increasing exchanges with North Korea—which both Park and Chun had tried—and normalization of South Korea's diplomatic relations with the Soviet Union, China and Central and Eastern Europe—which Chun had also considered.[21] But Roh gave concrete shape to *Nordpolitik* and actively pursued exchanges, which his predecessors had failed to do. He put this policy at the centre of South Korea's foreign policy, in contrast to Park and Chun. And crucially, Roh did so from a position of strength vis-à-vis North Korea and at a time when it was feasible for South Korea to actually pursue its goals.

Roh was also tapping into South Koreans' wish to improve relations with their northern neighbour. Calls for reconciliation came from opposition parties, student groups, the feminist movement and myriad activist groups that no longer saw North Korea as an enemy. Roh was acutely aware of South Koreans' changing attitudes, and he sought to change South Korea's education system to focus on unification rather than anti-communism. He also made it easier for information about North Korea to circulate.[22] In this context and coupled with South Korea's already obvious diplomatic and economic ascendance over North Korea, *Nordpolitik* was a no-brainer.

With Seoul 1988, an economy three times bigger than North Korea's and Pyongyang's supposed communist allies having used the Olympic Games to initiate contacts with South Korea, Roh put his plan in motion. In February 1989, Hungary became the first country from Central and Eastern Europe to establish diplomatic relations with Seoul. By 1993, almost all of the former and current communist countries had followed suit. The Soviet Union itself did so in September 1990. China as well, in August 1992. In contrast, no new Western country established diplomatic relations with North Korea. With the end of the Cold War and communist regimes rapidly folding across the world, South Korea was the present and future, its economic allure obvious for all to see. North Korea was the past, a remnant of a Cold War that everyone wanted to leave behind.

Kim Il-sung sought to counter South Korea's obvious success with Seoul 1988 and rapprochement with the communist bloc by hosting the Thirteenth Festival of Youth and Students. With the event scheduled for July 1989, the Kim regime doubled down on its efforts to upstage its southern neighbour following the Olympic Games. In May, the Rungrado 1st of May Stadium opened. Officially seating 150,000 people, it was the biggest stadium in the world. Pyongyang was in no mood to spare any cost. It reportedly spent a quarter of its annual budget on preparing the festival. But shortly after the event was over, the protests leading to the end of communism in Central and Eastern Europe erupted. And North Korea had anywhere between US$4 and 9 billion in debt to pay.[23] If anything, the festival made the disparity between South and North even more obvious.

It was in this context that Roh moved ahead with his push to improve relations with North Korea. In September 1991, both

Koreas joined the United Nations as independent countries.[24] In December, the two Koreas signed the Agreement on Reconciliation, Non-Aggression and Exchanges between South and North Korea (also known as the Basic Agreement). The declaration reaffirmed the three principles of the 1972 joint communiqué. Its first article stated that the two Koreas recognized each other and their systems. The second then established that they would not intervene in each other's affairs. Reunification remained the ultimate goal.[25] But separate UN membership and the Basic Agreement recognized the reality of a divided Korean Peninsula with two different systems. The two Koreas had to coexist peacefully. And, ultimately, the agreement was recognition that rich, prosperous and democratic South Korea had left the North behind.

Shortly afterwards—in January 1992—Seoul and Pyongyang signed the Joint Declaration of the Denuclearization of the Korean Peninsula.[26] A few weeks earlier, the United States had removed its tactical nuclear weapons from South Korea as part of US President George W. Bush's policy of withdrawing them from across the world.[27] This declaration also fitted with Roh's *Nordpolitik*, which promised to reduce tensions between the two Koreas. Pyongyang, of course, would go on to break the promise contained in the declaration. Seoul did not. South Korea had its alliance with the United States. It was the richer country, which allowed it to have a more powerful army than the North. And it was a democracy and respected member of the international community, not in the game of breaching such an important agreement.

In the following years, the gap between South and North only grew. It was not only that the South Korean economy continued to grow and that its democracy continued to consolidate. It is also that tragedy hit North Korea. Kim Il-sung passed away in July 1994.[28] This might have been a disaster for the North Korean people in and of itself, since many of them genuinely loved the founding father of their country. But the real tragedy was only starting to hit North Koreans. Between 1994 and 1998, an acute famine, leading to mass starvation, hit the country. The Soviet Union—North Korea's main economic benefactor—had collapsed. China—which had replaced the Soviet Union as North Korea's main food provider—had to reduce aid to North Korea due to its own shortfalls. Floods and droughts then hit North Korea, leading to a sharp decline in food production. Faced with these pressures, North Korea's centralized distribution system collapsed. Estimates suggest over two million North Koreans died from malnutrition and hunger-related illnesses during the five years of the famine.[29]

South Korea and other countries offered food aid, but North Korea's distribution system and misappropriation by the North Korean authorities meant that little reached the North Korean population. Kim Jong-il, who had replaced his father as the country's leader, continued to use repression to keep the population under control.[30] It was not only that South Korea had won its competition with North Korea; the North Korean authorities had tragically failed their own population.

### Civilian government, civic nationalism

Kim Young-sam became South Korea's first civilian president in over thirty years after winning the December 1992 election. He was also the first of the Three Kims to succeed in his quest to lead the country. As the candidate of the DLP, he received Roh's support. Running on a conservative platform, Kim Young-sam won 42 per cent of the total vote. Kim Dae-jung came second, receiving almost 34 per cent. Hyundai founder Chung Ju-yung also ran for president, getting a share slightly over 16 per cent.[31] Kim Young-sam's victory against the very popular leader of the liberal opposition and arguably the most famous *chaebol* chairman gave him further legitimacy. Roh had implemented a raft of policies taking South Korea down a freer and more liberal path. Kim would double down on his predecessor's approach upon his inauguration in February 1993.

Kim's election coincided with a period in which South Koreans' ideas about what being (South) Korean meant were in flux. *Minjok* continued to be central to South Korean identity. All Koreans were still part of a unique race with a centuries-old history as a single country. One day, they should reunify.[32] But South Korea was now developed and democratic. South Koreans were able to vote for their own president, who in a sense truly represented the people because he was not ruling them without their consent. And the president would be replaced when voters chose a different one after five years. Ultimately, the people had the power. Not the president. So, yes, race continued to be crucial. But were South Koreans really the same as North Koreans just because they shared the same race? By the time Kim took office, the fortieth anniversary of the end of the Korean War was only months away. The forty-fifth anniversary of Korea's division into two was also close. A growing number of South Koreans had been born after Korea's division. They had no recollection of a unified Korea. They had been born and lived as South Koreans. Dictatorial leaders could not represent them, or their country. But that was the past. Democracy had arrived. Perhaps their country increasingly shared more with other advanced democracies than with the poor dictatorship on the other side of the thirty-eighth parallel.

South Koreans therefore started to develop a new civic nationalism. Arguably driven by the 386 generation and its generally left-leaning worldview, this new civic nationalism was bringing about a new *South* Korean identity. They were Koreans. They belonged to a single race. But they were also South Koreans. And South Korea was a separate country from North Korea.

And what was the meaning of civic nationalism? It was a commitment to nation-building, to the well-functioning of the modern South Korean state that the people had built.[33] For South Koreans, their nation was Korea. But their state was South Korea. *Minjok* still mattered of course. Pride in their traditional Korean culture remained. But this pride in Korean traditions was being adapted to suit the modern South Korean state and modern lifestyles.[34] Increasingly, it would have to coexist with a civic nationalism that was equally important to growing numbers of South Koreans.

This changing mentality informed demands for a more egalitarian society. Most South Koreans were now middle class and could satisfy their basic needs. Income inequality was among the lowest in the developed world. But there were inequalities. Most obviously, women were still not equal to men. The peak of the birth sex ratio imbalance had come in 1990. Abortion of female foetuses was not as widespread as in years past, but it was not uncommon either. Open debate about this reality took off in the mid-1990s.[35] Confucian-infused ideas informed a patriarchal approach to family and society that many South Koreans still shared.[36] These ideas prioritized men as the family head and confined women to housework upon marriage whether they liked it or not.

The government stepped in. Change in the legal status of women started with the Roh government's revision of the Family Law in 1989, with new provisions being included that brought the legal status of women to the same level as that of men. Women could now succeed men as the family head and had equal rights to property and child custody rights after a divorce. In 1994, the Kim government passed the Act on the Punishment of Sexual Crimes and Protection of Victims. This was followed in 1997 by the Act on the Prevention of Domestic Violence.[37]

Equally important, Kim worked to ensure that the legal changes enacted by Roh and by his own government were implemented.

The judiciary stepped in as well. Throughout the 1990s, several court judgments ruled unconstitutional aspects of the Family Law discriminating against women. Most notably, in 1997 the Constitutional Court ruled that the prohibition of marriage within one's clan was unconstitutional.[38] In a sense, the government and the courts were catching up with a society where women continued to suffer discrimination—particularly in the workforce but also in terms of expectations about their role within the family—yet that was also changing. Most notably, the sex ratio at birth started to move into a more natural trend as industrialization and urbanization brought a new mindset among South Koreans.[39] And by the mid-1990s, the number of women joining more socially prestigious careers traditionally dominated by men like medicine, law and academia was also on the rise.[40]

Corruption was another area in which the new egalitarian ethos led the Kim government to seek change. Between January 1993 and June 1995, the Wooam arcade building crumbled, the Mugunghwa-ho train rolled over near Busan, Asiana Airlines Flight 733 crashed in the South Jeolla Province, the MV *Seohae* ferry sank in the West Sea, the Seongsu Bridge crossing the Han River collapsed, there was an explosion in a Daegu subway construction site and the Sampoong Department Store gave in. Together, these incidents caused over a thousand deaths—more than half of them in the Sampoong disaster. In most cases, it turned out that different government officials had received bribes, allowing for existing construction, maintenance and regulatory standards to be ignored.[41] Furthermore, close links between the government and the *chaebol* continued to be a concern. The Kim Young-sam government launched an anti-corruption drive with scores of investigations and high-profile arrests. But in May 1997, Kim's own son was arrested on bribery and tax evasion charges.[42] To many South Koreans, the arrest showed that the wealthy were still playing by different rules.

One area the government did not address, but that highlighted the changes underway in South Korea, was the formation of the country's first gay and lesbian organization in 1993: Chodonghwe. One year later, the organization dissolved and two new ones were launched: Chingusai for gay men and KiriKiri for lesbians. Advocating the human rights of LGBTQ+, the organizations spearheaded a movement that soon spread to universities in Seoul. In 1997, the LGBTQ+ movement became more visible. To begin with, the South Korean capital hosted the country's first Korean Queer Film Festival, even though the authorities shut it down on the first day. In addition, the Union of College Lesbians and Gays (Daedongin) was launched. Finally, the first demonstration explicitly focusing on LGBTQ+ rights was held.[43] They were baby steps, but they signalled that South Korean society was evolving.

The changes in South Korean society were inevitably reflected in its culture. In March 1992, Seo Taiji and Boys debuted their first song, 'I Know' ('Nan Arayo'). Initially panned by critics, the song became wildly popular. The video clip was fresh and innovative. Seo Taiji and 'his boys' were wearing the coolest of clothes. They danced and shook their bodies in a new way. Mixing the traditional Korean ballad with US influences including rap and rock, Seo Taiji and Boys had just inaugurated K-Pop.[44] They became known as the first 'boy group' in the K-Pop industry. And they paved the way for a new style that paid homage to South Korea's traditional music while infusing it with elements from other countries that South Koreans now saw as their equals. A transposition of civic nationalism to culture, so to speak.

For the 1990s were the years when Generation X came of age in South Korea. Born in the 1970s and reaching their twenties in the 1990s, this generation was able to enjoy South Korea's prosperity and freedom. They did not have the economic power of the 386 generation, for they were just joining university or starting their careers. They were not active participants in the democratic struggle of the 1980s, when they were still in school. But they shared the civic nationalism ethos of the 386 generation.[45] (Without abandoning *minjok* either.) And many young people saw culture—its creation and its consumption—as the way to experiment, in the way one could do in a country where dictatorial-era censorship was fading away.

Seo Taiji and Boys were tapping into this thirst for experimentation. But they were not the only ones; merely the most famous. Hongdae—a neighbourhood named after Hongik University, one of South Korea's top fine arts colleges—became one of the key centres of this new culture. New sounds, new cultural expressions and, ultimately, new ideas about what being South Korean meant started to emerge from the cheap flats, music venues and independent cafés and shops in the area.[46] Hongdae symbolized both what South Korea had become and where it was heading. Decades later, one can still walk around the neighbourhood and enjoy live music, cool bars and the latest fashion trends.

*Revisiting the dictatorial past*

South Korea's reckoning with its dictatorial past was inevitable. In a context in which South Koreans were developing a new civic nationalism and were increasingly proud of their democratizing institutions, there were calls for politicians and prosecutors to investigate the worst aspects of the country's history. After the opposition won a majority in 1988, the National Assembly launched the 'Fifth Republic Hearings'. The investigation focused on the Gwangju Uprising and subsequent deadly repression, ultimately laying the blame at Chun. The former president was forced to apologize in November. But investigations into the

127

Chun era also unearthed massive corruption among the former president's family and top officials. Several of them went on trial, and Chun himself vowed to return his ill-gotten gains. Chun then retreated to the Baekdamsa Buddhist temple in the Seorak Mountain for two years before returning to Seoul.[47]

South Koreans' push to investigate the country's dictatorial past took another turn after Kim Young-sam took office. The president launched an anti-corruption campaign, which also targeted Chun and Roh, shortly after his five-year term began. In June 1993, the Kim government reopened anti-corruption cases against the two former presidents.[48] And in 1993 as well, none other than Chung Sung-hwa—the army chief of staff when Park had been assassinated who Chun had then had arrested during his coup—led a group who brought a complaint against the former president on a host of charges, including treason.[49] But Roh had supported Chun's coup. So the president who had only recently stepped down was also included in the complaint, along with several more of Chun's supporters. Would the young democracy prove resilient enough to investigate its two most recent presidents?

The answer was yes. The chief prosecutor saw enough evidence that Chun and Roh had been involved in mutiny and treason in relation to the '12.12 Military Insurrection'. These charges were added to that of corruption. In March 1996, South Koreans had to rub their eyes as Chun and Roh entered the Seoul District Court building to go on trial. They were convicted in August and sentenced to life imprisonment in the case of Chun—after his original death sentence was commuted—and seventeen years in prison in the case of Roh—after he appealed his original sentence of twenty-two and a half years. Kim would pardon both of them in December 1997 in the name of 'national unity'.[50] But South Korea had shown that it was not afraid to investigate, prosecute and—if found guilty—imprison its former presidents. A remarkable achievement considering that many established democracies still baulked at pursuing corruption cases against their former leaders.

Kim also targeted the ANSP as part of his drive to move the country further away from its past history as a dictatorship. In 1994, he worked with the ruling and opposition parties in the National Assembly to set up an Information Committee to redefine the role of the agency. As a result, political neutrality was enshrined in its charter. Furthermore, the ANSP was removed from politics and the scope of its activities was revised to focus more heavily on the collection of intelligence to protect South Korea from international threats.[51] The ANSP would sometimes continue to meddle in politics. But following from the 1994 reform, South Koreans felt that the intelligence services would no longer engage in random arrests or try to shape the direction their country was taking.

*Washington visits the South Korean economy*

The Washington Consensus. An economic reform package promoted by the IMF, the World Bank and the US Department of the Treasury. Three institutions sitting within a fifteen-minute walk radius, a stone's throw from the White House. These institutions had been pushing this reform package throughout the 1980s, especially in Latin America. This was a package that the Chun government had also found appealing but did not ultimately fully embrace. With the end of the Cold War, the three institutions pushed these policies across Central and Eastern Europe, Russia and Sub-Saharan Africa. As well as East Asia. At the core of the package lay three neoliberal principles that had remained unchanged since the 1980s: deregulation, privatization and liberalization. Principles that proved fatal for countries across the world, causing financial crises and job losses. But in the

1990s and as communism collapsed, the Washington Consensus was seen as the undisputed, single road towards development.

South Korea had previously refrained from fully adopting policies associated with the Washington Consensus. On balance, its economic development model had been based on the very visible hand of the state working together with private firms. By the 1980s, however, the *chaebol* especially, and other firms were becoming too big for the state to guide. And by the early 1990s, South Korea was on the cusp of consolidating its democracy. Political freedom. Could South Korea really keep economic interventionism as part of its policy toolkit when politics had been fully liberalized? Should the economy not be fully liberalized as well? After all, did rich countries such as the United States, those in Western Europe and Japan not have liberal economies? These were the questions that Roh and, especially, Kim, had to confront. And they decided to go down the liberalization route. The Washington Consensus set the path that South Korea should walk.

In 1991, Roh launched a plan to deregulate interest rates. A first step on the road down a more liberal economy with less state intervention. But with economic growth falling to 'only' slightly above 6 per cent in 1992,[52] the scene was set for full-scale reform. That same year, the South Korean Ministry of Finance presented a new 'blueprint for comprehensive liberalization of the financial sector' to the US Department of the Treasury. The blueprint was a neoliberal's dream: interest rate deregulation, monetary policy liberalization, the launch of short-term money markets and liberalization of the capital account and foreign exchange transactions.[53] Over the next few years, the Kim Young-sam government slowly but steadily built on the blueprint and introduced reforms that were meant to change the face of the South Korean economy. The market, not the state, would be in charge of growth.

The Kim government doubled down on its neoliberal agenda by dispensing with the five-year plans that had defined South Korean economic policy-making from the moment Park Chung-hee had consolidated power in the early 1960s. Roh's seventh five year-plan, announced in 1992 and scheduled to end in 1996, was South Korea's last.[54] And Kim distanced himself from the plan upon entering office anyway, deciding against carrying it through. In 1994, the Economic Planning Board was unceremoniously abolished as an independent unit and its remnants placed within the Ministry of Finance.[55] From Kim's perspective, the South Korean economy would only be able to deal with a new world economy defined by globalization (*segyehwa*) if the central government stepped aside.

Kim also sought to devolve power to South Korean cities and regions. In 1995, Busan, Daegu, Daejeon, Gwangju and Incheon were re-designated as Metropolitan Cities. Ulsan would follow suit in 1997. These were South Korea's six biggest cities, after Seoul. Kim thought that the central government and Seoul-based bureaucrats could not decide what was best for the whole of the South Korean economy from their cosy offices in the bustling capital. Local policy-makers and local businesses working together would know better. The state had to move out of the way.

Kim then took the ultimate step to cut ties between the government and the private sector. He launched an anti-corruption drive, targeting politicians, bureaucrats and businesspeople. Above all, Kim set up an extremely popular 'real name' bank account and financial transaction policy. With the new policy, bank accounts and transfers could only be set up under someone's real name. Until then, it had been possible to use a false name, which had helped facilitate illegal payments from businesspeople to politicians and bureaucrats. Other popular anti-corruption measures followed, including a 'real name' property ownership policy, as well as a public service act forcing a larger number of officials to disclose their assets. The Kim years were also marked by high-profile investigations, charges and prosecutions of several *chaebol* owners. These included Samsung's Lee Kun-hee, Daewoo's Kim Woo-chung and Hyundai's Chung Ju-yung.[56]

Kim's liberalization drive came as South Korean businesspeople were themselves pushing for change in their business model. Growing labour costs were leading to lower profits, at a time when many already saw China's opening up and cheaper workforce as an existential threat. South Korean *chaebol* doubled down on a shift towards innovation and high-tech exports. Electronics, automobiles and ships were South Korea's main exports by value throughout the 1990s. In terms of technology, South Korean *chaebol* were already starting to catch up with competitors in the United States, Western Europe and Japan.[57] But they could still produce these high-tech goods more cheaply than their peers. This—and not cheap goods—would sustain economic growth.

Samsung's Chairman Lee Kun-hee, however, had loftier ambitions. He wanted Samsung to be known as a world-class innovator and pioneer. In 1993, he exhorted Samsung's executives to 'change everything but your wife and your children'. The 'New Management Initiative' was born. Samsung units had to innovate.[58] Executives had to try new things. Employees—whisper it—should be allowed to come up with their own ideas. This was a shock to the system. Like all other *chaebol* and most other South Korean firms, up until then decisions at Samsung came from the top and only after careful consideration. But this was no way of driving innovation, Lee thought. For decades to come, the 'New Management Initiative' underpinned Samsung's rise to the upper echelon of global firms. Other *chaebol* would also adopt similar processes, slowly loosening South Korea's hierarchical and rigid corporate structure.

But this was not enough to continue to propel economic growth. In 1994, South Korea's Presidential Advisory Council on Science and Technology marvelled at the movie *Jurassic Park*. Sure, those special effects were awesome. But there was something even more astonishing about the movie: in one year, it had made as much money as Hyundai selling 1.5 million cars.[59] That—and not the dinosaurs—was the most terrifying aspect of Steven Spielberg's hit movie. Should South Korea not also try its luck at making similar entertainment products that could be exported all over the world?

Thankfully for the government, South Korean entrepreneurs were already aware of the profits one could make from popular cultural goods. SM Entertainment, YG Entertainment and JYP Entertainment were founded in 1995, 1996 and 1997 respectively. (SM Entertainment traced its origins to 1989.) They would become the 'big three' firms propelling K-Pop's phenomenal success in the following decades. South Korean filmmakers also started to think big. If American filmmakers could produce hit movies, why not them? Kang Je-gyu was writing *Shiri*, the story of a North Korean assassin tracked by two South Korean agents. Samsung and other firms provided enough funding to make it the most expensive South Korean movie ever produced. Upon its release in 1999, it became South Korea's highest-grossing movie ever until then.[60] It also became a hit across several countries in East Asia. Culture, some dared to think, had the potential to become another growth engine for South Korea.

Kim's economic policy prescriptions seemed to be working. Economic growth went above the 9 per cent mark in 1994 and 1995.[61] Unemployment went down from almost 3 per cent of the workforce in 1993 to barely 2 per cent in 1996.[62] And inequality remained low.[63] South Korea seemed on the verge of becoming a developed economy, with diversified products and exports ranging from high-tech ships to original K-Pop bands.

*A developed nation*

On 12 December 1996, South Koreans thought they had indeed arrived. Lee Si-young, their ambassador to France, deposited South Korea's instruments of ratification in Paris to become the twenty-ninth country to join the OECD—only the second East Asian country to do so, after Japan. Both the government and the people celebrated accordingly. 'Joining the OECD is an honour for the Korean people', said Kim shortly after the ratification instruments were deposited.[64] KBS opened its 9pm news with footage of the ambassador signing the documents that confirmed South Korea's membership of the OECD.[65] His broad smile represented the smile on the faces of the government officials and millions of South Koreans who had worked so hard for this moment to arrive. Their country had moved from economic shrimp to whale.

The Kim government continued South Korea's relentless push to make the country a *seonjinguk*. And even though the consolidation of South Korea's democracy was a crucial element, so was the continuous move of the country's economy up the value-added chain. To this end, the Kim government focused on what it thought would allow South Korea to compete with other developed countries: highly skilled human capital formation and a leading role in new technologies.

In late 1993, the World Bank had published 'The East Asian Miracle'—a report analysing the drivers of South Korea's and other East Asian countries' economic development from the 1960s onwards.[66] Among other things, the report emphasized a relentless focus on education as the key driver behind the formation of highly skilled human resources. But the Kim government thought that the South Korean education system should be reformed as befitted a democratic and economically developed country. Labelling himself an 'Education President', Kim introduced an astonishing 120 educational reforms from 1995 to 1997. The Kim government thus overhauled South Korea's education system from top to bottom, focusing on the decentralization of the education system, boosting English language and IT education, increasing university education opportunities with a special focus on women, enhancing the accountability of schools and increasing cooperation between education providers and industry.[67]

As a result of these reforms, literacy and numeracy became almost universal in South Korea. In fact, 63 per cent of high school graduates were going on to university by 1997. Back in 1991, the university enrolment rate was just under 49 per cent.[68] It was under the Kim government that women's access to university education received a significant boost. Furthermore, the government promoted English language-taught classes. And both political mobilization and military officer training were abolished in South Korean universities.[69] These measures helped to further increase enrolment. Kim was laying the foundations of the contemporary South Korean university that domestic and foreign students alike would enjoy in decades to come—including the author of this book.

The 1990s were also the years when South Koreans' 'education fever' went universal at all levels, from middle school to university. Whether due to Confucian ideas about the value of education to achieve a higher social status, or a desire to become better educated to improve employment prospects, South Korean families had been spending heavily on education for decades. Following Seoul 1988, travel restrictions were lifted. As a result, a growing number of South Korean families started to emigrate or send their children to the United States or Canada for their high school studies—later moving on to university education there.[70]

The government also started to allow private tuition from university students in 1989. This market subsequently boomed, particularly tuition to achieve a high score in the annual university entrance exam that determined much of a student's future.[71] In addition, from 1991 private educational institutions (*hagwons*) were allowed to offer tuition to middle and high school students. *Hagwons* had a long history, predating the division of Korea. Family spending on them ballooned following the 1991 decision. In 1995, family spending on education was estimated at seventeen trillion won—slightly above the budget allocated to the Ministry of Education the year before.[72] (South) Koreans had traditionally attached great importance to education as the way to improve their life chances. They were willing to spend to make sure that their children could fulfil their potential.

Making South Korea a world leader in the newest technologies was the other key focus of the South Korean government throughout the 1990s. The Kim government bet big on telecommunications and set out to create the conditions for South Korea to become a world leader in this sector. In 1995, the government passed the Framework Act on Informatization Promotion. The act aimed to promote the use of the internet and mobile phones among South Korean consumers, with the government laying out the infrastructure and launching R&D projects,[73] while private providers competed against each other to offer the best-quality and cheapest products possible.

The private sector was responding in kind to the government's push to develop the internet and mobile phone sectors. In 1994, online gaming giant Nexon was established. One year later, Daum was launched; it would go on to open an internet portal and search engine. One year later, antivirus software AhnLab was also established. In 1997, NCSoft—another game developer—was born. Two years later, another online platform was launched—Naver. These firms would lead South Korea's IT and internet revolution in the years to come. They were joined by *chaebol* and privatized firms that soon came to dominate the mobile phone sector in South Korea. These were the years when Samsung and LG started to dabble in this sector, laying the groundwork for their global expansion from the 2000s onwards.[74] The private sector thus worked together with the government to make South Korea an ICT leader.

## The 'IMF crisis'

On 3 December 1997, Minister of Finance and Economy Lim Chang-yuel and Governor of the Bank of Korea Lee Kyung-shik signed the most humiliating letter any South Korean had had to prepare on behalf of their country's young democracy. It was a Letter of Intent from the South Korean government to the IMF.[75] The dull, bureaucratic title betrayed a painful reality for the Kim government and the South Korean population at large. South Korea was giving away its sovereignty in exchange for a US$57 billion bailout package. The IMF's largest-ever at the time it was approved. Two days later, the IMF and South Korea agreed an arrangement that made the humiliation official.[76] Not only that, South Korea was about to hold its five-yearly presidential election. The IMF forced all candidates to endorse the arrangement,[77] essentially leaving the incoming president hostage to an agreement he had had no say in. South Korea could still make its own decisions about its economic path. But at least in the short term, in theory the IMF would be able to veto any decision that it disliked.

The pain was further compounded by the behaviour of IMF Managing Director Michel Camdessus. To many, Camdessus embodied the worst of the 'white man's burden' cliché: the rich, wise white man saving the poor, foolish Asian country. Camdessus—and the IMF team sent to Seoul for discussion with the South Korean government at large—portrayed the bailout package as an opportunity for South Korea to reform its financial sector, liberalize the capital account and, more generally, further develop the economy. The 'benevolent' IMF would hold South Korea's hand as it became more 'developed' (i.e. as it implemented the economic policies then prevalent in Europe and the US). The IMF managing director would continue to insist on this message for years.[78] A picture of Camdessus with a broad smile on his face as Lim Chang-yuel signed the bailout package document was the last thing South Koreans needed to see.

What is generally known as the Asian Financial Crisis is thus known as the 'IMF Crisis' in South Korea. For the IMF's 'structural adjustment' programme would contribute to hundreds of thousands of job losses, the first drop in income for South Koreans since the 1950s, *chaebol* bankruptcies and the fire-sale of South Korean banks to foreign financial firms.[79] And how had South Korea reached the point of needing the biggest bailout in history? By following the Washington Consensus policies espoused by the IMF. Indeed, the crisis that hit South Korea in 1997 was essentially the result of the country's neoliberal turn throughout the 1990s coupled with the failure to address domestic corruption. A combination of domestic and foreign factors doomed the South Korean economy.

It was actually OECD membership that precipitated the financial crisis, by turbocharging the implementation of neoliberal policies. Having joined the organization, Seoul had to adhere to its Code of Liberalization of Capital Movements. Financial system liberalization measures included allowing domestic firms and banks to issue foreign-currency denominated debt without government approval, allowing foreign investors to purchase won-denominated bonds and removing limits on the ability of foreigners to buy shares in South Korean firms. OECD membership forced the South Korean government to implement these changes, but many officials serving in the Roh Tae-woo and Kim Young-sam governments actually supported them because they thought they would benefit the country's economy. The immediate result, in any case, was that South Korean banks and firms started to issue large amounts of short-term debt denominated in US$ to finance long-term domestic projects.[80] Never a good combination.

At the same time, corruption continued to be a problem. Links between the government and the *chaebol* were far from over. In fact, the son of Kim Young-sam was arrested in May 1997 on bribery and tax evasion charges related to the Hanbo scandal. The president and other high-ranking executives from South Korea's second-largest steelmaker would be found guilty of providing payments to Kim's son as well as several government officials including a minister and several presidential aides.[81] Even though Kim Young-sam himself was not directly involved, the Hanbo scandal showed that the government and the *chaebol* remained too close to each other. The South Korean government had been unable or perhaps unwilling to root out corruption.

Furthermore, many *chaebol* received easy credit from banks thanks to the cosy relationship between the two. Or due to government pressure, since neither the Roh Tae-woo nor the Kim Young-sam governments could resist the links between easy credit, *chaebol* investment and economic growth. For the Hanbo scandal ultimately involved corrupt government officials forcing banks to provide the steel giant with cheap loans. With banks providing credit to *chaebol* of their own volition or due to government pressure, and OECD-induced reforms leading to an influx of foreign capital into South Korea, the South Korean economy was heading down an unsustainable path.

The signs of trouble became obvious in January 1997, when Hanbo filed for bankruptcy after it became clear that it would be unable to service its debts of almost US$6 billion. Sammi Steel, beverage firm Jinro, carmaker Kia, Ssangbang Wool and several other *chaebol* would follow suit, either declaring bankruptcy or calling for a government bailout. In fact, the Kim government had brought together thirty-five banks to set up an anti-bankruptcy facility.[82] It was becoming clear that the South Korean economy as a whole was at stake. As a growing number of conglomerates and firms were going public with their debt financing problems, South Korea was on the verge of a structural crisis.

The final blow came from Thailand. In July 1997, the South East Asian country suffered a sudden capital withdrawal. As had been the case in South Korea, Thai banks and firms had been issuing short-term US$-denominated debt. But the Thai baht had been suffering speculative attacks. On 2 July, the government had no option but to float the country's currency. It had run out of money to maintain the peg in the value of the baht against the US$. Investors took their money out of the country. Unable to service their short-term, US$-denominated debt, Thai banks and firms collapsed one after the other.[83] Scared, foreign investors started to look at other countries that could suffer the same fate. The Philippines and, especially, Indonesia were next in line. Then came South Korea's turn.

As investors started to pull their money out of South Korea, the country's government, banks and firms watched powerless from their offices dotted around Seoul and other cities across the country. Firm bankruptcies were leaving banks with mounting non-performing loans. Short-term borrowing by banks denominated in US$ had to be repaid. The Bank of Korea was in danger of running out of reserves to defend the value of the won against the US$. If the central bank could not maintain the peg between the two currencies, banks—and firms—would have no hope to pay off their debts; the declining value of the won would have made it impossible to pay US$ to foreign lenders. On 21 November, the Kim government wrote to the IMF to request its assistance.[84] The rest, as they say, is history. Or a bad dream, from which South Koreans hoped to wake up with the election of their country's first liberal president since the early 1960s.

1. Gyeongbokgung, originally built in 1395, was the main royal palace of the Joseon Dynasty, and continues to sit at the centre of Seoul.

2. Koreans celebrate in the streets of Seoul during Korean National Liberation Day, 15 August 1945. This date marked the end of Japanese occupation and the beginning of the modern history of Korea.

3. Ceremony of inauguration of the Republic of Korea, 15 August 1948, the day South Korea was established.

4. Korean refugees crossing the thirty-eighth parallel dividing the two Koreas during the Korean War, 8 December 1950. Drawn by two US army officers, the parallel artificially divided Korea into two and remains the dividing line between them, as of 2022.

5. Korean War orphans in front of a US M-26 tank, June 1951. One of the most famous pictures of a war that caused one and a half million civilian deaths, over a million military casualties, left hundreds of thousands of orphans and an unknown number injured.

6. Korean War armistice signing, 27 July 1953. The armistice ended the Korean War de facto, but not de jure; the South Korean government refused to sign the armistice in the hope of taking over the whole of the Korean Peninsula.

7. Rhee Syngman, first President of South Korea (1948–60). Initially supported by the US, he won the first elections in Korean history, but his regime turned increasingly authoritarian and he was forced to resign and go into exile.

8. Park Chung-hee (centre, wearing sunglasses) and fellow soldiers on the day of their military coup, 16 May 1961. Implicitly accepted by the US, Park's coup put an end to a period of political instability and slow economic growth.

9. Park Chung-hee, third President of South Korea (1961–79), portrait, 1963. Under Park's leadership, South Korea achieved one of the highest economic growth rates in the world but also became a repressive dictatorship.

10. Statue of Jeon Tae-il on a bridge in Seoul. Jeon was a garment worker whose self-immolation in 1970 is credited with helping to spark South Korea's labour movement and slowly improve working conditions.

11. Hyundai Pony factory, 1970s. The Pony was South Korea's first exported car; though initially criticized for its low quality, it was improved and went on to sell hundreds of thousands of units.

12. Protesters are taken by the army during an uprising that took place in the southwestern city of Gwangju. The Gwangju Uprising, 18–27 May 1980, was part of a set of demonstrations demanding the democratization of South Korea.

13. Chun Doo-hwan, fifth president of South Korea (1980–87) attending a military briefing, 1985. Chun's government, marked by violence and repression as South Koreans demanded democratic elections, also saw high rates of economic growth.

14. Funeral of university student Lee Han-yeol, attended by over a million people, 9 July 1987. Lee was struck by a tear gas shell on 9 June 1987 during pro-democracy protests and remained unconscious until his death a month later. A picture taken of him after being struck helped to fuel the June Democratic Struggle, which resulted in the Chun government agreeing to free democratic elections.

15. Seoul Olympic Games opening ceremony, 17 September 1988; the Olympic Games served as South Korea's 'coming out' party, taking place only a few months after its democratization and showcasing a modern economy.

16. A stall holder's 'IMF sale' during the 1997–98 Asian financial crisis, Seoul. The 'IMF Crisis' resulted in South Korea's biggest recession since the Korean War and the highest unemployment rate in decades.

17. Kim Dae-jung (right), eighth president of South Korea (1998–2003), greets Kim Jong-il (left) upon landing in Pyongyang for the first-ever inter-Korean summit, 13 June 2000. The summit, which followed years of severe economic crisis in North Korea, brought hopes of reconciliation and potentially even reunification between the two Koreas.

18. South Korea supporters in front of Seoul City Hall, World Cup 2002. The national football team was the first from Asia to reach the tournament's semi-finals, boosting patriotism and civic nationalism.

19. Park Geun-hye at a press conference in the German Chancellery in Berlin, 26 March 2014. Park, Park Chung-hee's daughter, was the first female president of South Korea (2013–2017), but also the first to be impeached on corruption charges.

20. The headquarters of Samsung Electronics Co. in Seoul. By the 2010s, Samsung was the biggest company in South Korea and had become one of the biggest tech firms in the world, symbolizing the country's status as a developed economy.

21. Candlelight protest against President Park Geun-hye, 19 November 2016. The protests of up to one million people symbolized the power of the South Korean people to hold their leaders accountable, ultimately leading to Park's impeachment and removal from power.

22. Figure skater Kim Yu-na before lighting the cauldron at the PyeongChang 2018 Winter Olympic Games, 9 February 2018. Nicknamed 'Queen Yu-na', she was the first South Korean figure skater to win an Olympic gold medal and represented a younger generation of South Koreans competing with the world's elite.

23. BTS on *Good Morning America*, 15 May 2019. The most popular boy-band in the world in the late 2010s and early 2020s, they represented the globalization of K-Pop in particular, and *Hallyu* and the South Korean arts in general.

24. *Parasite* director Bong Joon-ho and cast members at the Oscars, 9 February 2020. The movie made history as the first foreign language winner of the Best Picture Oscar. It represented the globalization and success of Korean cinema.

5

## THE LIBERAL DECADE
## 1998–2007

*A peaceful transition, an economy in tatters, a new economy*

In February 1998, Kim Dae-jung was inaugurated as South Korea's first liberal president post-democratization. Kim won a majority or plurality of the vote in every single province in the western half of South Korea, including Seoul and his home region of Jeolla—where he received over 90 per cent of the vote. His main opponent, conservative Lee Hoi-chang, won the most votes in the eastern half. As a result, Kim won by a slim margin of just under 2 per cent.[1] But fears that South Korea would be plunged into a political crisis or that the conservatives or perhaps even the military would refuse to acknowledge Kim's victory quickly proved unfounded. On the night of the election, Kim received a flower bouquet from Lee.[2] A bouquet that symbolized the remarkable maturity of a democracy barely a decade old. With Roh Moo-hyun replacing Kim in 2003, South Korea was about to start a decade of liberal rule—the longest such period in its history.

To a large extent, Kim's victory was the result of the 386 generation flexing its political muscle. Its members saw their liberal values reflected in a man who had been working tirelessly for democracy since the 1960s. And they did not see any danger in electing 'a leftist'. The threat of a North Korean takeover—or South Korea falling under the spell of communism—did not cross their minds. Having grown up in a prosperous South Korea, the 386 generation now wanted a leader who would press ahead with political and social reform. Kim held the promise of bringing the change that the 386 generation thought their country needed. And he brought this promise on TV screens. A highly gifted orator, Kim won South Korea's first real TV election.[3]

Kim's first task, however, was to put an end to the IMF Crisis and reform the economy to ensure sustainable growth. In 1998, GDP plunged by 5 per cent.[4] This was South Korea's biggest recession on record. The unemployment rate shot up from under 3 per cent in October 1997 to over 8 per cent in July 1998.[5] This was unheard of since the Park Chung-hee government inaugurated the era of rapid economic growth. But the IMF was clear: its bailout package came with strings attached, and South Korea had to implement painful measures to receive the funding it was due. With an almost non-existent social safety net, unemployment often meant having to rely on family, friends or NGOs. In the worst cases, unemployment was a direct route to poverty. In a country used to high rates of employment—especially for men—and jobs (almost) for life, this was a very bitter pill to swallow.

But the South Korean economy bounced back swiftly and strongly. GDP went up by over 11 per cent in 1999 and a further 9 per cent in 2000.[6] The unemployment rate decreased rapidly, reaching a post-crisis low of 3 per cent in September 2002.[7] A boost to exports—supported by a weaker won after its value plunged during the crisis—was a key driver behind the recovery. The Kim government also moved quickly to improve the health of the banking sector. In a period of just three years, it spent KRW29 trillion (around US$26.2 billion) in writing off bad loans, plus a further KRW44.3 trillion (around US$40 billion) in fresh cash.[8] This served to quickly restore lending. Twelve out of the thirty-two biggest banks were either closed or restructured.[9] And the stock exchange staged a swift turnaround, with the value of many firms surpassing pre-crisis levels in 1999.[10] They were buoyed by both domestic and foreign investors seeking to grab a bargain.

But the Kim government had bigger and bolder reforms in mind, for which the IMF bailout package offered excellent cover. By the end of Kim's first year in office, eleven of the thirty biggest *chaebol* were allowed to go bankrupt. Venerable names including Halla, Hanwha and Kia were among the casualties.[11] Other *chaebol* were forced to slim down, disinvesting from many of the dozens of sectors that were non-core business. Kim met with chairmen to plead the case for the merger of units from different *chaebol* competing directly against each other and for *chaebol* to swap units with each other so that none lost out. Kim's efforts were partially successful at best. More effective was his push to make bank lending more transparent and closely aligned to market principles.[12] Credit certainly continued to flow to *chaebol*. But decisions about loans were increasingly the result of a careful consideration of business plans rather than a handshake in a dark room or—worse—a bribe.

Overseen and mandated by the IMF, Seoul also opened up the banking sector, the property market and several other sectors to foreign investors. But there were limits to the extent to which South Korea was willing to allow foreign investment. When

Ford announced its interest in buying Kia in mid-1998, both the South Korean government and its industrial leaders worked to ensure that the carmaker remained in domestic hands. In the end, Hyundai bought Kia.[13] They had seen Central and Eastern European states asset-stripped following the fall of communism in the early 1990s and IMF- and World Bank-mandated privatization. They had read about similar stories in Latin America, as the countries in the region suffered a spate of crises throughout the 1980s and the 1990s. Understandably, South Koreans sought to protect the firm they had built. Hyundai therefore received support to acquire Kia, a partnership that only ten years later would become the fifth-largest carmaker in the world.[14] And, crucially, that would continue to employ or support hundreds of thousands of jobs across South Korea.

Taking another leaf out of the IMF's book, the Kim government also liberalized the job market. Again, the IMF bailout package offered cover for a measure that the government may have wanted to implement anyway. Laws and regulations were changed so that it became easier for firms to hire and fire. This included measures to facilitate short-term contracts at the expense of permanent contracts. In subsequent years, the share of temporary contracts hovered around 20 to 25 per cent. This was towards the higher end among OECD countries.[15] Meanwhile, the share of part-time jobs crept up as the years went by. Even though part-time employment was lower than the OECD average,[16] this was unwelcome news for the many South Koreans accustomed to full-time jobs allowing the breadwinner to provide for his family. Similarly, youth unemployment went up and remained stuck around 10 per cent for years. Even though this was not particularly high compared to other OECD countries,[17] the days when graduates could choose between a number of job offers as soon as they were done with their degrees were gone. Overall, the liberalization of the job market helped keep unemployment low but created a set of issues that future governments had to confront.

Less noticed at the time was the Kim government's push to promote entrepreneurship and start-ups. The dot-com bubble was in full swing in the United States by the late 1990s and yet to result in one of the biggest crashes Wall Street would ever see. Why could South Korea not replicate the success of the United States in fostering innovation among its young people? This would help growth and, more importantly for Kim and successive South Korean governments, create jobs. Starting from its first year in office, the Kim government launched three governmental venture capital firms, introduced tax incentives and regulatory changes to make it easier to launch and invest in start-ups and established iParks overseas to support the internationalization of South Korean start-ups.[18] The government also continued to build the necessary infrastructure to facilitate access to the internet and expand the telecommunications sector. By 2001, South Korea had one of the highest broadband penetration rates in the world.[19] This helped start-ups to reach out to customers without having to spend large amounts on office or shop rent.

In this environment, South Korean entrepreneurship started to flourish. Launched in 1999, Naver was the country's first-ever portal website with its own search engine.[20] Daum, another search engine that launched shortly before the financial crisis, would grow rapidly.[21] In 2002, biopharma firm Celltrion was established. It would go on to become one of the biggest firms in the sector worldwide.[22] South Korea was breeding a new wave of 'self-made' businesspeople who could count on government support to put their ideas to work and make them grow. This symbiotic relationship between entrepreneurs with original ideas and a government willing to fund them would become a feature of the South Korean economy from then on.

*Building a more liberal society*

Voted in with a mandate to enact more liberal politics and policies, Kim set about strengthening the rights of South Korean citizens vis-à-vis the state and other authorities. Fulfilling a campaign pledge, Kim launched the National Human Rights Commission of Korea (NHRCK) in November 2001. An independent agency, it was tasked with protecting and improving the individual rights of South Koreans as well as helping safeguard the country's democracy.[23] The focus on *individual* human rights was deliberate. In the past, South Korean leaders had appealed to the common good of the country to justify the oppression of individual South Koreans. Furthermore, during the 1990s there had been a debate among leaders across Asia over whether the 'Western' values of democracy and individual human rights were suited to the supposedly 'collectivist' and 'authoritarian' Asian mindset. In a well-known article with the title 'Is Culture Destiny? The Myth of Asia's Anti-Democratic Values', Kim made clear that Asians—and by extension, (South) Koreans— also cherished their individual rights.[24] Once in power, Kim sought to turn his words into action.

Over the next two decades, the NHRCK would go on to investigate and handle hundreds of thousands of counselling requests and tens of thousands of complaints.[25] The commission was also instrumental in shaping South Korean policy through its opinions. Most notably, in April 2005 it issued an opinion supporting the elimination of capital punishment.[26] Kim Daejung had enacted a moratorium on executions upon taking office. The NHRCK's opinion gave further weight to this moratorium. Even though capital punishment continued to be legal in South Korea, executions were de facto abolished once Kim took office and the NHRCK issued its opinion.[27] The commission's opinions and investigations on a range of matters such as the right to conscientious objection to military service, the protection of irregular workers and human rights abuses in professional sports shaped debate in South Korea in the direction of greater individual freedoms—as well as towards holding the powerful accountable.

Kim also prioritized the reform of institutions and practices that his voters—and many other South Koreans—loathed. Top of the list was reform of the old ANSP, which twenty-five years earlier—when it was still known as the KCIA—had been within minutes of throwing him from a boat off the coast of Japan. Kim Young-sam had already introduced reforms to transform the ANSP into a more traditional intelligence gathering agency. In 1999, Kim renamed the agency as the National Intelligence Service (NIS). The NIS became accountable to the National Assembly, rather than the president alone. It also lost the power to make arrests without following legal procedures.[28] Roh Moo-hyun would later introduce further reforms upon his election in 2003, eliminating many of the grounds for domestic intelligence surveillance—including suspected anti-communism—and transferring many other surveillance activities to the police forces.[29]

Kim also pressed ahead with changes to policing practices to move them away from their previous authoritarian and confrontational approach, which the new president had personally experienced during his time as an opposition activist. Anyone witnessing a South Korean demonstration can attest that they are fairly peaceful compared to demonstrations elsewhere. Starting from the Kim government, instead of tear gas police forces brought lipstick to demonstrations and protests. Yes, lipstick. Euphemistically called 'the lipstick line', protesters were now greeted by a line of police women dressed immaculately and invariably wearing lipstick. The message was clear. Police forces were not there to repress and beat demonstrators. They were there to serve South Korean citizens, like any other public servant. Certainly, the riot police were still dispatched whenever necessary. But they were hidden behind cute cartoon police mascots, to underscore their friendliness and public service ethos. These simple practices changed the dynamics of demonstrations in South Korea, which became far less violent.[30] The goal was to calm tensions if they arose, rather than violently disperse the demonstrators. Together with Kim's election itself, this change was a key reason behind the development of a non-violent protest culture in South Korea from the late 1990s that continues at the time of writing.

Both Kim and later Roh also prioritized addressing one of the root causes of the IMF Crisis: corruption. In 1999, a presidential Special Committee on Anti-Corruption developed an Integrity Assessment and the government ratified the OECD Anti-Bribery Convention. And in January 2002, the Kim government upgraded a presidential advisory committee to the Korean Independent Commission Against Corruption (KICAC). The commission was tasked with the development of anti-corruption policies, handling cases of potential corruption and promoting transparency and ethics in both the public and private sectors.[31] More generally, KICAC was a clear statement that the fight against corruption was at the top of the Kim government's agenda. It was also a statement that the goal was not only to punish corruption but also to prevent it from happening in the first place. At a more practical level, public procurement was made electronic to advertise contracts, facilitate the submission of proposals and allow citizens to track and monitor procurement processes.[32]

Roh doubled down on this anti-corruption drive by expanding the mandate of KICAC to ensuring integrity in the public administration. His government also signed the UN Convention against Corruption in 2003. And the president was personally invested in ensuring that the National Assembly passed acts to increase information disclosure standards from public institutions, to allow individual investors to bring class action lawsuits against firms if they felt that corruption had affected their economic interests and to force private firms into greater information disclosure and improved corporate transparency.[33] In line with his 'participatory government' ethos, the Roh government also involved civil society in crafting policies and informing legislation to fight against corruption.[34] For the first time, the people ultimately affected by corruption in the public and private sector were active participants in trying to find a solution to this problem. Corruption did not disappear from public life. But South Korea was becoming a country where corruption was not tolerated for the sake of economic growth.

*Making history: the first-ever inter-Korean summit*

It is a sunny morning in Seoul. The morning of 13 June. At 8am, the doors of the main entrance to the Blue House are opened. Out comes Kim Dae-jung with his wife, Lee Hee-ho, and five advisors. Kim and his wife sit on the back seat of the presidential car. Their driver starts the engine to take them to Gimpo International Airport. Tens of thousands of South Koreans line the streets between the presidential residence and the airport, waving South Korean flags. They are excited. And full of dreams. Kim gives his pre-departure speech behind a podium on the airport's tarmac: 'To my beloved and respected fellow citizens. I am leaving today to spend the next two nights and three days in Pyongyang. The road to an inter-Korean summit that seemed as if it would be blocked forever has been opened.'[35]

Words that capture the mood and hopes of the moment. Kim, Lee and the presidential delegation board the plane, which takes off as the delegation waves from the windows. The pilot flies above the West Sea. Within thirty-five minutes, the plane has crossed into North Korean territory. Twenty-five minutes later, one hour after leaving Seoul, the plane touches ground in Pyongyang International Airport. The delegation claps. Excitement builds up inside the plane as it moves along the tarmac and the delegation sees dozens of North Korean military officials and other dignitaries waiting to receive them.[36]

But, internally, Kim Dae-jung has his doubts. How will the summit go? How important is the meeting for North Korea? Is its leader Kim Jong-il really invested in improving inter-Korean relations? The answer comes right before Kim Dae-jung leaves the plane.[37] Unexpectedly, Kim Jong-il appears and walks all the way to the front of the plane's airstair, where he stands. Waiting for his guest. Kim Dae-jung comes out of the plane, looks at Kim Jong-il, takes a look at the clear sky around the airport and looks at his host again. 'I am glad to see you.' 'I had wanted to see you.' The leaders of the two Koreas exchange pleasantries and shake hands.[38] The delegation is greeted by dozens of North Koreans waving and cheering, men wearing suits and women wearing traditional *hanboks*. The two Kims and their entourages then watch and listen as the (North) Korean People's Army plays the 'Parade and March of the People's Army'. The highest honour afforded to visiting foreign dignitaries. Completely breaking with protocol, Kim Jong-il then gets into the car that is going to take Kim Dae-jung to Paekhwawon Guest House—the residence of the South Korean president during his stay in Pyongyang. As the car drives off to the guest house, the two Kims hold hands and wonder. They wonder why this meeting has had to wait for almost fifty years.[39]

From a South Korean perspective, the summit was a success. Kim Dae-jung had come to power promising a 'Sunshine Policy' to promote inter-Korean peace. The two Koreas had reached an agreement in 1998 for the South to provide aid to the North. That November, Pyongyang had opened Mount Kumgang

(Diamond Mountain) to tourists from South Korea. But in 1999, there had been an artillery exchange between the two Koreas in the West Sea.[40]

Relations had improved again, however, in early 2000. Representatives from the two Koreas had started to make contact in February. One month later, Kim had delivered his 'Berlin Declaration' in the German capital, establishing four points to underpin inter-Korean relations: direct dialogue and cooperation, an end to Cold War confrontation and settling for peace, the reunion of separated families and the exchange of special envoys. By April, the South Korean government was ready to make the announcement that the two Koreas would hold a summit. On 13–15 June, the summit took place.[41] Fifty South Korean journalists were allowed into North Korea to document the event. To put an end to the summit, the two Koreas issued the '6.15 Joint Declaration' laying out five principles: independent reunification, reunification along confederation or loose form of federation formula, the reunion of separated families, cooperation in fields ranging from culture to the environment and the establishment of a dialogue to implement the agreement.[42] Kim's popularity soared in the weeks after the summit. And in December he was awarded the Nobel Peace Prize 'for his work for democracy and human rights in South Korea and in East Asia in general, and for peace and reconciliation with North Korea in particular'.[43] Recognition for a life fighting for his (South) Korean dream.

The summit was also followed by a flurry of meetings. Ask any South Korean who lived through those months. Many thought that reconciliation and, perhaps, reunification were a certainty. Between June and December, the two Koreas held four ministerial-level talks, discussions between Red Cross representatives, one defence minister meeting, two working-level meetings focusing on economic cooperation and a working-level military discussion. Seoul also approved a food loan for Pyongyang. And the two Koreas agreed to reopen their Liaison Office at Panmunjom, which the North had closed in 1996 in the midst of its famine, to open working-level talks in a wide range of fields and to rehabilitate the railway line connecting Seoul with Sinuiju—the city sitting on the south bank of the Amrok River separating the North from China.[44] On 15 September, the two Koreas marched as one to a standing ovation at the Sydney Olympic Games opening ceremony.[45]

Above all, reunions between separated families took place for the first time since 1985. Starting on 15–18 August 2000 and all the way until 2007, there were nineteen family reunion meetings, fifteen of them in person and four via video communication. Four more meetings would be held in 2009–15, when the conservatives returned to power in South Korea and inter-Korean relations would sour once again. In total, 20,604 people would have the opportunity to briefly meet their loved ones. A further meeting would be held in 2018.[46] Each meeting was a bittersweet occasion. Elder Koreans from South and North separated for decades would meet for a few days or, sometimes, for only a few hours. They knew that they were seeing each other for the last time, for as time went by the prospect of reconciliation seemed evermore elusive.

Relations between the two Koreas deteriorated in the years after the summit. Kim's 'Sunshine Policy' had been greatly facilitated by Bill Clinton's decision to seek US–North Korean rapprochement in 1999–2000, towards the end of his presidency. However, in November 2000 George W. Bush won the US election. Upon his inauguration in January 2001, he shifted Washington's approach towards North Korea, moving away from Clinton's pro-engagement policy. In a meeting in March, Kim learnt first-hand that Bush had little time for engagement with North Korea. Following the 11 September terrorist attacks on

New York and Washington, DC and the subsequent 'War on Terror', Pyongyang was included in an 'Axis of Evil' also including Iran and Iraq. Eventually, the Bush administration would engage North Korea in the multilateral Six-Party Talks also involving the two Koreas, China, Japan and Russia.[47] But it was too late for Kim, who had left office by then.

Kim was also criticized domestically by conservatives who thought that he was giving too much in return for too little. Indeed, economic projects were the most tangible result of the summit. Foreign tourists had already started to be allowed to visit Mount Kumgang in the North two years before the summit. 'I wish that I had been born in Korea so that I could see the Diamond Mountains in person!', wrote Chinese scholar Su Shi in the eleventh century. For centuries, the mountain had a reputation as the most beautiful in the whole of Korea.[48] Following the inter-Korean summit, North Korea opened a special tourist region to facilitate tourism from South Korea. The opening of the special region boosted tourism from the South. And in 2004, the Kaesong Industrial Complex bringing together the South's capital and know-how with the North's labour opened north of the DMZ.[49] For the first time ever, South and North Koreans would be working hand-in-hand to manufacture Korean products.

But in 2003 a scandal broke out following reports that Hyundai had paid half a billion dollars to North Korea in advance of the 2000 inter-Korean summit.[50] And in sharp contrast to economic cooperation projects that mainly benefitted the North Korean government, security discussions were proceeding very slowly and the North often dragged its feet regarding family reunions. For a growing number of South Koreans, Kim Jong-il was simply using their money to strengthen his domestic position. The Hyundai payment scandal was particularly damaging for Kim Dae-jung, since it came as he was about to leave office and tarnished both his 'Sunshine Policy' and his image as a fighter against corruption. The dream of reconciliation was fading only three years after it had started.

## The 2002 Korea/Japan World Cup and growing South Korean pride

It is 22 June 2002. A red wave has taken over the whole country. Millions and millions of people. Wearing red, to the last person. The colour that now represents their own country. *Be the Reds* emblazoned on their chests. Proudly and cheerfully singing *Dae-han-Min-guk*! The metonym South Koreans use to refer to their country, especially during sporting events. Millions of people are staring at giant TV screens. They account for well over half of the South Korean population, also watching their TV sets up and down the country. They are joined by 40,000 lucky South Koreans sitting—well, standing for the most part—at Gwangju World Cup Stadium.[51] The Red Devils are about to take on the Red Fury. South Korea versus Spain. The quarter-final of the World Cup. Surely South Korea cannot defeat a third European powerhouse in a row, following victories against Portugal and Italy? But two hours later all those people clad in red will still be singing. Following the penalty shoot-out that decides the match, they will have two new heroes. Lee Woon-jae, who saved Spain's fourth kick from the penalty spot, and Hong Myung-bo, who scored the fifth and final South Korean kick to take his country to the semi-finals.[52] Together with the rest of the men's national football team, they helped boost South Koreans' pride in their own country at a time when memories of the IMF Crisis still hurt and when the excitement of the first inter-Korean summit was waning.

This pride was not only due to South Korea's improbable run to the semi-finals—the first Asian country to achieve this feat.

Incheon International Airport had opened in March 2001, becoming the main gateway for international flights in and out of South Korea.[53] Someone landing at the airport in late 2002 or early 2003 would have marvelled at its clean and modern facilities. This person could have then taken one of the ubiquitous buses to anywhere in Seoul or Gyeonggi Province. Inside the bus, that person would have watched a TV screen. On the screen, that person would have watched the Red Devils scoring goal after goal. And they would have watched footage of South Koreans cheering, of modern football stadiums, of a nation enthralled by the World Cup co-hosted by South Korea and Japan. The World Cup was arguably the first mass event in which South Koreans cheered for, well, *South* Korea. Not for Korea. Not because they had unshackled themselves from an oppressor, be it Japanese colonialists or South Korean dictators. Cheering because they were happy for their own country. For the World Cup gave a significant boost to South Korea's civic nationalism. To the pride in being South Korean.

Civic nationalism continued to go from strength to strength during the 2000s.[54] With a president representing their views in power, members of the 386 generation certainly felt proud of their country. The inter-Korean summit had surely boosted *minjok*. But Kim Jong-il's inability or unwillingness to fully reciprocate Seoul's openness underscored how different their countries were. In fact, South Koreans had long stopped comparing their country to North Korea. A more apt comparison was with other OECD members, fellow developed and democratic countries with their positives and negatives. This was quite remarkable to foreigners who may have been interested in South Korea because of the division with North Korea. For growing numbers of South Koreans, North Korea was a non-issue. Improving their country was all that mattered.

This trend towards greater civic nationalism was reinforced by the coming of age of millennials. Entering university from the late 1990s and early 2000s, this was a generation with barely any memories of the struggle for democracy of the 1980s. This was also a generation with no direct relatives in North Korea.[55] For many, their first clear memory was probably related to the 1988 Olympic Games, South Korea's coming out party on the global stage. And it was the first South Korean generation that had grown up accustomed to international travel, a generation with friends and sometimes family spread around the world. Their outlook went far beyond the confines of the Korean Peninsula. Reunification was not really something they thought about. Some of them were actually quite open about their doubts regarding the desirability of reunification, a process that would be costly and could reduce job opportunities. As they entered university, the student movement was already moving away from demands for reunification.

One of the most conspicuous changes brought about by the new civic nationalism was an interest in Korea's cultural heritage. This might have seemed paradoxical, given that South Korea was more outward-looking and modern than it had ever been. But as is often the case, foreign travel and living can make people think about the uniqueness of things back at home. Many South Koreans underwent this process throughout the 2000s. They realized that South Korea was not backward compared to fellow developed countries. It was different. Each country had its own history and culture. (South) Korea was no different. At the time, many younger South Koreans wished that people from their own country and overseas would understand the beauty of traditional Korean culture. For it is beautiful indeed.

Bukchon Hanok Village was the prime example of this trend. Located in central Seoul, within walking distance of

Gyeongbokgung, Bukchon is a 600-year-old residential district lined with narrow streets filled with *hanok*—the traditional Korean house with a tiled, curvy roof. By the late 1990s, most of the district had been torn down and only about 1,000 *hanok* remained. But starting from 2001, a preservation project led by the Seoul Metropolitan Government began to restore the *hanok*. Their price immediately shot up, as it started to become trendy to live or stay in one of them.[56] One could still visit Bukchon without the crowds that one day would flock to the neighbourhood. It was clear, however, that the preservation project was going to change it for the better. This preservation movement spread across the country, along with an interest in Korea's traditional *ondol* floor-heating system, furniture and other crafts. These were uniquely Korean, and South Koreans who had travelled the world were proud that their country could preserve and even revive them.

## *A year of anti-Americanism*

Relations between Kim Dae-jung and US President George W. Bush continued to be rocky as policy differences between Seoul and Washington over North Korea policy were aired publicly. In this context, any real or perceived slight by the United States threatened to raise tensions between the two allies. In July 2000, for example, the US military was forced to apologize after admitting that it had dumped 228 litres of a highly toxic chemical in the Han River. The actions by US military personnel led forty-eight South Korean policy-makers to issue a statement demanding a revision of the Status of Forces Agreement (SOFA) that set out the regulatory framework for American troops stationed in South Korea.[57] The policy-makers believed that SOFA essentially gave US troops carte blanche to behave in any way they pleased while performing official duties, for they were beyond the jurisdiction of the South Korean judiciary. Tensions eventually simmered. But they were not completely gone.

It was the death of two fourteen-year-old schoolgirls in June 2002 that finally triggered the biggest wave of protests against the US military presence in South Korea in decades. Walking home along a road near Yangju—a mid-sized city in Gyeonggi Province—the two girls were struck and killed by a US armoured vehicle. This resulted in a bout of anti-American protests.[58] Three weeks after the fatal incident, the two soldiers manoeuvring the vehicle went on trial. But SOFA stipulated that US military personnel who had committed a crime would face a US military court if the crime took place while performing their official duties. Given the seriousness of the crime, South Korea's Ministry of Justice requested that jurisdiction be transferred to South Korean courts, which SOFA allowed for. The US military declined this request, a decision that further increased anti-American sentiment. Bush called Kim to express his regrets for the killing of the two schoolgirls, and the US military had to issue several apologies.[59]

In November, however, the US military court found the two soldiers not guilty of the charge of 'negligent homicide'. This caused anti-American sentiment to grow to new levels.[60] From the perspective of many South Koreans, US soldiers could kill two of their own—even if accidentally—and escape punishment for their actions. And the South Korean judiciary had no say on whether the accused were guilty or not. In a sense, many South Koreans thought, their country was in no better position than in the late nineteenth century, when unequal treaties imposed on Korea allowed foreigners to behave without concern or regard for local laws. Weeks of protests ensued, including outside Yongsan Garrison. Located near central Seoul, this was the main base for US soldiers stationed in South Korea.

The killing of the two schoolgirls had come only a few months after a South Korean speed skater had been disqualified having apparently won the gold medal for the 1,500-metre short track competition at the Salt Lake City 2002 Winter Olympics. His disqualification had allowed an American rival to claim gold.[61] The killing also happened only a few months before US Congress passed the Iraq Resolution, which allowed the Bush administration to invade the Middle Eastern country. In common with many countries around the world, South Korea was gripped by anti-war sentiment.[62] Combined, these three events ensured that anti-American sentiment spread beyond its usual left-wing base.

In this context, Roh Moo-hyun took office on a platform openly arguing for the renegotiation of the South Korean–US alliance to make it more balanced. Even though the alliance itself was never in doubt, Roh's public questioning of the prevailing state of South Korean–US relations created considerable frictions between the two countries.[63] Many South Koreans believed that Seoul's subordinate position to Washington curtailed their country's sovereignty. Eventually, anti-American protests subsided. But in December 2003, South Korea joined many other countries in banning imports of US beef as a result of cases of mad cow disease. For some, this was the peak of anti-Americanism, since South Korea flatly rejected the Bush administration's calls not to ban imports outright.[64] The beef ban became symbolic of the strain in South Korean–US relations. It would come back to haunt future president Lee Myung-bak shortly after his inauguration in 2008.

## Hallyu *arrives*

*Hallyu* came as a shock to most South Koreans. K-Pop acts were becoming ubiquitous at university festivals across the country.

Those attending these festivals could be witnessing the next megastar. But few were willing to predict that *Hallyu* would take off outside the country. For the first time ever, South Korea was cool. Not only cool. It was becoming the coolest country in Asia, a spot long reserved for Japan. *Hallyu*'s literal meaning—Korean Wave—aptly described this phenomenon. (South) Korean culture started to sweep China, Japan and Taiwan from the late 1990s. In fact, the term *Hallyu* was originally coined by Chinese media, before being adopted by the South Korean government and people themselves.[65] Dramas, pop music and movies were becoming popular among Chinese and Japanese of all ages, whether young boys seeking to imitate the looks of the latest pop star or middle-aged women waiting for the latest heartthrob arriving at the local airport.

The emergence and eventual success of South Korean cultural products was a testament to the continued push for innovation and the booming creativity of the country's people. By the mid-1990s, Hollywood had successfully lobbied the US government to press South Korea to open up its film market. As a result, American movies had gained an 80 per cent share of the market, displacing South Korean movies that local moviegoers found unappealing.[66] Meanwhile, the South Korean government was lifting restrictions on the import of Japanese cultural goods.[67] Back then, movies, pop or anime from South Korea's neighbour were seen as more attractive by many South Koreans. South Korea's creative industries were at risk of suffering a second, devastating blow.

South Koreans decided to compete head-on with the US and Japanese cultural industries, rather than simply accept their seemingly preordained fate. Unhindered by the censorship and the budgetary constraints of the past, many South Korean filmmakers sought to create both blockbusters and auteur films that could attract a wide following. The success of *Shiri* had shown that South Korean moviegoers would flow en masse if they were offered what they wanted to see.[68] Thus, *Joint Security Area*, *My Sassy Girl*, *Silmido*, *Memories of Murder*, *Taegukgi* and *The King and the Clown* became instant blockbusters. Straddling historical drama, comedy and action movies, South Korean filmmakers showed that they could captivate domestic audiences. And foreign audiences too. A romantic comedy telling the story of a college student who falls in love with a girl whose name remains unknown throughout the movie, *My Sassy Girl*—which opened in 2001—was a hit across East Asia.[69] South Korean audiences laughed and cried throughout the movie—before falling in love with the heart-warming ending. It was also the movie that showed that South Korean stories could transcend the country.

But it was *Oldboy* that showed that South Korean directors could speak to the tastes of a wider international audience and foreign critics as well. Several South Korean directors had been winning awards at the Berlin and Cannes film festivals. But it was Park Chan-wook's masterpiece exploring the depths of the human soul that won the Grand Prix at the 2004 Cannes Film Festival, the second-highest honour.[70] In this way, Park opened the doors for the many South Korean filmmakers that would receive international acclaim well beyond East Asia in the years that followed. His success showed that South Korean stories were, well, not 'simply' South Korean anymore.

South Korean dramas became widely popular across East Asia, before also jumping to South Asia, the Middle East and beyond. Like the country's movies, South Korean dramas encompassed a wide range of genres including love stories, historical dramas and comedies. Above all, there was *Winter Sonata*, which aired in South Korea in 2002. Bringing together a love story, great acting, memorable tunes and breath-taking scenery, the drama prompted Japanese Prime Minister Koizumi Junichiro to quip in jest that its main character was more popular than he was.[71] It was the first South Korean drama to truly affect fashion trends across East Asia and to attract fans from across the region to its filming locations. Nami Island, in particular, became a tourist hotspot for international travellers. (In my view, best enjoyed in the autumn when red and orange leaves cover the whole island.)

And then along came pop. Or K-Pop, as it came to be known outside South Korea. Boybands, girlbands and solo stars started to become popular in South Korea and across East Asia. Some of them were nurtured by the 'Big 3' agencies: SM Entertainment, YG Entertainment and JYP Entertainment.[72] Launched in the mid-1990s, these three labels helped to evolve the style pioneered by Seo Taiji and Boys by mixing it with pop sounds to broaden its appeal. In 2000, H.O.T. was the first South Korean band to sell out a concert overseas—in Beijing.[73] From the early to mid-2000s, bands such as TVXQ, Super Junior, Big Bang, Wonder Girls and Girls' Generation became popular across East Asia. Employing catchy lyrics, powerful dance routines and an impeccable image, K-Pop bands became the entry point into *Hallyu* for many teenagers—and, increasingly, youngsters and adults. The bands went on tours across the region, performing in front of sold-out crowds of tens of thousands.

Soloists also joined the Korean Wave. In fact, BoA was the first South Korean musician to top the Japanese music charts. Released in 2002, her debut album *Listen to My Heart* became an instant hit. BoA's popularity then spread to China, Taiwan and South East Asia.[74] There was a good reason why she came to be known as the 'Queen of Pop'. Similarly, soloist Rain became popular across the region upon the release of his album *Bad Guy*. A former member of an unsuccessful boyband, Rain also helped pioneer the phenomenon of former band members launching their solo careers.[75]

The South Korean government helped to spread the reach of *Hallyu*. From the mid-1990s, the government boosted the budget of the Ministry of Culture and Sports, which was rebranded as the Ministry of Culture and Tourism in 1998. There soon followed departments of cultural industry across South Korean universities, cultural festivals inside and outside the country and the promotion of the Korean language in partnership with other government agencies.[76] The Kim Dae-jung government, in particular, saw the promotion of South Korean culture overseas as a way to boost economic growth following the 1997–8 financial crisis.[77] It was a case of South Korean talent and hard work meeting a determined government that started to make the country's image be defined by *Hallyu*. The people with the help of the government created a cultural juggernaut. A cultural whale.

### Power to the 386 generation

December 2002 was a moment of truth for the 386 generation. The opposition Grand National Party (GNP) had defeated Kim Dae-jung's rebranded Millennium Democratic Party (MDP) in the legislative elections held in 2000, as well as the local elections of June 2002. GNP candidate Lee Hoi-chang, narrowly defeated by Kim in the 1997 election, was leading the polls to win the presidential election. Roh Moo-hyun—his MDP opponent—was a surprise candidate. The MDP had run open primaries to select its candidate for the first time ever. Affable and a veteran of the Fifth Republic Hearings, Roh was not expected to win the primaries. But he did. He then trailed Lee in the polls for most of the presidential campaign.[78] By the time the election came, Roh and Lee were running neck and neck. But older voters—most leaning conservative—had traditionally been more willing to actually cast their vote.

On the day of the election, the 386 generation did turn out to vote for their preferred candidate. But Roh received an 'unexpected' boost from South Korea's very own Generation X, as well as millennials. Born in the 1970s, Generation X was more liberal than the 386 and previous generations. They were not particularly enamoured with Kim Dae-jung. His fight against South Korea's dictatorship was not really their fight, for it was a past event when they were still children or teenagers at most. But they wanted a continuation of his liberal reforms, which Roh promised to deliver.[79] Millennials, born from the 1980s onwards, meanwhile, had the more liberal values that university student groups were imbuing in students. Usually considered politically apathetic, they were mobilized through online news, via text message and an incipient social media.[80] Foreigners arriving in the country and only starting to understand the power of the internet may have been surprised at how this new medium was shaping politics in ways then unimaginable in their own countries. But it was. In fact, Roh was arguably the world's first 'internet president'. For online newspaper OhmyNews—launched in 2000 and the first South Korean newspaper to accept articles from readers—had built a huge following among the 386 generation, Generation X and, especially, younger millennials. Few doubted that this young newspaper had helped sway the election.[81]

Roh's victory over Lee put an end to the 'Three Kims Era'. And the new president worked to address two issues of utmost concern to the constituencies that had elected him: inequality and the work–life balance. With regard to the former and along with more traditional policies such as tax reform and the expansion of the welfare state, Roh put on the table a debate over the relocation of the administrative capital away from Seoul and further south in Chungcheong Province.[82] The South Korean capital had become a megalopolis. Together with its surrounding region, it was home to well over a third of South Korea's population, and it was also the country's undisputed economic and cultural powerhouse.

Moving the capital away from Seoul, the thinking went, would serve to boost economic opportunities elsewhere and support more balanced growth. Facing fierce opposition from conservative policy-makers but also from many liberals, Roh pressed ahead nonetheless. In 2007, his government founded Sejong Special Self-Governing City as the new administrative capital. For the Constitutional Court had ruled in 2004 that moving the capital away from Seoul would violate the constitution.[83] In the end, conservative President Park Geun-hye would start to move most government agencies to Sejong from 2012 onwards. Roh's plan would eventually be embraced by the opposition after all.

The new president also introduced the five-day workweek shortly after his inauguration as a way to improve the work–life balance of South Korean workers. Plus, he expanded the welfare state to cushion the impact of joblessness while seeking to boost South Korea's meagre public pension system.[84] South Koreans were working some of the longest hours among OECD citizens,[85] while the country's jobseekers' allowance and state pensions were inadequate at best. The old model of large families living under the same roof with a sole, male breadwinner providing for his family was becoming less relevant to most South Koreans. Clans were becoming less important as extended families spread across the country—or across the world—and more liberal values took hold. At the same time, living in a developed country meant that many South Koreans wanted to have enough time to enjoy the fruits of their work. Roh was aware of these realities, and his government sought to tackle them.

Roh also believed that South Korea had not done enough to address its colonial and dictatorial history. In December 2005, his government established a Truth and Reconciliation Commission to investigate collaborators with the Japanese colonial authorities, massacres committed during the Korean War and state-sponsored killings and torture during the dictatorship years. Controversially, however, the commission covered a period stretching all the way until 1993.[86] Many liberals refused to acknowledge Kim Young-sam as South Korea's first legitimate post-democratic transition president. Also, the commission implicitly targeted Park Geun-hye by investigating her father's— Park Chung-hee's—time serving in the Imperial Japanese Army. The result was that the commission unveiled many crimes and incidents in twentieth-century (South) Korean history.[87] But it also became mired in controversy.

For the Roh government arguably proved to be much more divisive than the three preceding ones. There was farmer unrest, as the government pressed ahead with controversial negotiations with Chile to sign a free trade agreement. Farmers feared that the South Korean market would be flooded with cheaper agricultural products from the Latin American country. The agreement was finally signed in February 2003.[88] In March 2006, railway workers went on strike due to the increasing use of short-term contracts.[89] These had become more prevalent since the IMF Crisis. The Roh government reacted by declaring the strike illegal, leading to the arrest of hundreds of workers. And that same year, farmers led strikes against a proposed free trade agreement with the United States.[90] The government went ahead and signed the agreement—known as KORUS—in June 2007.

As Roh channelled the hopes of the 386 and younger generations but also became embroiled in controversies, the GNP engaged in a discussion over the best way to regain the presidency. In March 2004, the GNP had made the strategic mistake of pushing an impeachment vote against Roh for allegedly interfering in the upcoming legislative election. The vote backfired, and Roh's newly formed Uri Party won the April legislative election while the Constitutional Court reinstated the president one month later. But the GNP had appointed Park Geun-hye as its chairwoman shortly before the election. She went on to receive the nickname 'Queen of Elections'.

The GNP's loss in the legislative election was narrower than many thought following from the unpopular impeachment process—and a corruption scandal involving former presidential candidate Lee Hoi-chang—and the party then went on to win the 2006 local elections.[91] With Roh's popularity at record lows, by 2007 it was a foregone conclusion that the GNP candidate would win the next presidential election. Roh held an inter-Korean summit of his own in October 2007, but this failed to reverse the fortunes of the liberals. After all, North Korea had conducted its first-ever nuclear test in October 2006. The mood between the two Koreas had clearly changed. Amid the lowest turnout in history for a South Korean presidential election—as the 386 generation and younger cohorts stayed home, put off by the controversies surrounding Roh—GNP candidate Lee Myung-bak easily won the December 2007 vote.[92]

*Social change and the end of the* hoju *system*

The liberal decade coincided with profound social changes in South Korea, sometimes supported by the Kim and Roh governments but mainly driven by an evolving society itself. Above all, the role of women within society underwent dramatic changes. The legislative changes introduced in the mid-1990s to prevent discrimination against women in relation to succession rights or rights following a divorce had an immediate effect. The divorce rate more than doubled between the early 1990s and 2007,[93] Roh's last full year in office. The fertility rate, meanwhile, continued its downward trend.[94] At the same time, the average age for women to get married increased from under twenty-six to over thirty-one years of age between 1997 and 2007.[95] It also became acceptable for women to state outright that they did not intend to get married. And single motherhood—if certainly not common—ceased to be taboo.[96] In short, by the mid-2000s South Korean women were behaving in the same way as women in other developed countries rather than in the way that old Confucian values mandated. And this situation was here to stay, as anyone attending university at the time and listening to female students could attest.

Change also came to the workplace. '*Ajumma* jobs' continued to exist, but many married middle-aged women aspired to something different. The number of female employees taking maternity leave grew from under 20 per cent in 2003 to over half in 2007.[97] Furthermore, a growing number of women re-joined the workforce after having children. And the percentage of female managers went above 10 per cent for the first time in 2006.[98] That same year, Han Myeong-sook became the country's first-ever female prime minister, the second-highest political position in South Korea. And the percentage of female National Assembly members reached an all-time high of 10 per cent following the 2004 legislative election. Low—or rather, very low—in relation to comparable countries, but an improvement nonetheless. In other words, change was slowly creeping into society, the workplace and politics.

But this did not mean that women were treated equally to men. Many women were still forced to leave their jobs upon getting pregnant and sometimes even after they got married. Women also accounted for a larger share of temporary contracts and part-time jobs.[99] And the percentage of female managers and National Assembly members remained very low, even if those with more traditional views believed that these jobs should be reserved for men to begin with. But the change in mentality was inexorable. Most notably, by the early 2000s the centuries-old preference for boys over girls was no more. By 2007, the sex ratio at birth had reached a natural range.[100] Talking to the 386 and younger generations, it was clear that it no longer mattered whether their children were male or female. And politicians and the courts tried to keep up, spurred by women's groups and society at large. The Kim Dae-jung government established the Presidential Commission on Women's Affairs in 1998. It would be replaced by the Ministry of Gender Equality in 2001, a first in South Korean history.[101] The ministry would address issues such as sexual and domestic violence and discrimination against women in the workplace.

Greater political and legal change, however, took place between 2005 and 2008, when South Korea abolished the *hoju* system. In February 2005, the National Assembly revised the Civil Code to abolish *hoju*, along with the prohibition of marriage between a woman and a man with the same surname and ancestral seat. The latter had been declared illegal by the Constitutional Court in 1997.[102] And in January 2008, the Constitutional Court ruled that *hoju* was also unconstitutional, for it violated the 2005 revision to the Civil Code. With the stroke of a pen and the knock of a gavel, politicians and judges had put an end to decades of legal discrimination against women.

Another important change also took place during the liberal decade. In 2000, the Daehangno neighbourhood near central Seoul hosted South Korea's first Queer Culture Festival, marking another step forward in the visibility of the LGBTQ+ community. The inaugural festival attracted around fifty participants.[103] That same year, actor Hong Seok-cheon became the first South Korean celebrity to come out as homosexual. He promptly lost his acting roles and his endorsements.[104] But the Queer Culture Festival continued, and only grew in size. By the mid-2000s, it had a festive atmosphere, helping to broaden its appeal. And Hong resumed his acting career while also launching a series of successful restaurants. At the same time, the

NHRCK issued recommendations to eradicate homophobic language and the Supreme Court declared transgender sex change legal.[105] Very slowly but inexorably, society was becoming more accepting of different sexual orientations. Indeed, whereas 89 per cent of South Koreans believed that homosexuality was 'never justifiable' in 1990, by 2001 that figure had plunged to 53 per cent.[106]

Throughout the 2000s, South Korea also started to see a relatively large influx of immigrants, at least by the country's past standards. Foreign workers from East Asian countries such as China and Mongolia and also from South Asian nations such as Bangladesh were flying into South Korea in droves. Most were taking jobs that South Koreans no longer wanted to do: fruit picking, fishing, construction work and the most repetitive jobs in factories. These were the so-called 3-D jobs: dirty, difficult and dangerous.[107] In addition, women from countries such as China and Vietnam were flocking to the countryside to marry South Korean men.[108] The gender imbalance resultant from the previous preference for boys over girls was being accentuated by South Korean women shunning life in the countryside and moving into cities. For women from poorer countries in East Asia, the opportunity to marry South Korean farmers offered life chances unavailable in their home countries.

All these societal shifts were bringing structural changes that the central and local governments sought to tackle. Incentives were introduced for parents to have multiple children. There were discussions about raising the retirement age. There were reforms to the tertiary education sector to encourage more vocational training. And migration policy was changed to make it easier to bring over foreign workers or spouses.[109] In other words, politicians were trying to change some of the realities that they were facing but also acknowledging these realities.

These trends further undermined traditional understandings of family, clan and other types of social relations, leading to an emerging divide between those longing for a Confucian-informed past and those who had a more liberal outlook. But the second group had time on its side, for, in general, older generations were more conservative whereas younger ones were more liberal.[110] As a result, by the time that Lee Myung-bak won the 2007 election that put an end to a decade of liberal rule, South Korean society had changed. It was becoming more open-minded.

# 6

# GLOBAL SOUTH KOREA
## 2008–23

*The return of conservatism*

Lee Myung-bak was unlike any other South Korean president. Born in Japan when it was still Korea's colonial master, his family returned to his parents' motherland after independence. Imprisoned for five months for leading demonstrations against the normalization of relations between Seoul and Tokyo, Lee took a different route upon his release. In 1965, he joined Hyundai Construction. By the age of thirty-five, he was South Korea's youngest-ever CEO. At forty-seven, he was appointed as the chairman of Hyundai Construction. During his time with the firm, he earned the nickname 'bulldozer'. Lee then decided to become a politician and was elected to the National Assembly. But he rose to national prominence when he became the mayor of Seoul in 2002. As mayor, the 'bulldozer' launched a major urban regeneration project to make the city greener. By then, he was also known as a devout Protestant who doubled as a church elder. Upon his inauguration in February 2008, Lee was both South Korea's first-ever president with a background as *chaebol* 'quasi-royalty' and the most religious president since Rhee Syngman.[1] After ten years of liberal rule, South Koreans were unsure what to make of their new president.

Many South Koreans soon took a negative view of Lee. The reason? Beef. In April—merely two months after his inauguration—Lee announced that his government had agreed to lift the ban on US beef imports that had been in place since 2003 due to concerns over mad cow disease. Lee was immediately accused of bowing to US pressure and putting the relationship with Washington ahead of the health of the South Korean population. In particular, many South Koreans thought Lee had only agreed to lift the ban to get US Congress to approve KORUS. Hundreds of thousands of South Koreans took to the streets. Several ministers offered their resignation. Lee's approval rating plummeted below 20 per cent in a matter of weeks. And the president apologized for, in his words, ignoring the concerns of the South Korean population.[2] The ban was eventually lifted, but initially with a number of restrictions to assuage public health concerns.

As the beef protests subsided, Lee could focus on the main selling point of his campaign: his promise to restore high rates of economic growth. By the time of Lee's inauguration, the South Korean economy was growing at an annual rate of 4 to 6 per cent.[3] While high by the standards of a developed economy, this seemed low to many South Koreans accustomed to much higher rates. As a former CEO, Lee had the credibility that many other politicians lacked when it came to driving economic growth. He thus launched his '747 plan' to achieve 7 per cent annual economic growth during his five years in office, boost per capita income to US$40,000 and make South Korea the seventh largest economy in the world.[4]

In a departure from South Korea's previous economic policy, Lee promised to privatize hundreds of public firms, together with other market-friendly measures. But 'Mbnomics'—as Lee's economic policy was dubbed—had to confront the aftermath of the global financial crisis that hit the United States and Europe—two key South Korean markets and investment sources—in 2007–8. Lee thus followed a more orthodox and better-known South Korean policy of private–public cooperation. However, the Lee government's attempt to reduce taxes for wealthier South Koreans reinforced the president's reputation among liberals as someone who did not care for ordinary people.[5]

For the Lee years revealed a big split between older, generally more conservative South Koreans who put economic growth above all else and younger, usually more liberal South Koreans who believed that addressing social problems was a bigger priority. This division became poisonous in May 2009, when Roh Moo-hyun committed suicide. The former president and his family were under investigation for corruption, accused of having received payments from a businessman close to the family. Roh's supporters claimed that the investigation was politically motivated, and the former president's suicide led them to direct their anger towards Lee Myung-bak. Shortly after, in August, Kim Dae-jung died of natural causes. With his death coming so shortly after Roh's, liberals were without their two most prominent leaders. This only increased their opposition to the Lee Myung-bak government.

As Lee's term was coming to an end, attention shifted towards the candidates for the next presidential election. In September 2012, Moon Jae-in won the primary for the just-launched liberal Democratic United Party. Moon was Roh Moo-hyun's former chief of staff, and his victory showed the enduring popularity of the late president. But Moon would be facing a formidable opponent: none other than Park Geun-hye, selected as the candidate for the (rebranded) conservative Saenuri Party the month before.[6] Park was still considered one of the most powerful South Korean politicians and had only narrowly lost the conservative party's primary to Lee Myung-bak in 2007. And indeed, this time she would win the primary by a crushing margin and then go on to defeat Moon Jae-in in the general election with more than 51 per cent of the vote. This was the highest-ever share that a presidential candidate had received since the restoration of democracy, demonstrating her popularity as well as the enduring appeal of the conservatives. But Moon received a 48 per cent share of the vote, the highest among all second-placed candidates since South Korea's transition to democracy.[7] This demonstrated both the growing appeal of the liberals and the split cutting right through the middle of South Korean society.

Indeed, regional cleavages were becoming less important in South Korea compared to generational differences. Moon did win the traditional liberal stronghold of Jeolla by a wide margin. But the biggest split in South Korean politics was by age. Park received overwhelming support from the over-fifties. In particular, the 'new 386' generation gave her a big boost. Born in the 1930s, in their eighties by the time of the election and having gone to university in the 1960s (or at least the men in this generation), this group mobilized en masse during the election. The under-forties, meanwhile, decisively broke in favour of Moon but did not vote in sufficient numbers to allow him to win the election.[8]

This generational division masked an incipient divide between young men and women. A growing number of younger men in their twenties believed that the 386 generation represented by Moon did not pay attention to their plight. Highly educated but finding it more difficult to get jobs straight out of college compared to previous generations, some young men resented both those South Koreans who had grown up in a dictatorship but had had an easier professional career—and women who, they thought, if anything had an easier time finding jobs because they did not have to complete compulsory military service. Talking to younger men during this time, one could see that they did not feel that women were disadvantaged like previous generations had been. The most extreme among these young men turned to Ilbe Storehouse, an alt-right website launched in 2009 and then relaunched in 2010, in which they criticized both liberals and women.[9] Young men with more traditional conservative values helped Park to win the election with their votes.

In February 2013, therefore, Park became South Korea's first female president. She was the closest thing South Korea had to royalty. And this was the criticism that liberals—as well as some of her conservative opponents—levied against Park. The new president was accused of being out of touch and taking decisions in a secretive manner and without consultation.[10] And indeed, one day Park's disconnect from the general public and secretive decision-making process would be her downfall.

But Park enjoyed a honeymoon period during her first few months in office. She successfully sought to distance herself from internal divisions, and indeed even embraced Roh Moo-hyun's policies to address inequality. Most notably, Park's time in office was marked by the relocation of thirty-six ministries and public institutions to address regional inequalities.[11] In contrast with Lee, Park emphasized the themes of happiness and self-fulfilment above growth at all costs. And in May, Park travelled to the United States, where she gave a rare and well-received address to a joint session of US Congress. This further boosted the new president's image back home. By the summer, her approval rating was well above 60 per cent.[12] Park may have been a conservative, but she was a conservative with a human face compared to Lee, and seemingly bent on bridging the divide with the other aisle. Even some liberals approved of this at the time.

# SHRIMP TO WHALE

*South Korea goes global*

The Lee and Park governments coincided with South Korea becoming a leading global powerhouse. Undoubtedly, *Hallyu* was the key reason behind the country's newfound place in the world. Throughout the 2000s, South Korea's thriving contemporary culture had taken over Asia. By the end of the decade, *Hallyu* was making inroads into Latin America and the Middle East.[13] Younger people were watching K-Pop songs online and some K-dramas were becoming instant sensations overseas.[14] For example, the historical drama *Jumong*—depicting the life of the founder of Goguryeo—was watched by over 80 per cent of viewers in Iran.[15] Many overseas audiences were attracted by the way that Korean dramas portrayed social and family relations—which they could relate to—as well as the lack of nudity compared to Western dramas.

Meanwhile, K-Pop bands started to tour Europe, Latin America and the United States, and the South Korean government chipped in by organizing and supporting K-Pop and South Korean culture festivals around the world.[16] In the case of the United States, Korean Americans initially and the Asian American community at large also propelled the popularity of South Korean culture. In 2012, California hosted the first-ever KCON, a festival for K-Pop fans to connect with their idols. Over 10,000 people attended. The following year, 20,000 did. One year later, over 40,000 fans packed the festival.[17] *Hallyu* was not yet mainstream in the United States. But it had moved well beyond a niche interest for a few fans even in the world's cultural powerhouse.

And then along came 'Gangnam Style'. In his mid-thirties, best known for his humorous video clips and eccentric choreographies, Psy was not your average K-Pop star. And while popular in South Korea, he had not found fame across Asia in the same way as many other K-Pop acts. But everything changed in the summer of 2012. 'Gangnam Style' became a global phenomenon: number one in over thirty countries, the first video to reach one billion views on YouTube and a dance that not even UN Secretary-General Ban Ki-moon or US President Barack Obama could resist. Not to mention the tens of thousands of people joining 'Gangnam Style' dance mobs in South Korea, the rest of Asia and beyond.[18] Psy was a global sensation, the first K-Pop solo act who could claim mainstream global fame. His hit single helped open the doors for other South Korean artists who would eventually follow him in taking over the world.

The South Korean government also wanted the country to be better known globally. Lee Myung-bak even dubbed his foreign policy 'Global Korea'. In his view, it was time for South Korea to move beyond what he deemed to be a narrow focus on the Korean Peninsula and North East Asia. South Korea had to take on the world. And the timing was auspicious. South Korea was a founding member of the G20, the forum to address global economic imbalances upgraded in 2008 due to the Global Financial Crisis.[19] It had a seat at the top economic policy-making table. But for Lee, it was not enough to have a seat at the table. South Korea had to lead.

And lead it did. In November 2010, the impressive COEX Convention & Exhibition Center in Gangnam hosted the first G20 summit in Asia and in a non-G8 country. World leaders descended into the South Korean capital to discuss the state of the global economy and to push ahead with sustainable and balanced growth.[20] It is fair to say that South Korea had never hosted such an important meeting. 'Gangnam Style' had put the wealthy district south of the Han River on the lips of countless people around the world. The G20 summit now attracted the world's most important leaders to the district.

But Lee's ambition did not stop there. Also in 2010, he launched the Global Green Growth Institute, which two years later would become an international organization under the aegis of the United Nations.[21] In July of the following year, South Koreans celebrated as Pyeongchang was awarded the Winter Olympic Games at the third time of asking. Pyeongchang had very narrowly lost the vote to host previous games first to Vancouver and then to Sochi. But it won the 2011 vote by an overwhelming majority against its German and French opponents.[22] South Korea was going to become the second Asian country to host the Winter Olympic Games after Japan, just as it had done with the summer games. Three months later, in October, the United Nations Office for Sustainable Development opened not far away from the international airport in Incheon.[23] And less than half a year later, in March 2012, the COEX centre would once again receive dozens of world leaders as Seoul hosted the second edition of the Nuclear Security Summit, an initiative launched by Obama two years before.[24]

As impressive as these cultural and diplomatic accomplishments were, for most South Koreans it was a different event that made them proud of the global standing of their country. In February 2010, a young South Korean not even in her twenties entered the ice rink in Vancouver, home to the Winter Olympic Games. South Koreans knew that she was good. She was ranked first in the world after all. And ice skating was quite popular in South Korea, for the country's speed and short track skaters were among the best in the world. But this was different. This skater was a figure skater, a sport in which South Koreans had never previously excelled. In fact, this skater had grown up practising in public ice rinks—South Korea did not have the necessary facilities for skaters to train properly. So eventually this skater had had to move to Canada to improve her skills.[25]

Kim Yu-na was her name. And when she took to the ice rink in Vancouver for the first time to complete her short programme, South Korea noticed. When she returned to complete her free skate routine, South Korea simply stopped. Kim shattered the world record. She won South Korea's first-ever Winter Olympic Games gold medal outside of speed and short track skating.[26] 'Queen Yuna'. An instant celebrity in South Korea. The best athlete in the world in a discipline hitherto dominated by other countries. A global icon for a global (South) Korea.

### A new Kim, the same old North Korea?

Things were very different on the other side of the DMZ. In dramatic contrast to South Korea, North Korea became more reclusive and confrontational during this period. Throughout 2008, there were rumours about Kim Jong-il's health. This included reports about one or more strokes, which not even public appearances by Kim were able to quell. In fact, there were claims that some of Kim's pictures during his public appearances had been doctored.[27] Pictures of Kim at the time certainly show his physical deterioration. This only served to fuel further speculation about his health.

While rumours swirled, North Korea became more bellicose. Pyongyang conducted its second nuclear test in May 2009, shortly after Obama's inauguration and even though the new president had promised that he would continue the Six-Party Talks diplomatic process launched by his predecessor. What is more, North Korea conducted a record number of missile tests in 2009.[28] This included several tests of mid-range missiles that put the whole of Japan—and the American troops stationed there—within the range of a potential North Korean attack.

In 2010, the North Korean government upped the tempo and showed that, from its perspective, relations with South Korea were essentially broken. In March, a North Korean torpedo sank the ROKS *Cheonan* off the South Korean west coast. Forty-six of its 104 seamen were killed.[29] It is difficult to exaggerate the impact this had on the country. Since all South Korean men have to complete mandatory military service, all South Korean families know what it is to have a husband, father, son or other male relative serve in the armed forces. Any of the dead could have been their family. And in November, the North Korean military launched an artillery attack on Yeonpyeong, an island near the disputed border between the two Koreas in the West Sea. Two civilians and two soldiers were killed.[30] The North Korean armed forces had deliberately attacked South Korean civilians. Tensions between the two Koreas escalated to their highest point in decades, but the situation seemed to be improving throughout 2011.

And then, Kim Jong-il passed away. In December 2011, well-known North Korean news anchor Ri Chun-hee announced that Kim had died. Within a few days, it had become clear that his son would succeed him. Kim Jong-un headed the funeral committee paying respects to his father, and within months he had formally become the new leader of North Korea.[31] But such was the opacity of North Korea that there were no recent pictures of the new North Korean leader, and his age was unknown. It is believed that he was slightly under thirty by the time he took office, making him the youngest head of government in the world at the time. And it was also known that he had studied in Switzerland during his childhood, using a different name. Some analysts hoped this would lead Kim to set North Korea on a different path. Some even thought that the young North Korean leader might launch a Chinese- and Vietnamese-style economic and diplomatic opening up process.[32]

Alas, that was not to be the case. Kim Jong-un resumed North Korea's missile launch campaign in 2012 after a two-year hiatus under his late father. From 2014 and until 2017, North Korea would conduct a record number of tests every year. North Korea also conducted a new nuclear test in February 2013, which would be followed by three more in 2016 and 2017.[33] And this was accompanied by a brutal purge campaign the like of which the country had not seen since his grandfather's days. Most shockingly, Kim had his uncle Jang Song-thaek executed in December 2013, only a few days after his public arrest at a party meeting was broadcast on North Korean TV.[34] Even though the reasons for his execution will probably never be known, it was rumoured that Jang was too close to China and prioritized economic reforms. Whatever the truth, his purge showed that Kim would be ruling with an iron fist.

In this context, relations between the two Koreas continued to be marked by a deep freeze. Both Lee Myung-bak and Park Geun-hye left the door open to engagement with North Korea. Crucially, however, they supported inter-Korean negotiations as long as Pyongyang ceased development of its nuclear weapons programme. And both presidents supported the sanctions regime that the international community had been reinforcing since 2006 to stop North Korea's development of the programme. The Park government went even further. In March 2016, the National Assembly passed the North Korean Human Rights Act at the behest of the ruling Saenuri Party.[35] For Park and her party, South Korea needed to make a stand against the North Korean government's human rights abuses.

Even the symbols of inter-Korean cooperation launched at the turn of the century suffered. Tours to Mount Kumgang departing from South Korea ground to a halt after a tourist was shot in July 2008, never to be resumed. Family reunions between Koreans on both sides of the border became few and far between. Four meetings took place in 2009, 2010, 2014 and 2015, respectively. They continued to be poignant occasions, but the numbers were too small for the tens of thousands of elderly South Koreans aching to see their long-lost loved ones. And in early 2016, the Kaesong Industrial Complex was shut down. A rocket launch by North Korea had been the last straw, prompting the Park government to take this decision. The North Korean regime alleged that it had been a satellite launch.[36] But it did not matter. Relations between the two Koreas had become almost non-existent throughout the Lee and Park years. For conservative politicians, kinship was no reason to continue cooperating with North Korea simply for the sake of it. For South Koreans at large, North Korea was either an irritant or something they did not think much about. Most continued to support reunification. But a growing number had second thoughts, given North Korea's behaviour and the costs that reunification would entail.[37] In a sense, the North Korea policy of the Lee and Park governments was not out of touch with public opinion.

*Big firms, small firms, one innovative economy*

By the time Lee Myung-bak took office in February 2008, China had been a member of the World Trade Organization for seven years and its firms had started to move up the value-added chain. The days when South Korea could rely on the export of cheap goods to boost economic growth were over. But what if China was able to build semiconductors, smartphones, modern cars or high-tech ships cheaper than South Korea? And what if *Hallyu* was replicated by other countries such as China or Thailand that also had a thriving pop music scene?

Clearly, Lee thought, the South Korean economy could only thrive through innovation. This would prevent Chinese firms from catching up with their South Korean counterparts, while the latter would be able to compete head-to-head with their Japanese peers. South Korea would not become a shrimp again, sandwiched between lower-cost China and higher-tech Japan. Instead, South Korea should strive to become an innovation powerhouse. Not an original idea, for South Korean policy-makers and businesspeople had already been looking for ways to make their country's economy more innovative.[38] But an idea that seemed closer to fruition by the time Lee took office. Indeed, the 2009 International Innovation Index had ranked South Korea as the most innovative large economy in the world—second only to Singapore overall.[39] Travelling across the country, one could encounter and talk to entrepreneurs dreaming of making it big.

Lee made low-carbon green growth the centrepiece of his innovative economic growth policy from the moment of his inauguration.[40] His belief was not only that South Korea could rely on the export of green growth technologies to boost exports but also that a transition to a low-carbon economy would help clean up the country's air. For the latter had become a political issue, since particles coming from China—especially—coupled with South Korea's own emissions had led to a deterioration in air quality, particularly in Seoul and the surrounding area.[41] Innovation could therefore drive growth and improve the quality of life of the South Korean population.

But how could South Korea maintain its position as a world-class innovative nation? Education was key. Starting from 2000, the OECD had been conducting the Programme for International Student Assessment (PISA) study to assess the performance of high school students in the areas of maths, science and reading. Students across dozens of countries were presented with a set of tasks to which they applied their knowledge creatively to solve them. And South Korean pupils came top or very close to the top in each PISA test.[42] They were both knowledgeable and creative. Yet, they also studied for long hours. Herein lay a dilemma with no easy answers, for South Korea's innovation came on the back of long hours of study. Plus the dreaded *Suneung*: the nine-hour university entrance exam that all school leavers had to take, which paralyzes traffic and flights to avoid disturbances and determines the future of many South Koreans. This dilemma remained unsolved.

Yet the school system was one of the institutions in which South Koreans placed their trust to act in the best interest of society.[43] And indeed, South Koreans showed relatively little concern about educational inequality compared to people in other parts of the world.[44] Plus, the PISA study did show that South Korean students fared very well regardless of socio-economic status.[45] Simply put, students from both richer and poorer backgrounds performed very well by international standards. Which in turned helped propel South Korean innovation.

South Korea's highly educated workforce would go on to join the *chaebol*, smaller firms and research centres developing new products. But would others buy them? The Lee government built on his predecessor's trade policy by negotiating a bilateral trade agreement with the EU and renegotiating the controversial KORUS. The former entered into force in July 2011, with the latter following suit in March 2012.[46] With the strokes of two pens, South Korean firms had easier access to two of the three biggest economies in the world compared to their competitors across East Asia. Government and the private sector in a symbiotic relationship. The hallmark of South Korea's economic policy had evolved, but it certainly remained alive.

Park Geun-hye also believed in the need for South Korea to innovate to maintain its economic edge. But in a clear break with Lee, she put start-ups and SMEs at the core of South Korean innovation. Park's Creative Economy Action Plan, introduced only a few weeks after her inauguration, sought to create the conditions for cities across South Korea to develop their own entrepreneurial ecosystems.[47] Park was harking back to the Kim Dae-jung and Roh Moo-hyun years. Both presidents had heavily supported entrepreneurship and start-ups, and even though Lee Myung-bak had not left them aside, his economic policies relied strongly on the *chaebol*.[48] Park did not seek to undermine the country's big conglomerates—no South Korean president really does—but she wanted entrepreneurs and start-ups to make a greater contribution to economic growth and job creation.

The Creative Economy Action Plan thus resulted in a raft of initiatives to support entrepreneurs. The government established eighteen Creative Economy innovation centres up and down the country, with each of South Korea's nine provinces hosting at least one—and all of them having a *chaebol* as a partner. Visiting them, one could talk to entrepreneurs, government officials, mentors and *chaebol* representatives working together in search of the next product or service that South Korean consumers might want. The government also launched funds to support domestic entrepreneurs and attract foreign ones, set up Born2Global and other initiatives to support the internationalization of SMEs, and opened KONEX in 2013—one of the first stock exchanges in the world specifically targeting start-ups. The Park government also sought to attract foreign venture capital firms and other sources of funding. And the president herself went on TV and up and down the country to promote entrepreneurship. Park made it easier for younger South Koreans to tell their parents and grandparents that they wanted to launch their own start-up rather than join a *chaebol*. And foreigners also bought in. Capital—including from innovation hotspots such as Silicon Valley and Israel—and entrepreneurs started to flow from overseas. In a reversal of South Korea's migration history, many of them were Korean Americans and South Koreans who had lived overseas but who now wanted to try their luck in South Korea.[49]

To top it off, Google opened its first Asia campus in Seoul.[50] Not only in the South Korean capital but in Gangnam of all places. For Daejeon aside, the Seoul district of Psy fame had become the centre of innovative start-ups in South Korea. All along the area, one could find start-ups, incubators, venture capital firms and all the necessary elements of an entrepreneurial ecosystem. Seoul did not aspire to become a new Silicon Valley, for no other city in the world came close to matching the Californian innovation mecca. But during the Park years, Seoul did become one of Asia's innovation hotspots. Complete with the in-house baristas and slick barbeques that start-ups across the world aspire to.

Indeed, it was during this period that South Korea truly started to develop an open innovation system. Government research institutes and universities had traditionally worked together with *chaebol*. But *chaebol* had often been accused of 'stealing' innovative ideas and products from SMEs. This was now changing. Not only were *chaebol* nurturing start-ups and SMEs through the Creative Economy innovation centres but Samsung, Hyundai and others were buying up innovative SMEs whose owners wanted to benefit from the scale that large firms brought.[51] And on top of that, South Korea had by far the largest number of researchers moving from industry to academia among the most innovative countries in the world, as well as a fairly large share of people making the move in the opposite direction.[52] The private and public sectors were developing a symbiotic relationship underpinning South Korea's open innovation. Year after year, the Bloomberg Innovation Index named South Korea the most or one of the most innovative countries in the world.[53] (South) Korea Inc. had evolved and was ready to take on the other economic powerhouses of the twenty-first century.

### Two disasters, one revolution

It is a freezing Saturday evening in central Seoul. It is similarly cold across the whole of South Korea. But that does not stop over two million people from taking to the streets once more. Carrying candles, which have become the symbol of a protest movement sweeping the country. It is the evening of 3 December 2016.[54] The sixth Saturday in a row that South Koreans have taken to the streets to protest against Park Geun-hye, the embattled president. A protest movement that started in the scorching heat of the previous July, when thousands of students at Seoul's Ewha Womans University had taken over their campus to hold their own protests against a new degree programme. The programme would have offered degrees in health, beauty and fashion to students who had not had any prior experience of higher education. The programme had been quickly withdrawn, but the protests had served to unearth the favouritism shown by the university to the daughter of Choi Soon-sil. Choi herself, it turned out, had been providing advice to Park Geun-hye and had been given access to secret government documents even though she did not hold any official position. Late in the afternoon of 25 October, Park had admitted Choi's role in supporting her presidency. Within minutes, the terms 'impeachment' and 'resignation' were trending on social media. On 29 October, the first organized protest had taken place, with some 20,000 people joining in. Park's approval rating had already fallen to 17 per cent. By the time of the 3 December protest, it is down to 5 per cent. Six days later, on 9 December, the National Assembly will vote to impeach Park.[55] Six weeks from a social media trend to reality. The people will have won. South Koreans will have shaped their country's politics once more, holding their leader accountable. The Candlelight Revolution. A new source of pride for South Koreans.

The Candlelight Revolution was directly linked to the Choi scandal. But it came against the backdrop of a more general questioning of Park's conduct as president. Many South Koreans felt that Park was behaving in a way more reminiscent of her father's dictatorial rule. Shortly after the 2012 election, prosecutors had accused the NIS of a smear campaign against Moon Jae-in—Park's liberal opponent in the election—to sway the vote.[56] Many liberals saw this as proof that there was a 'deep state' bent on preventing their movement from holding power again. Even though it was unclear whether Park knew of the campaign, that it had taken place during Lee Myung-bak's presidency only served to raise suspicions of collusion between the conservative party and the NIS. Furthermore, there were also suspicions that the Park government was trying to silence its critics. And indeed, in late 2016 South Korean media and investigators unearthed a list of 10,000 left-leaning artists, journalists and other public figures who had been blacklisted by the government.[57] In addition, Park was seen as unwilling to submit herself to the scrutiny of media and public opinion. And to top it all, the president was seen as distant and her administration as incompetent. This was the result of Park's and her government's response to two disasters that hit South Korea in less than a year.

The first disaster could more accurately be characterized as a tragedy. A tragedy that played out live on TV sets across the country. On the morning of 16 April 2014, the MV *Sewol* ferry on its way from Incheon to Jeju took a sudden sharp turn, capsized after a few minutes and started sinking. A distress call went out. Fishing boats, commercial vessels and the coast guard rescued 172 passengers during two days of frantic searching. But over 300 people died, including some of the boat's crew and many of its passengers, most of whom were teenage students from Danwon High School, as well as rescue divers and emergency workers.[58] It was South Korea's biggest ferry tragedy since 1970.

Lax regulation enforcement, overloading and the behaviour of the crew were the direct causes of the *Sewol* ferry disaster. It turned out that the ferry had not undergone the necessary checks to ensure that it complied with existing regulations. It was also carrying over three times its cargo limit on the day of the accident. And the crew had asked the passengers to stay put even as water made it on to the boat while the captain and some crewmembers themselves abandoned ship.[59] South Koreans were rightly outraged. Those passengers—those children—could have been their relatives. Their government had failed them.

And Park, their president, had failed them too. It took seven hours for Park to show up at the disaster control centre. It was unclear where she had spent the morning while the *Sewol* sank. It turned out that she had spent most of the time in her bedroom. Park had also summoned Choi to the Blue House and met with her some four hours after the ferry had sank. She had then had her hair styled by a hairdresser before finally leaving for the control centre. The whole truth of Park's whereabouts was only uncovered during her impeachment trial.[60] But South Koreans were incensed by Park's absence from public view while the tragedy unfolded. And their anger only grew stronger in the following days when they learnt about Park's meeting with her hairdresser and the president displayed little empathy towards the grieving parents and relatives of the victims.

The second disaster unfolded a little over a year later. On 20 May 2015, a man who had recently returned from the Middle East was diagnosed with Middle East Respiratory Syndrome (MERS). The MERS coronavirus had first been identified in Saudi Arabia three years earlier, in April 2012. It was under control. But that first case in South Korea sparked an outbreak across the country. Between May and July, a total of 186 cases were confirmed, with thirty-eight deaths being recorded.[61] In retrospect, not many cases compared to the suffering and death that COVID-19 would unleash worldwide five years later. But a disaster for South Korea nonetheless, as it became the country with the second highest death total as a result of MERS.

That disaster again had the government as a key culprit. The Ministry of Health and Welfare initially withheld information from the public, including crucial details such as the transfer of MERS patients between medical facilities. When this information came to light, South Koreans became scared of visiting medical centres. Furthermore, MERS patients were initially free to move around. There was no isolation system in place. Nor a track and tracing system to know who had been in touch with those infected with the virus.[62] Once again, South Korea's lax regulatory standards had resulted in avoidable deaths. And at a time when the people needed reassurance, Park was again nowhere to be seen. This only made South Koreans more mistrustful of their president and the government at large.

A zombie movie released in July 2016 captured the public mood. *Train to Busan* told the story of a zombie apocalypse in South Korea. Lax regulation had resulted in a chemical leak. As zombies took over the country from the north in Seoul to the south in Busan, the government withheld information and failed to contain the crisis. The parallels with the *Sewol* and MERS disasters were obvious.[63] And South Koreans responded. *Train to Busan* became the highest-grossing movie of 2016, with over eleven million tickets sold.[64] Zombies are not real. But for many South Koreans, the failings of the Park government were.

It is in this context that the Candlelight Revolution swept the country. Park's impeachment was confirmed by the Constitutional Court in March 2017, in a unanimous eight to zero vote.[65] Protests continued until the very end of the impeachment process, in a display of civic nationalism not unlike that which the country had witnessed several times since the early 1990s. Even liberal–conservative divisions were put aside for a few months. Most notably, Park's Saenuri Party split into two as many of its National Assembly members voted for her impeachment, while counter-protests organized by Park's supporters only attracted a fraction of the attendees of the candlelight protests.[66] Park's approval rating by the time of her impeachment said it all.

*Liberals return to power*

Moon Jae-in became South Korea's new president in May, at the second time of asking and after winning the election following the confirmation of Park's impeachment. Moon captured slightly over 41 per cent of the vote, easily beating Hong Jun-pyo from the conservative opposition on 24 per cent and the centrist Ahn Cheol-soo on slightly more than 21 per cent.[67] Moon came top across the whole of the country except for parts of Gyeongsang in the south-west. But the strong showing by Ahn—founder of antivirus software firm AhnLab before moving into politics as a centrist candidate—indicated that many South Koreans were wary of the liberal–conservative divide in the country.

Moon's victory confirmed the ascendance of liberals in South Korean politics. A human rights lawyer who had been involved in labour law cases in the 1980s, one of the co-founders of South Korea's pre-eminent liberal newspaper *The Hankyoreh* in 1988 and Roh Moo-hyun's close aide during his presidency, Moon was a representative of the 386 generation.[68] His victory in the presidential election came one year after the Democratic Party's (DP) defeat of the Saenuri Party in the National Assembly elections of April 2016. Founded in 2014 as the main liberal party, the DP allowed liberals to retake the legislature for the first time since 2004. The DP would also go on to win the June 2018 local elections, clinching eight governorships and six metropolitan mayorships against two for the Liberty Party, the new name of the Saenuri Party.[69] The liberals were on a roll.

The new president had been elected under the promise of *jeokpye cheongsan* (disposing of the accumulated ills). According to Moon and the DP, the scandals of the Park Geun-hye years were not a one-off but rather the result of inappropriate government–*chaebol* links, a disinformation campaign by conservative forces and a slowdown if not a rollback of civil liberties.[70] And indeed, in

August 2017 the NIS admitted that it had launched a pro-government and anti-opposition disinformation campaign throughout the Lee Myung-bak and Park Geun-hye governments.[71]

Meanwhile, South Korean prosecutors and the courts were busy dealing with the misdeeds of previous years. In August 2017, Samsung heir Lee Jae-yong was sentenced to five years in prison after being convicted of paying bribes to Choi Soon-sil.[72] That same month, former NIS director Won Sei-hoon was sentenced to four years in prison for ordering a smear campaign against Moon and the liberal party.[73] In March 2018, Lee Myung-bak was arrested on charges of graft, embezzlement and abuse of power.[74] One month later, Park Geun-hye was sentenced to twenty-four years in prison for abuse of power and corruption stemming from the Choi scandal.[75] (She would be pardoned by Moon in December 2021 in the name of 'national unity' as well as for health reasons.)[76] In October, Lee was sentenced to fifteen years in prison as a result of the charges levied against him.[77] Several other businesspeople and former officials connected to these scandals were also sent to prison.

In the meantime, the Moon government introduced policies to reduce inequality. By global standards, South Korea had relatively low income inequality. And in fact, the Lee Myung-bak and Park Geun-hye governments had expanded the welfare state to mitigate the impact of unequal incomes.[78] Yet, South Koreans remained among the most concerned people in the world regarding this type of inequality.[79] And even though South Korea also had fairly high levels of social mobility,[80] South Koreans also expressed their concern about the lack of it.

Moon's signature measure was raising the minimum wage by over 16 per cent in 2018 and by almost 11 per cent in 2019.[81] South Korea's minimum wage relative to average wages was already among the highest in the developed world, but these increases further reduced the difference between both.[82] In addition, the government reduced the maximum length of the working week from sixty-eight hours to fifty-two. South Koreans worked some of the longest hours in the OECD and this reduction started to bring the country closer to its developed peers.[83] Unsurprisingly, many South Koreans were more than happy to work fewer hours and spend their salaries on their hobbies. Meanwhile, the government also boosted the number of public sector jobs as a way to increase employment, in a country that had the second lowest government employment as a percentage of total employment across the OECD.[84] These measures indeed led to a decrease in income inequality,[85] as well as more free time for workers. And South Korea's unemployment rate crept down, including the youth unemployment rate.[86] However, the incidence of temporary and part-time employment went up.[87]

In other areas, Moon's policies were actually indistinguishable from those of his conservative predecessors. A promised *chaebol* reform failed to materialize. The new president launched the world's first Ministry of SMEs and Start-Ups, but his policies to promote growth-inducing innovation followed those of Park and also involved the *chaebol*.[88] And the new government's push to promote green growth was similar to that of the Lee government.[89] To a large extent, the consensus that had dominated South Korea's economic policy for decades was not transformed following the shift from nine years of conservative rule to a liberal government.

The biggest change that Moon introduced related to North Korea policy. The new president took advantage of the PyeongChang Winter Olympic Games in February 2018 to extend an olive branch to Kim Jong-un.[90] And Kim responded in kind. The two Koreas marched under one flag in the opening ceremony, to the sound of 'Arirang'. Meanwhile, a delegation led by his sister Kim Yo-jong—albeit nominally led by head of state

Kim Yong-nam—visited South Korea during the Games. Kim was the first member of her family to set foot in the South.[91]

What followed was a whirlwind of diplomacy. Moon and Kim Jong-un held the first inter-Korean summit in almost eleven years in April 2018. Moon and Kim drew gasps by crossing over the demarcation line separating both Koreas across the DMZ. It was a delight to witness such a historic moment. They then met again the following month, in a summit arranged at only twenty-four-hours' notice. In June, Kim met US President Donald Trump in Singapore. This was the first time in history that a sitting US president had met his North Korean counterpart. It was followed by another inter-Korean summit in September, this time in Pyongyang and with Moon addressing some 120,000 North Koreans at the Rungrado 1st of May Stadium. But inter-Korean relations then deteriorated once more. Although Kim and Trump met again in Hanoi in February 2019, they failed to reach any kind of deal. Moon, Kim and Trump held one impromptu meeting at the DMZ in June 2019, following a trademark tweet by the US president while visiting Japan. The meeting marked the first time that a sitting US president had set foot in North Korea. But nothing came of it.[92] By 2020, the inter-Korean and US–North Korean rapprochement processes had stalled. Moon's signature foreign policy was in tatters.

In sharp contrast, however, Moon's domestic agenda took on a new lease of life in April 2020. The DP and its satellite Platform Party won a landslide in the National Assembly election, winning 180 out of the 300 seats. This was the largest number of seats that any party had won since the transition to democracy, on the back of the highest turnout for a legislative election in twenty-eight years. Voters had rewarded the Moon government's competent response to the COVID-19 pandemic—which had first hit South Korea in late January—as well as the government's relatively scandal-free rule since taking office.[93] It was the fourth electoral victory in a row for the liberals, an unprecedented feat for any party since South Korea regained its democracy. Lifted not only by the votes of the 386 generation but also Generation X,[94] the DP won the necessary three-fifths super-majority required to fast-track legislation without the need of support from opposition members of the National Assembly. The liberal movement had a once-in-a-generation opportunity to try to transform South Korea. Talking to liberals at the time, one could sense that they knew that history beckoned.

Moon and the DP took the opportunity they had been presented with in earnest. During the second half of 2020, the government introduced hundreds of laws that would fundamentally transform the character of the South Korean state. In the first week of December alone, the DP passed 130 laws. The liberal legislative blitz covered the strengthening of labour rights, cracking down on corruption, addressing the allegedly uncompetitive practices of the *chaebol* and reducing inequality.[95] Corruption had actually been declining for a decade and was neither higher nor lower than in other OECD countries.[96] But high-profile cases demanded further measures to address this issue. Meanwhile, the government also revived a plan to move the administrative capital from Seoul to Sejong. South Koreans were among the most concerned in the world regarding regional inequality.[97] This concern was warranted, since by 2019 and for the first time ever over half of the South Korean population was living in Seoul and the surrounding area.[98] In fact, driving out of Seoul it had become easy to miss where the city proper finished and satellite cities started. The government hoped that moving the capital would help to address this type of inequality.

In addition, the minor liberal Justice Party proposed an anti-discrimination bill in July. This was the seventh attempt by the liberal movement since 2007 to pass a law banning discrimination on the basis of gender, disability, age, sexual orientation, country of origin or any other reason. Previous attempts had failed, mainly due to opposition led by Christian groups that considered homosexuality sinful.[99] In addition, the government committed South Korea to carbon neutrality by 2050 in an effort to improve the country's air quality and combat climate change.[100] And by 2021, South Korea was openly debating the introduction of a universal basic income as the liberal governor of Gyeonggi Province Lee Jae-myung had implemented this measure to address the loss of income that many people had suffered as a result of the COVID-19 pandemic.[101] South Korea was being transformed by a liberal movement that reflected the changing nature of the country's society.

*Civic nationalism, liberal values and societal change*

South Korea was indeed becoming more liberal, as notions about the meaning of (South) Koreanness continued to evolve and downplay—but not abandon—*minjok*. Civic nationalism continued to become more powerful. Almost twice as many South Koreans considered citizenship more important than race for their own identity.[102] For most South Koreans, having a Korean bloodline or having been born in South Korea—in other words, *minjok*—were less important than civic nationalism in being a member of the South Korean family.[103] South Koreans took pride in their state and in their contribution to it. But at the same time, individualism was creeping in. More and more South Koreans were willing to defy traditional, Confucian-informed expectations about their role in society. Which brought a new open-mindedness and acceptance of differences within society. Most tellingly, over 90 per cent of South Koreans supported an anti-discrimination bill.[104] Where most politicians hesitated, the people almost universally had no doubts: all of them were equal regardless of gender, sexual orientation, religion or any other characteristic. Founded in 2012, the Justice Party was the first to openly give voice to the South Korean people by making minority rights a centrepiece of its platform.

It was in this context that feminism became an even stronger force. South Korean women continued to suffer from discrimination, particularly in the workforce. Compared to other developed countries, women participated slightly less in the job market and had one of the biggest pay gaps.[105] And for many firms, giving birth or sometimes even marriage continued to be a sign that it was time for a woman to leave work and stay at home. Talking to women at the time, it was clear that many felt frustrated. Careers mattered as much as motherhood to many of them. And there should be nothing wrong with that. As these conversations were taking place, the May 2016 murder of a young woman in a public toilet, at the hands of a man who was simply looking for a woman to kill, triggered a re-awakening of discussions about the treatment of women in South Korean society.[106]

In addition, a sexual harassment case brought against Seoul's mayor Park Won-soon in July 2020 showed that the attitudes of many men remained unchanged. The three-term mayor was an icon for liberals, given his progressive views even when compared to other members of the DP. But that month, Park's former secretary brought sexual harassment claims against him. The mayor committed suicide shortly afterwards and months later an investigation determined that the claims were true.[107] This case came on top of another sexual harassment incident involving the mayor of Busan, Oh Keo-don, also from the DP. In April 2020, he had been accused of sexual assault by two employees. Oh admitted the charges and resigned that same month. He would go on to be indicted in January 2021.[108] For many women, Park's behaviour as well as Oh's was the ultimate proof of the unsafe environment in which they lived.

SHRIMP TO WHALE

Two writers gave voice to the angst that many women felt. The novelist Cho Nam-joo published *Kim Jiyoung, Born 1982* in October 2016. It told the story of an ordinary woman—Kim Ji-young being a common South Korean female name—and the hardships and discrimination she had suffered from her childhood in the 1980s up to and during her marriage in the 2010s.[109] And in December 2017, poet Choi Young-mi published 'Monster', a poem denouncing sexual harassment at the hands of national hero Ko Un—none other than 'the poet of (South) Korea'.[110] Cho and Choi inspired many more women to speak up.

Seo Ji-hyun—a prosecutor—was one of the first to do so. And she was the one with the biggest impact. In January 2018, the prosecutor wrote in her work's intranet about the sexual harassment that she had suffered at the hands of a senior prosecutor. A few days later, Seo was invited to *JTBC Newsroom*, South Korea's flagship news programme. During the interview, Seo explained how she had been molested by her senior in public and surrounded by other prosecutors, yet no one had done anything about it. And she also explained how her career had suffered as a result of raising the issue at the Prosecutors' Office.[111] A few days after Seo's interview, Choi Young-mi also appeared on *JTBC Newsroom* to talk about 'Monster'. She discussed how she had suffered sexual harassment at the hands of a number of cultural figures when she was younger.[112] These interviews triggered the #MeToo movement in South Korea. Women in fields ranging from politics and journalism to sports and religion came out publicly with their stories of sexual harassment. Thousands also took to the streets to demand change. In the past, they would have hesitated to do so out of fear of losing their jobs. But times were changing. Now they would not be silenced. And then Seo's sexual harasser was sentenced to prison for abuse of power.[113] Women started to think that justice could be served.

And indeed, change was coming. After all, South Koreans had elected their first female president when they voted Park into office. Democracies with a much longer history were yet to vote for a female leader. Growing numbers of women were also shunning marriage and parenthood, instead choosing to focus solely on their careers. As a result, South Korea's fertility rate plummeted to 0.84 children per woman in 2020, one of the lowest in the world yet in line with declining fertility rates elsewhere.[114] Some decried this trend, especially as South Korea suffered its first-ever population decline in 2021.[115] But the truth was that South Korean women increasingly had a choice. Whether due to the costs of raising children, as some surveys showed, or for other reasons, women were taking the decision to have fewer children.[116] And men's attitudes were changing too. As a case in point, growing numbers of fathers were taking leave to take care of their children. Traditionally, this would have been seen as both a lack of commitment by a father to his job—and almost as an abandonment of her 'duties' by the mother. But by 2020, over 24 per cent of parents taking leave were men, with the figure being above 30 per cent for people in their twenties.[117] Make no mistake. Walking around South Korean parks or shopping malls during normal working hours, one would still come across many more mothers with their children than fathers. But little by little, one could see more fathers taking care of their children as well. Attitudes were evolving.

Politicians also modernized the law to accommodate the changing role of women in society. In 2015, adultery was legalized. Introduced in the 1950s, anti-adultery laws were originally intended to protect women against men seeking to have more than one wife. But twenty-first-century women did not need this protection, so the law was abolished.[118] A more seismic change took place in 2019, when the Constitutional Court ruled that South Korea's abortion ban was illegal.[119] Even though abortion was widespread, it was only permitted under special circumstances. Thanks to the Constitutional Court's ruling, South Korean women would be free to choose to have an abortion without fear of being prosecuted. Thousands celebrated in streets up and down the country. Slowly but surely, women were becoming freer.

Views of the LGBTQ+ community also became more liberal, even if prejudice certainly still remained. In October 2014, Park Won-soon became the first mainstream politician to openly support same-sex marriage. The following year, he allowed the Queer Festival parade to set off from Seoul Plaza in front of City Hall.[120] One cannot exaggerate the importance of this gesture. One could walk to the centre of Seoul, only a ten-minute walk from Gwanghwamun, and see the festival in all its glory. Christian groups complained. Seoulites shrugged their shoulders and more and more of them joined the parade with each year that passed. By 2020, over half of South Koreans in the thirty to forty-nine age bracket and almost 80 per cent of their counterparts under thirty agreed that society should accept homosexuality.[121] Overall, the percentage of South Koreas who thought that homosexuality was 'never justifiable' had declined to 24 per cent.[122] This was a seismic change for a country where many in the 1990s still claimed that no South Korean was a homosexual. Indeed, when Ahn Cheol-soo—now running for Seoul mayor before later on once again running for president—claimed that some people could be offended by the sight of the Queer Festival in central Seoul, he was roundly criticized and forced to apologize.[123] He looked out of touch with modern South Korea.

Yet, there were limits to the extent that society had changed, as symbolized by the tragic fate of Byun Hui-su. Born a man, staff sergeant Byun underwent gender reassignment surgery in November 2019. She was discharged from the army within two months. But Byun launched a public campaign to be reinstated. Her patriotism was obvious for everyone to see. 'I want to show everyone that I can also be one of the great soldiers who protect this country', she said. But the army did not baulk and refused her reinstatement in July 2020. Suffering from depression, Byun committed suicide the following March. The NHRCK honoured her bravery in pushing for the rights of transgender people. The army offered its condolences, after its initial message indicating that it had nothing to say drew severe criticism.[124] Calls for the passage of the anti-discrimination bill only grew louder. Byun only wanted to serve her country. For many South Koreans, that was all that mattered.

The 2010s were also the years when the term 'multiculturalism' made its way to South Korea. In 2000, less than 1 per cent of the country's residents were of foreign origin. The percentage had grown to slightly above 1 per cent by 2010, before increasing to over 3 per cent in 2019—around two million people.[125] This was mainly due to migration. Immigrants from China, Vietnam, Thailand and other Asian countries flocked to South Korea. The two main reasons were work and marriage, as immigrants continued to take jobs that South Koreans shunned and a growing number of South Koreans married foreign spouses—by the late 2010s, 10 per cent of marriages in the country were between a South Korean and a foreigner.[126] Many Chinese migrants were of Korean origin; people moving to their parents' or grandparents' motherland in search of a better life. Growing numbers of migrants from the United States, Europe, Canada and Australia were moving to South Korea too.[127] Along with those moving for work or marriage, Westerners also included second-generation migrants moving to South Korea in search of better job prospects. In the Yongsan district, for example, one could visit the Seoul Global Start-Up Center and meet hundreds of mainly Westerners trying their luck at launching their own firm from the South Korean capital. And while different groups certainly had very diverse experiences in adapting to South Korea, that tens of thousands moved to the country every year was proof that a more multicultural, inclusive, liberal and rich South Korea was increasingly appealing to foreigners.

This included North Koreans, record numbers of whom escaped their country and ended up in South Korea in the 2010s. By 2021, over 33,000 North Koreans were living in the South.[128] And the main reason they were moving from the North to the South was similar to that of other migrants: better life prospects. As more North Koreans learnt about the much better living standards in South Korea thanks to dramas and movies smuggled into their country, many decided to leave. Talking to some of them, it was actually a K-drama or a South Korean movie that had convinced them to try to move to the South. Average South Koreans were living in what looked like luxury apartments and driving what seemed like luxury cars well beyond the grasp of all but North Korean elites. Many North Koreans wanted that for themselves. Their settlement experience in the South of course was different depending on the person. But, in general, younger North Koreans fared better. And a growing number of them found love and married South Koreans.[129]

Young South Koreans were at the forefront of the increasing civic nationalism and liberalism driving change in their country. For older South Koreans, regional origin remained a strong predictor of their stance in the liberal–conservative divide—including their choice of political party. Their anti-communism also continued to have some influence on their political stance. But for younger South Koreans, region mattered less than their perception of whether policies and political parties were liberal or not.[130] And the threat of a communist takeover from North Korea was, essentially, a non-factor. It was hard to find a young South Korean who thought that the North could make theirs a communist country. So the biggest divide in South Korea was generational. The 386 generation and, especially, Generation X and millennials were much more accepting of diversity than the over-sixties. In 2017, they popularized the *honjok* lifestyle: willingly doing activities such as eating out in restaurants or singing at a *noraebang* alone. Even the number of single-person households ballooned to reach nine million people as 2021 drew to an end.[131] For younger South Koreans, people should be free to live their lives as they pleased. In fact, South Korea had one of the biggest gaps in the world in terms of the acceptance of homosexuality.[132] Likewise, these generations were far less religious than their elders. Again, South Korea had one of the largest generational gaps in the world in this area.[133] And younger South Koreans wanted their country to mimic the social democracies of northern Europe: an equal society with a strong welfare state, rather than the cut-throat capitalism usually associated with Anglo-Saxon countries.

For many younger South Koreans, their views were informed by a new attitude to life. Many believed that their society was becoming more unequal and exercised huge pressure on them. They rejected the '*pali pali*' culture that they thought fostered unhappiness and contributed to the pressure they were suffering. Symbolic of this pressure and inequality was the nut rage scandal of December 2014. Sitting on a flight from New York, Korean Air Vice President Heather Cho had assaulted the cabin crew chief after a flight attendant had served a bag of nuts to first-class passengers without using a plate. She made the plane taxi back to the gate at JFK airport before forcing the cabin crew chief to disembark. After his dismissal, he went public, leading to a public outcry and the trial of Cho.[134] For many young South Koreans, this incident showed the inequality of their country and the abuse of power by those in large firms. From 2015, these disaffected youth popularized the term 'Hell Joseon' to express their frustration. And South Koreans were in fact among the most concerned about generational inequality in the world.[135]

From 2017, the term *sampo* generation became popular. Introduced a few years earlier, the term referred to those who had given up on dating, marriage and children due to their precarious socio-economic position.[136] Certainly, most young South Koreans would not define themselves as belonging to this generation. But enough did to make this a popular term.

Kim Ou-joon gave voice to liberal South Koreans seeking change. Already a popular radio presenter, he launched the political podcast *Naneun Ggomsuda* (I'm a weasel) along with four colleagues in 2011. The podcast touched a nerve among liberals critical of the Lee Myung-bak government. It made Kim a celebrity, leading to more podcasts and even a TV show. But above all, Kim's popularity allowed him to launch *News Factory*. This became South Korea's most popular radio show and made Kim the country's most influential journalist. Millions of people listened every day, as Kim helped to tilt public opinion towards more liberal ideas.[137] Arguably, Kim became the voice of the direction of travel that South Korea was taking.

But there continued to be some divisions among young South Koreans along gender lines regarding which party best represented their interests. By 2021, the percentage of South Korean men in their twenties who said they supported the conservative party was similar to that of men and women over sixty. And most men in their thirties also supported the conservatives. Some commentators called them the 'ilbe generation'. In contrast, most women in their twenties and thirties supported the liberal (Democratic) party.[138] Even though both men and women held similar liberal values and views about fairness, men still thought that the 386 generation did not understand their economic plight. Furthermore, many still resented having to spend some eighteen months in compulsory military conscription, from which women were exempt. This led them to reject the feminism of the liberal

DP, which they thought disadvantaged men who had to 'waste' a year and a half of their twenties due to conscription.[139]

More broadly, South Koreans in general were not simply going to side with the liberal DP no matter what. Thus, after four consecutive elections, the party suffered a resounding defeat in the Seoul and Busan mayoral by-elections held in April 2021. South Korea's two largest cities went to the polls following Park Won-soon's and Oh Keo-don's respective sex scandals. The DP had seen its usual lead in the Seoul polls cut due to the sex scandal and it was trailing in Busan—a conservative bastion under normal circumstances. Then a massive real state scandal engulfed the government. Coming on the back of soaring house prices in the country's two main cities, the scandal made voters decisively turn their backs against the liberals.[140] From the moment the scandal broke, the rebranded People Power Party (PPP) candidates were overwhelming favourites to win the Seoul election—Busan had already been a given. And win they did, taking the Seoul and Busan city governments by overwhelming majorities: almost twenty points in the case of the South Korean capital and slightly under thirty points in the country's second largest city.[141]

The PPP's victory came only eleven months ahead of the presidential election scheduled for March 2022. South Koreans may have become more liberal in their values. But they wanted fairness, whether between men and women or between rich and poor. The party that did not give it to them could not expect to be elected. As the presidential election approached, the DP and PPP candidates—Lee Jae-myung, now the former Gyeonggi Province governor, and former Prosecutor General and political outsider Yoon Suk-yeol, respectively—were neck and neck in the polls. In the end, Yoon won the election with 48.5 per cent of the vote against Lee's 47.8. The conservative candidate won by the smallest margin in the history of South Korean presidential elections. Yet, Yoon's victory showed that, for many South Koreans, conservatives could represent fairness as well as or even better than liberals.

Shortly after Yoon's inauguration, on the night of 29 October 2022, disaster hit South Korea once more. Tens of thousands of South Koreans and foreigners were celebrating their first Halloween post-COVID-19 pandemic in the popular Itaewon neighbourhood, just north of the Han river in Seoul. Shortly after 10pm, there was a crowd crush. One hundred fifty-nine people died, mainly young people simply trying to enjoy a night out. It was South Korea's deadliest incident since the 2014 ferry disaster. Yoon convened an emergency meeting shortly after reports of the crush started to emerge. But the disaster made many South Koreans once again wonder whether they could trust their leaders.

## *World-leading South Korea*

It is already 16 March 2021 in South Korea. The seven boys take to TV screens and livestreams at the very end of the nearly four-hour award show. Primetime. They are arguably the biggest draw for a global music audience. For they are the most famous boyband in the world. Performing a number-one hit that has taken that same world by storm. They go on top of a skyscraper overlooking Yeouido, Seoul's financial district. Spectacular views. For a spectacular group of musicians. But by then they have already become much more than musicians. They are artists. They are icons. They sing to the hearts of their generation. With its joys, its fears, its sufferings. They are also UN spokesmen.[142] They are the voice of a generation coming of age, even if their fans span all ages. From Seoul to São Paulo. From Los Angeles to London. Their stage is the world. And the Grammys' organizers have finally caught on. They know what a global audience wants. And they give it to them, broadcasting their live performance from that Yeouido skyscraper. As the COVID-19 pandemic still rages. When many people are still in lockdown, in their homes, in search of reasons to believe in a better future. A song and a band that gives hope to these people. 'Dynamite', the latest hit from BTS.[143]

The rise of South Korea's first truly universal music act came in the midst of an astonishing transformation in perceptions of South Korea across the world. Up until the 1980s, South Korea was either largely unknown or known as a fairly poor country due to *M\*A\*S\*H\**. Even as the country transitioned into a democracy and became a rich, technologically advanced nation towards the end of the twentieth century, perceptions of South Korea did not catch up. But this had changed throughout the first and, especially, second decades of the twenty-first century. Thanks to *Hallyu*. Thanks to Samsung, LG and other globally recognized *chaebol*. And from 2020, thanks to its response to the COVID-19 pandemic. South Korea was seen as modern, likeable and cool. For the first time in its history, South Korea was a world-leading country. A true whale.

*Hallyu*, certainly, continued to go from strength to strength. K-Pop was everywhere. BIGBANG, EXO, Girls' Generation and Twice were internationally successful. Blackpink had become the biggest girlband in the world. BTS topped them all. Before the pandemic, these bands were performing to sell-out crowds across the Americas, Europe and Asia. BTS and Blackpink topped charts, had billion-viewer hits and each one of their members was a star in their own right.[144] At the end of 2020, there were at least 1,835 K-Pop-related fan clubs with over 104 million members.[145] Products endorsed by K-Pop stars immediately sold at an exponential rate. BTS alone were worth US\$4.65 billion to the South Korean economy in ticket sales, tourism revenue and product sales.[146] This was bigger than the size of the economies of Barbados or Fiji. Inevitably, construction of a *Hallyu*

K-Culture Valley started with a completion date of 2024, to capitalize on the success of BTS and other K-Pop acts.[147]

But of course it was not only about K-Pop. In February 2020, Bong Joon-ho took to the Oscars stage not one, not two, not even three, but four times. Including to collect the award for Best Picture. The first movie not in English to receive this honour. And only the second movie ever to collect both the Palme d'Or at the Cannes Film Festival and this Oscar. Plus a box office hit, making over US$250 million worldwide.[148] Celebrations ran wild in South Korea when Bong's movie received its four Oscars. *Parasite* was a global phenomenon. A very South Korean story, dealing with very universal themes, gaining recognition from critics and audiences everywhere.

Recognition for South Korea's film and TV industry was not confined to Bong and *Parasite*. Movies such as *Burning*, *The Handmaiden* and *Train to Busan* received critical acclaim. Dramas such as *Crash Landing on You*, *Itaewon Class* and *Mr Sunshine* became global hits. Both Asian and Western firms competed to place their products in the latest drama, a sure way to boost global sales.[149] *The Masked Singer*—a show where celebrities sing music hits while wearing imaginative costumes and masks—became an international sensation, with over fifty countries producing their own versions.[150] And the 2021 Oscars brought more reasons for South Koreans to cheer. *Minari* was nominated for the Best Picture award. Shot almost entirely in Korean and directed by Korean American director Lee Isaac Chung, it told the story of South Korean immigrants moving to rural Arkansas. South Korean icon Youn Yuh-jung—who had shot to fame five decades earlier as the titular character in *Jang Hui-bin*—was nominated for a Best Supporting Actress award and Seoul-born Steven Yeun became the first Asian American actor to be nominated for a Best Actor award.[151] And when Youn won the Oscar, seemingly every South Korean celebrated as if they had received the golden statue themselves. The same South Koreans who were astonished by the success of *Squid Game*, a South Korean drama about inequality and class struggle released in late 2021 and watched by over 140 million households.[152] South Koreans and their stories were taking over the world.

For one of the most interesting aspects of South Korean culture's global success is that the country's artists decided to stick to their Korean roots. BTS, Blackpink and other bands embraced Korean culture and sang predominantly in Korean.[153] South Korean movies and dramas told distinctly local stories referencing domestic developments. Webtoons, increasingly popular on the screens of smartphones across the world, spoke to a South Korean audience first and foremost.[154] Certainly, there were influences from foreign art ranging from hip-hop to Hollywood. Many South Korean filmmakers were spending time overseas while learning their craft, absorbing from the best film schools across the world. And K-Pop bands had become international operations, with songwriters and band members from across Asia, Europe, the United States and elsewhere. But the essence was distinctly (South) Korean.

In fact, the internationalization of South Korean culture came as South Koreans' pride in their own roots continued to grow. The number of *hanok* continued to increase, as more South Koreans embraced the country's traditional housing style, albeit equipped with modern appliances.[155] It became common to meet South Koreans expressing their wish to try living in a *hanok*. More women took to wearing *hanbok*-inspired clothes in their daily life.[156] It was not uncommon to meet South Korean women discussing the virtues of this comfortable and colourful clothing. *Trot*—folk ballads dating back to the Japanese colonial period— made a strong comeback.[157] Older South Koreans talked excitedly about attending their last or next *trot* performance. And *kim-jang*—the art of making kimchi at home—reclaimed its popularity as busy city dwellers travelled to rural towns to prepare their own Korean staple.[158] Many South Koreans spoke about how this communal activity brought them warm childhood memories. In my view, one should strive to try *kimjang* at least once to connect more deeply with this Korean staple.

The roots of this pride were of course not new. They preceded the Lee Myung-bak and Park Geun-hye governments and had continued to strengthen during their time in office. In 2009, Lee had inaugurated a statue dedicated to the most revered figure in Korean history: King Sejong. On the 563rd anniversary of the official invention of Hangeul, its inventor had his 6.2-metre high statue unveiled in Gwanghwamun—unmissable when strolling down central Seoul, right between Admiral Yi Sun-sin's statue and Gyeongbokgung.[159] And then the admiral himself became a box office hit. The 2014 epic *The Admiral: Roaring Currents*, depicting Yi Sun-sin's victory over Japanese invaders in 1597, became the highest-grossing movie of all time in South Korea. *The Admiral* sold an astonishing seventeen million tickets at a time when South Korea's population was slightly over fifty million.[160]

While looking at the past, it was South Korea's forward-looking attitude that was propelling it into world-leading country status. Pyeongchang is a small county with a population slightly above 43,700 people. When ice skating icon Kim Yu-na lit the Olympic cauldron on 9 February 2018 to inaugurate the 2018 Winter Olympic Games, the world's eyes were fixed on the county. So the South Korean government and the country's firms took the opportunity to showcase the future: 5G, AI, self-driving buses, robot guides, 360-degree virtual reality cameras ... the whole lot.[161] South Korean tech had become crucial to the world economy: the most advanced semiconductors along with Taiwan's, the largest cargo ships ever seen and the first foldable phones all hailed from South Korea. By 2020, it was once again ranked as the most innovative country in the world.[162] That October,

Samsung president Lee Kun-hee passed away. No one had done more than this visionary to make that happen.[163] Fittingly, he would be honoured almost as a head of government.

And then along came COVID-19. Located right next to China, South Korea was one of the first countries to be hit by the pandemic. As the number of infections mounted, South Koreans feared that the lessons from MERS had not been learnt. But actually, they had. The government quickly deployed a world-class track and trace system, the private sector developed COVID-19 tests within weeks that were exported to the rest of the world and hospitals were equipped with the necessary negative-pressure rooms and hazmat suits to prevent infections.[164] South Korea had one of the lowest death rates from COVID-19 in the world. And it was the triumvirate of government, *chaebol* and start-ups that continued to drive South Korean innovation—including its exemplary response to the pandemic.

As Moon Jae-in put it, 'mutually beneficial cooperation between large firms and SMEs as well as government support' had been the main driving force behind South Korea's success.[165] A partnership not only for the benefit of South Korea but also for the rest of the world. As people across the globe were receiving their COVID-19 vaccines, they could thank SME Poonglim for the invention of new low dead space syringes, *chaebol* Samsung for scaling up production and the government for brokering a partnership between both. These new syringes and the SME–*chaebol*–government partnership allowed nurses and doctors to offer tens of millions more vaccine shots using the same number of vaccine vials.[166] South Korean innovation, simply put, allowed the world to be vaccinated more quickly.

By 2021, South Korea had become a trendsetter. The *New York Times*, *Washington Post* and other international media were moving to and hiring staff in Seoul as China approved a Hong Kong Security Law that limited freedom of speech in the city. The two

US newspapers even opened global hubs in the South Korean capital. South Korea was ranked as the country with the greatest press freedom in Asia, so the move was only natural.[167] And as the move took place, *mukbang* and *gongbang* were taking over the COVID-19 lockdown world: live streams of people eating (*mukbang*) or studying (*gongbang*) for hours on end that had become popular in South Korea in the 2010s and were spreading to other countries.[168] Meanwhile, KOSPI—South Korea's stock exchange—set new records by the end of 2020 and became the best performing stock exchange in the developed world, as local retail investors and foreign funds poured money into it.[169] At the same time, South Korean emigrants made their way back home, where they could get better healthcare and politicians who actually sought to protect their people against a pandemic.[170] And the number of students taking Korean lessons grew by the millions. For old and young alike, from Egypt to Mexico, from France to Vietnam, Korean was becoming an ever-more popular language.[171] To top it off, in February 2021 Marvel released its latest superhero: Taegukgi. Yes, a superhero named after the South Korean flag. Proudly wearing his country's flag on his chest.[172]

And the South Korean government and people felt vindicated as recognition was bestowed upon the country. In April 2021, Hyundai unveiled a Pony electric vehicle concept. The *chaebol* was paying homage to the car that forty-six years earlier had been treated as little more than a laughing stock. The verdict? A car showcasing 'the future of the automotive retromod industry'.[173] Hyundai was among the voices leading the conversation about the future of sustainable transportation. In June, Moon Jae-in beamed when he touched down in the United Kingdom to attend the G7 summit held in Cornwall. South Korea had been one of only four countries invited to join the meeting organized by some of the biggest economies in the world.[174] He represented an economy that deserved to be at the table; an economy that in fact brought prestige to this table. In September, BTS spoke about youth power at the UN General Assembly. Over one million people tuned in to watch the livestream.[175] These artists represented their generation globally like few others did.

In November, Blackpink delivered a message ahead of the annual UN Climate Change Conference to be held later in the year.[176] As the organizers knew, few could deliver a message to the younger generations as effectively as these four artists could. Also in November, Samsung leader Lee Jae-young—released from prison on parole the previous August—made a successful business trip to North America, where he announced the opening of a semiconductor factory in Texas.[177] In the second half of the twentieth century, US firms had set up shop in South Korea and helped the country's development. In the twenty-first century, South Korean *chaebol* were opening factories in the United States in sectors in which they were world-leading. And in December, Moon took the virtual stage at the Summit for Democracy convened by the United States. The South Korean president spoke at an exclusive twelve-leader plenary session hosted by US President Joe Biden.[178] On this occasion, the South Korean president represented one of the strongest democracies in the world.

South Korea's streak of success continued during the Yoon presidency. Blackpink's 2022–3 world tour became the highest grossing by a girlband ever. Plus, the four-member group became the first K-Pop act to headline the Coachella Music Festival in April 2023. Meanwhile, K-dramas such as *Extraordinary Attorney Woo* and *The Glory* were global hits. And Yoon himself cohosted the second Summit for Democracy in March 2023 and attended the Hiroshima G7 summit, in Japan, on 19–21 May of the same year.

A country whose politicians, business leaders and artists were speaking to global audiences, at the demand of these global audiences. The world, simply put, could not get enough of South Korea.

# EPILOGUE

## THE FUTURE OF SOUTH KOREA

Never make predictions. So goes the dictum. And yet, we can venture to suggest that South Korea will only continue to go from strength to strength for years to come. The country has never before been as globally recognized and admired as it is as of 2023. South Korea is one of the largest economies in the world, powered by high-tech products such as semiconductors, cars, ships, electric batteries and mobile phones. The country's trendsetting culture has become a staple in homes everywhere, leading millions of people to want to learn the language, to gain a deeper appreciation of its films, music and dramas. For South Korea is cool. It is fashionable. It is a place to be, a place to visit. Strolling down the Myeong-dong shopping district in central Seoul, one can hear excited tourists speaking in dozens of languages. Visiting Gyeongbokgung, one can see hundreds of foreigners having their pictures taken while wearing their preferred *hanboks*. And when South Koreans travel abroad, their hosts recognize their country. They know about it. Samsung, Hyundai, LG. Gangnam, Bukchon, Jeju Island. BTS, Blackpink, BIGBANG. *Oldboy*, *The Handmaiden*, *Parasite*. Choo Shin-soo, Kim Yu-na, Son Heung-min. South Korean firms, art, places and people that the world knows about.

At the same time, South Korea is grappling with several of the issues that also afflict many other countries across the world.

Economic inequality is not particularly high by global standards, but the gap is indeed wider than it was before the IMF or Asian Financial Crisis. Women are freer than in the past, but the gender gap is certainly yet to be closed. The country is becoming more multicultural, but not everyone welcomes the growing number of foreigners making South Korea their home. And while divisions between liberals and conservatives are often more about form rather than substance, there is certainly an ideological divide in South Korean society. Likewise, the gap in thinking between old and young can sometimes be exaggerated, but there is indeed a generational divide in South Korea. As the people and the country think about their future, these are issues that cannot be ignored.

### Shrimp among whales no more

Let's state the obvious: as of 2023, South Korea is not a shrimp about to have its back broken by whales. There are of course South Koreans who continue to believe that the fate of their country is in the hands of the United States, China, the competition between the two or some other external force. But a country that, at the time of writing, is a full and well-consolidated democracy,[1] is the tenth largest economy in the world,[2] has the sixth most powerful military,[3] ranks eleventh worldwide in terms of soft power,[4] tops any other Asian country in terms of press freedom, has a seat at the G20 table and has been invited to attend the G7 is no minnow. Dozens upon dozens of other countries across the world would love to be this type of 'shrimp'.

Certainly, South Korea has been crafting its own path for decades at the time of writing. Its economy continues to be largely trade-dependent. But this is because South Korea's innovative *chaebol* and SMEs provide the goods and the services that consumers across the world want to buy. And this will surely continue into the future. For the country is one of the largest R&D investors in the world and South Korean consumers are among the earliest adopters of new technologies. So whether it is 6G, AI, electric or hydrogen vehicles, quantum computing or robotic automation, there will be one or other South Korean firm that will compete at the cutting edge. And this firm could well be Samsung or Hyundai, but it could also be the next Celltrion or Nexon that a young South Korean entrepreneur is about to launch in Gangnam or Daejeon.

If anything, South Korea will continue to be a model and a funder of others' economic growth. Foreign policy-makers and development specialists from Latin America, South East Asia and Sub-Saharan Africa will continue to flock to South Korean universities or the public policy school of the Korea Development Institute—Asia's top economic think tank[5]—to learn the secret of how South Korea went from poor to rich in a remarkably short period of time. KOICA—South Korea's development agency—will continue to provide aid to support the social development and infrastructure building that less developed countries want. Indeed, South Korea was the first country to graduate from aid recipient to donor.[6] This is a source of pride that will continue to drive South Korea's provision of aid for years to come.

South Korea is even a model for fellow developed countries. It avoided an economic contraction during the Global Financial Crisis—one of only two OECD members to achieve this feat. It did suffer a recession as a result of the COVID-19 pandemic, but no other developed country weathered its economic hit as well. The way in which the competence of the South Korean government and healthcare professionals prevented anything close to the COVID-19 death tolls seen in Europe and the United States was widely praised. Less noticed, South Korea's position at the top of all OECD governments in terms of digital openness is also a model for more secretive governments to follow.[7] South Korea's place among the most competent and open countries in the world will surely continue. Its citizens will make sure that this is the case, as they have been doing for decades.

And let's not forget a crucial aspect to properly put South Korea's position in the world into perspective: there has been no real talk about 'competition' between the two Koreas for decades. North Korea, sadly, is a reminder of where South Korea could still be in the 2020s: impoverished, authoritarian, with few—if any—real friends and with a population yearning for a brighter future. While comparing the two Koreas is not really the most appropriate of exercises in the 2020s, because they belong in different leagues, it does serve to underscore that if any Korea may fear being a shrimp it is the one north of the thirty-eighth parallel. If full reunification happens, there is little doubt that it will be on South Korean terms.

## South Korea's changing nature and bright future

At the domestic level, South Korea is a country vastly changed from the one that opened to the world with the Seoul 1988 Olympic Games. And the changes of the past few decades allow us to project into the future. Starting with the diversified nature of lifestyles and career paths that South Koreans can take. The model of the male breadwinner clocking the hours in his office or factory while his wife takes care of the children—perhaps chipping in with her '*ajumma* job'—is a thing of the distant past. As of 2023, many South Koreans still aspire to get a job in a *chaebol*. Many others want to join the ranks of socially prestigious white-collar professions such as law, medicine or academia. But many others want to open their own business: a game developer, a robotics company, a biotech lab, an independent café, a boutique hotel ... After all, South Korea is one of the most entrepreneurial countries in the world.[8] Many South Koreans will continue to pursue the dream of being their own boss.

The position of women has been the biggest change in South Korean society in recent decades—with much more yet to come. Young and middle-aged South Korean women have expectations that their mothers and grandmothers could not even dream about. As the influence of Confucianism has declined, women have increasingly felt free to be themselves and do as they please. South Korean women aspire to fulfilling professional careers. If they get married, they expect their husband to share household chores. Traditionalists will decry this and blame women for declining marriage and birth rates. But marriage and birth rates will continue to remain below the levels of decades past because women—and indeed, men—have a choice, and many are perfectly happy with having one child or none at all. South Korea's government and society will have to adapt to this change.

At the same time, multiculturalism—or at least the growing presence of foreigners in South Korea—is here to stay. Mixed marriages are the result of South Korea opening up to the rest of the world and South Koreans broadening their horizons well beyond the confines of the Korean Peninsula. Migration happens mainly because there are jobs that South Koreans no longer want to do. And most foreigners living in South Korea are there out of their own volition. Barring a collapse of the South Korean economy unseen since the Korean War, South Korea will continue to attract foreigners who want to settle in the country. Some even think of migration as a way to address what they see as the problems derived from South Korea's low birth rate. More likely is that migration will help to redefine our understanding of what a South Korean is.

In the midst of this change, liberals and conservatives will continue to be divided. But this division ought to be qualified. Liberal views about the position of women in society, the treatment of the LGBTQ+ community and other minorities and the need to address inequality or overwork are increasingly mainstream—especially among younger South Koreans. So while a more liberal worldview does not automatically translate into a vote for a liberal party, conservative forces in South Korea increasingly adopt positions closer to those of their liberal counterparts. The expectation is that this will continue for the foreseeable future. For in South Korea, as in most other democracies, elections are still won by attracting moderate voters. And the number of these voters that will hold more liberal views will continue to grow.

Ultimately, the changing nature of South Korean society is informed by the move towards civic nationalism. *Minjok* is certainly not gone. It continues to be a strong driving force in how South Koreans see themselves. But the South Koreans of 2023 share the characteristics of citizens in fellow developed countries. And civic nationalism is a powerful force. One has to contribute to South Korean society, as well as to the South Korean state. But one also has to make sure that those in positions of power deliver. Koreanness has been redefined. Race matters, yes. But so does being a good citizen—and this often takes precedence. This evolution in thinking has probably reached the point of no return.

As South Korea and South Koreans evolve, one thing is clear: a bright future awaits the country. For South Korea is home to a strong society, which has forged and will continue to shape the country's path. And a strong society makes for a strong country. Which the South Korea of 2023 is. Proud of its heritage, yet unafraid to embrace the change that the future holds. Let's make this clear: South Korea has arrived; South Korea is here to stay.

# CHRONOLOGY

## 1945–2023

15 August 1945—Independence of Korea

8 September 1945—Establishment of the United States Army Military Government in Korea (USAMGIK) in south Korea

3 April 1948—Start of the Jeju Uprising

10 May 1948—First-ever elections in (south) Korea

24 July 1948—Rhee Syngman elected as the first president of south Korea

15 August 1948—Foundation of South Korea

1 December 1948—National Security Law approved by the National Assembly

10 March 1950—Promulgation of the Land Reform Law

25 June 1950—Start of the Korean War

5 August 1952—First-ever direct presidential election

27 July 1953—Korean War armistice

1 October 1953—Republic of Korea–US Mutual Defense Treaty signed

# SHRIMP TO WHALE

19 April 1960—Start of the April Revolution

29 May 1960—Rhee Syngman goes into exile

15 June 1960—Inauguration of the Second Republic

12 August 1960—Yun Posun elected as the second president of South Korea

16 May 1961—Coup d'état led by Park Chung-hee

13 June 1961—Korean Central Intelligence Agency (KCIA) established

5 January 1962—Announcement of Park Chung-hee's first five-year plan

17 December 1963—Inauguration of the Third Republic; Park Chung-hee inaugurated as the third president of South Korea

26 February 1965—Dispatch of the first South Korean troops to the Vietnam War

22 June 1965—Diplomatic normalization with Japan

1 April 1967—Completion of the Guro Industrial Complex

21 January 1968—North Korean assassination attempt on Park Chung-hee

1 April 1968—Establishment of the Pohang Iron and Steel Company (POSCO)

22 April 1970—Launch of Saemaul Undong (New Village Movement)

28 August 1970—Release of 'Morning Dew' by Kim Min-ki

13 November 1970—Self-immolation of labour activist Jeon Tae-il

4 July 1972—North–South Joint Communiqué

30 August 1972—Launch of Red Cross talk between the two Koreas

21 November 1972—Approval of the Yushin Constitution in referendum

27 December 1972—Inauguration of the Fourth Republic

23 March 1973—South Korean withdrawal from the Vietnam War

8 August 1973—Kim Dae-jung kidnapping and assassination attempt

15 August 1974—Killing of First Lady Yuk Young-soo after an assassination attempt on Park Chung-hee; opening of the Seoul Subway

26 October 1979—Assassination of Park Chung-hee

6 December 1979—Choi Kyu-hah elected as the fourth president of South Korea

12 December 1979—Coup d'état led by Chun Doo-hwan

18 May 1980—Start of the Gwangju Uprising

1 September 1980—Chun Doo-hwan inaugurated as the fifth president of South Korea

3 March 1981—Inauguration of the Fifth Republic

18 March 1982—Arson attack against the Busan American Cultural Service

30 June 1983—Start of the *Finding Dispersed Families* broadcast

1 September 1983—Korean Air flight shot down by the Soviet Union

# SHRIMP TO WHALE

9 October 1983—North Korean assassination attempt on Chun Doo-hwan

21–24 September 1985—First-ever inter-Korean family reunion

20 September 1986—Opening of the Asian Games hosted in Seoul

14 January 1987—Death of student Park Jong-cheol following his torture

9 June 1987—Fatal injury of student Lee Han-yeol

10 June 1987—Beginning of the June Democratic Struggle

29 June 1987—Special Declaration for Grand National Harmony and Progress Towards a Great Nation by Roh Tae-woo

29 October 1987—Democratic amendment to the South Korean constitution

29 November 1987—Bombing of a Korean Air flight by North Korea

16 December 1987—First truly free elections in almost three decades

25 February 1988—Inauguration of the Sixth Republic; Roh Tae-woo inaugurated as the sixth president of South Korea

17 September 1988—Opening of the Seoul Olympic Games

30 September 1990—Diplomatic normalization with the Soviet Union

17 September 1991—South and North Korea join the United Nations

13 December 1991—Agreement on Reconciliation, Non-Aggression and Exchanges and Cooperation between South and North Korea

# CHRONOLOGY

23 March 1992—Release of 'Nan Arayo' by Seo Taiji and Boys

24 August 1992—Diplomatic normalization with China

25 February 1993—Kim Young-sam inaugurated as the seventh president of South Korea

5 June 1993—Launch of the New Management Initiative by Samsung

26 August 1996—Chun Doo-hwan and Roh Tae-woo convicted for their role in the 1979 coup

12 December 1996—OECD membership

3 December 1997—IMF bailout of South Korea signed in the midst of the Asian Financial Crisis

25 February 1998—Kim Dae-jung inaugurated as the eighth president of South Korea

13–15 June 2000—First-ever inter-Korean summit

15–18 August 2000—First of nineteen family reunions held (until 2007)

8–9 September 2000—First Queer Culture Festival

10 December 2000—Nobel Peace Prize awarded to Kim Dae-jung

29 March 2001—Official opening of Incheon airport

25 November 2001—Establishment of the National Human Rights Commission of Korea (NHRCK)

14 January 2002—Release of *Winter Sonata*

31 May 2002—Start of the 2002 Korea/Japan World Cup

# SHRIMP TO WHALE

13 June 2002—Accidental killing of two schoolgirls by a US armoured vehicle

25 February 2003—Roh Moo-hyun inaugurated as the ninth president of South Korea

12 March 2004—Impeachment of Roh Moo-hyun by the National Assembly

14 May 2004—Roh Moo-hyun's impeachment overturned by the Constitutional Court

30 June 2007—South Korea–US Free Trade Agreement signed

2–4 October 2007—Second inter-Korean summit

1 January 2008—Abolition of the *hoju* system following a decision by the Constitutional Court

25 February 2008—Lee Myung-bak inaugurated as the tenth president of South Korea

24 May 2008—Start of the US beef protests

23 May 2009—Suicide of Roh Moo-hyun

26 March 2010—ROKS *Cheonan* sunk by North Korea

11–12 November 2010—Hosting of the Seoul G20 summit

23 November 2010—Yeonpyeong Island shelling by North Korea

22 November 2011—Ratification of the South Korea–US Free Trade Agreement by the National Assembly

25 February 2013—Park Geun-hye inaugurated as the eleventh president of South Korea

16 April 2014—MV *Sewol* Ferry disaster

29 October 2016—Start of the Candlelight Revolution

9 December 2016—Impeachment of Park Geun-hye by the National Assembly

10 March 2017—Park Geun-hye's impeachment upheld by the Constitutional Court

10 May 2017—Moon Jae-in inaugurated as the twelfth president of South Korea

9 February 2018—Opening of the PyeongChang Winter Olympic Games

6 April 2018—Park Geun-hye sentenced to prison on corruption charges

27 April 2018—Third inter-Korean summit; Kim Jong-un becomes the first North Korean leader to enter South Korea

19 September 2018—Inter-Korean summit

5 October 2018—Lee Myung-bak sentenced to prison on corruption charges

11 April 2019—Full decriminalization of abortion by the Constitutional Court

9 February 2020—*Parasite* wins the Oscar for Best Picture

21 August 2020—Release of 'Dynamite' by BTS

11–13 June 2021—Moon Jae-in attends the G7 as South Korean president

20 September 2021—BTS deliver speech at UN General Assembly

9 March 2022—Yoon Suk-yeol elected as the thirteenth president of South Korea

29 October 2022—Itaewon Halloween crowd crush

29–30 March 2023—Co-hosting of the Summit for Democracy

16 April 2023—Blackpink headlines Coachella Music Festival

# SELECTED KEY PEOPLE

Ban Ki-moon (b. 1944)—Eighth secretary-general of the United Nations (2007–16) and minister of foreign affairs and trade (2004–6).

BoA (Kwon Bo-ah) (b. 1986)—Internationally acclaimed singer known as the 'Queen of K-Pop'.

Bong Joon-ho (b. 1969)—Oscar-winning movie director who received the Best Picture Oscar for *Parasite* (2020).

BTS (formed 2010)—Internationally acclaimed seven-member K-Pop boyband who have topped music charts worldwide.

Byun Jin-seob (b. 1966)—Singer known as 'The Prince of Ballads' throughout the late 1980s and early 1990s.

Chang Myon (1899–1966)—Prime minister (1950–2, 1960–1) and vice president (1956–60) who opposed Rhee Syngman's authoritarianism.

Chey Jong-hyon (1930–98)—Businessman and entrepreneur who founded SK (1953) and made it one of the leading *chaebol*.

Choi Kyu-hah (1919–2006)—Prime minister (1975–9) and fourth president (1979–80) who sought to liberalize and democratize the country.

# SHRIMP TO WHALE

Chun Doo-hwan (1931–2021)—Fifth president (1980–8) who led the 12 December 1979 military coup as South Korean army general.

Chung Ju-yung (1915–2001)—Businessman and entrepreneur who founded Hyundai (1947) and ran for president (1992).

Han Myeong-sook (b. 1944)—Long-term pro-democracy activist and politician who became the first female prime minister (2006–7).

Hong Seok-cheon (b. 1971)—Actor and TV personality who became the first celebrity to come out as gay (2000).

Jeon Tae-il (1948–70)—Labour activist who self-immolated and whose death helped spark the workers' rights movement.

Kim Dae-jung (1924–2009)—Eighth president (1998–2003), Nobel Peace Prize winner (2000), long-term politician member of the 'Three Kims' and pro-democracy activist.

Kim Jae-gyu (1926–80)—Director of the Korean Central Intelligence Agency (1976–9) who assassinated Park Chung-hee.

Kim Jiha (1941–2022)—Poet, playwright and pro-democracy activist whose poem *Five Bandits* (1970) denounced the Park Chung-hee regime.

Kim Jong-pil (1926–2018)—Prime minister (1971–5, 1998–2000), long-term politician as part of the 'Three Kims' and pro-democracy activist.

Kim Ku (1876–1949)—Independence leader, politician and activist against the division of Korea.

Kim Kyu-sik (1881–1950)—Independence leader, politician and activist against the division of Korea.

Kim Min-ki (b. 1951)—Composer and singer whose song 'Morning Dew' became an anthem against the Park Chung-hee and Chun Doo-hwan dictatorships.

Kim Young-sam (1927–2015)—Seventh president (1993–8), first civilian president since 1962, long-term politician as part of the 'Three Kims' and pro-democracy activist.

Kim Yu-na (b. 1990)—Ice skater who won an Olympic gold medal (2010) and silver medal (2014); known as 'Queen Yuna'.

Koo In-hwoi (1907–69)—Businessman and entrepreneur who founded LG (1947) and provided funding to the independence movement.

Koo Ja-kyung (1925–2019)—Businessman and second chairman of LG who internationalized the *chaebol*.

Lee Byung-chul (1910–87)—Businessman and entrepreneur who founded Samsung (1938) and made it the biggest *chaebol*.

Lee Han-yeol (1966–87)—Student activist whose serious injury after being hit by a tear gas grenade, eventually leading to his death, helped spark the June Democratic Struggle (1987).

Lee Hyo-jae (1924–2020)—Professor and women's right activist who launched the country's first women's studies course (1977).

Lee Kun-hee (1942–2020)—Businessman and second chairman of Samsung who launched the 'New Management Initiative' (1993).

Lee Myung-bak (b. 1941)—Tenth president (2008–13), long-term businessman and mayor of Seoul (2002–6).

Moon Jae-in (1953)—Twelfth president (2017–22), long-term human rights lawyer and pro-democracy activist.

Park Chung-hee (1917–79)—Third president (1963–79) who led the 16 May 1971 military coup as South Korean army general and presided over a period of rapid economic growth.

Park Geun-hye (b. 1952)—Eleventh president (2013–17), first lady (1974–9) and first president to be removed from office following an impeachment.

Rhee Syngman (1875–1965)—First president (1948–60), independence leader and first and last president of the Provisional Government of the Republic of Korea (1919–25, 1947–8).

Roh Moo-hyun (1946–2009)—Ninth president (2003–8), long-term human rights lawyer and pro-democracy activist.

Roh Tae-woo (1932–2021)—Sixth president (1988–93), first president since the restoration of democracy and South Korean army general.

Seo Ji-hyun (b. 1973)—Prosecutor whose denunciation of sexual harassment helped spark the #MeToo movement in the country (2018).

Seo Taiji (1972)—Leader of Seo Taiji and Boys, whose song 'Nan Arayo' is credited with inaugurating K-Pop.

Sohn Kee-chung (1912–2002)—Marathon Olympic champion (1936) who carried the torch into the stadium during the opening ceremony of the Seoul Olympic Games (1988).

Yoon Suk-yeol (1960)—Thirteenth president-elect (2022), long-term prosecutor and Prosecutor General (2019-21).

Youn Yuh-jung (1947)—Actress who shot to fame in the 1970s and received the Best Supporting Actress Oscar for her performance in *Minari* (2021).

Yun Posun (1897–1990)—Second president (1960–2) who opposed Park Chung-hee's authoritarianism and ran for president against him (1963, 1967).

# NOTES

PROLOGUE

1. Hwang, Pae-Gang, *Korean Myths and Folk Legends*, trans. Young-Hie Han, Se-Joong Kim and Seung-Pyong Chwae, Fremont: Jain Publishing, 2006, pp. 1–12.
2. Ibid.
3. Kim, Jinwung, *A History of Korea: From Land of the Morning Calm to States in Conflict*, Bloomington: Indiana University Press, 2012, p. 10.
4. Shin, Michael D. (ed.), *Korean History in Maps: From Prehistory to the Twenty-First Century*, Cambridge: Cambridge University Press, 2014, p. 6.
5. Ibid., p. 13.
6. Lee, Ki-baek, *A New History of Korea*, trans. Edward W. Wagner with Edward J. Shultz, Cambridge: Harvard University Press, 1984, pp. 36–44.
7. Ibid., pp. 48–65.
8. Ibid., pp. 66–73.
9. Kim, *History of Korea*, pp. 91–100; Kim, Chong Sun, 'Silla Economy and Society', *Korean Studies*, Vol. 28, 2009, pp. 75–86.
10. Kim, *History of Korea*, pp. 108–11.
11. Ibid., p. 109.
12. Lee, *New History of Korea*, pp. 71–2.
13. Ibid., pp. 88–91.
14. Kim, *History of Korea*, pp. 115–18.
15. Ibid., p. 120.
16. Hwang, Kyung Moon, *A History of Korea*, London: Palgrave, pp. 30–1; Lee, *New History of Korea*, pp. 101–4.

17. Ibid., pp. 29–30.

18. Vermeersch, Sem, *The Power of the Buddhas: The Politics of Buddhism during the Koryŏ Dynasty (918–1392)*, Cambridge: Harvard University Press, 2008, pp. 151–2.

19. Ibid., pp. 358–9.

20. Song, Minah, 'The History and Characteristics of Traditional Korean Books and Bookbinding', *Journal of the Institute of Conservation*, Vol. 32, No. 1, 2009, p. 74.

21. Ibid.

22. Eckert, Carter J., Ki-baik Lee, Young Ick Lew, Michael Robinson and Edward W. Wagner, *Korea Old and New: A History*, Cambridge: Harvard University Press, pp. 76–7.

23. Hwang, *History of Korea*, pp. 44–7; Kim, *History of Korea*, pp. 168–9.

24. Hwang, *History of Korea*, pp. 44–7; Kim, *History of Korea*, pp. 182–3.

25. Eckert et al., *Korea Old and New*, pp. 99–100; Kim, *History of Korea*, p. 183.

26. Shin, *Korean History in Maps*, p. 81.

27. Ibid., p. 84.

28. Ibid., p. 82.

29. Kim, Bok Rae, 'Nobi: A Korean System of Slavery', *Slavery & Abolition*, Vol. 24, No. 2, 2003, p. 155.

30. Kim-Renaud, Young-Key (ed.), *King Sejong the Great: The Light of 15th Century Korea*, Washington, DC: International Circle of Korean Linguistics, 1992.

31. Ibid., p. 34.

32. Hwang, *History of Korea*, pp. 63–4.

33. Yi, Song-mi, 'Sin Saimdang (1504–1551): The Foremost Woman Painter of the Choson Dynasty', in Young-Key Kim-Renaud (ed.), *Creative Women of Korea: The Fifteenth through the Twentieth Centuries*, London: Routledge, 2003, p. 58.

34. Ibid., p. 59.

35. Shin, *Korean History in Maps*, p. 83.

36. Kim, *History of Korea*, pp. 229–34.

37. Ibid., pp. 237–9.

38. Howard, Keith, *Perspectives on Korean Music: Volume 1; Preserving Korean Music*; *Intangible Cultural Properties as Icons of Identity*, Aldershot: Ashgate, 2006, p. 85.

39. Shin, *Korean History in Maps*, pp. 93–4.

40. Even in the 1960s, diplomat and scholar Gregory Henderson would famously argue that Korean politics had been driven by divisions among ever-changing factions rather than group continuity for over a millennium and a half. Anderson, Gregory, *Korea: The Politics of the Vortex*, Cambridge: Harvard University Press, 1968.

41. Hwang, *History of Korea*, pp. 104–5.

42. Ibid., pp. 112–18.

43. Eckert et al., *Korea Old and New*, pp. 194–5.

44. Wang, Dong, *China's Unequal Treaties: Narrating National History*, Lanham: Lexington Books, 2005.

45. Beasley, William G., *The Meiji Restoration*, Stanford: Stanford University Press, 1972.

46. Ibid., p. 200.

47. Griffis, William Elliot, *Corea, the Hermit Nation*, New York: Charles Scribner's Sons, 1897, https://archive.org/details/coreahermitnation-00grif/mode/2up, accessed 27 Apr. 2021.

48. Lowell, Percival, *Choson, the Land of the Morning Calm, a Sketch of Korea*, Boston: Ticknor and Company, 1886, p. 7, https://archive.org/details/chosnlandmornin00lowegoog/page/n29/mode/2up?q=morning+calm, accessed 27 Apr. 2021.

49. Cumings, Bruce, *Korea's Place in the Sun: A Modern History*, updated edn, New York: W. W. Norton, 2005, pp. 120–1.

50. Ibid., pp. 124–5.

51. Ibid., p. 123.

52. Hwang, *History of Korea*, p. 126.

53. Ibid., pp. 119–23.

54. 'The Treaty of Portsmouth', 5 Sept. 1905, http://www.portsmouth-peacetreaty.org/process/peace/TreatyText.pdf, accessed 27 Apr. 2021.

55. Nobel Prize, 'Theodore Roosevelt: Facts', 2021, https://www.nobel-prize.org/prizes/peace/1906/roosevelt/facts, accessed 27 Apr. 2021.

56. Eckert et al., *Korea Old and New*, pp. 242–3.

57. Cumings, *Korea's Place in the Sun*, p. 145.

58. Kim, *History of Korea*, p. 320.

59. Schmid, Andre, *Korea between Empires, 1895–1919*, New York: Columbia University Press, 2002, pp. 173–5.

60. Cumings, *Korea's Place in the Sun*, pp. 148–9.

61. Seagrave, Sterling, and Peggy Seagrave, *Gold Warriors: America's Secret Recovery of Yamashita's Gold*, London: Verso, 2003, pp. 19–20.

62. Cumings, *Korea's Place in the Sun*, p. 145.

63. Gragert, Edwin H., *Landownership under Colonial Rule: Korea's Japanese Experience, 1900–1935*, Honolulu: University of Hawai'i Press, 1994, pp. 71–3.

64. Ibid., pp. 144–5.

65. Schmid, *Korea between Empires*, pp. 173–5.

66. Kim, *History of Korea*, p. 332.

67. Shin, Gi-Wook, and Rennie Moon, '1919 in Korea: National Resistance and Contending Legacies', *Journal of Asian Studies*, Vol. 78, No. 2, May 2019, p. 402.

68. Kim, *History of Korea*, p. 330.

69. Cumings, *Korea's Place in the Sun*, p. 159.

70. Kim, *History of Korea*, p. 346.

71. Ibid.

72. Shin and Moon, '1919 in Korea', p. 399.

73. Doherty, Thomas, 'Creating a National Cinema: The South Korean Experience', *Asian Survey*, Vol. 24, No. 8, Aug. 1984, p. 840.

74. International Olympic Committee, 'Kitei Son', 2021, https://www.olympic.org/kitei-son, accessed 28 Apr. 2021.

75. Hwang, *History of Korea*, pp. 135–7.

76. Kim, Sebastian C. H., and Kirsteen Kim, *A History of Korean Christianity*, Cambridge: Cambridge University Press, 2018, pp. 107–18.

77. Hwang, *History of Korea*, p. 142.

78. Ibid., pp. 141, 152.

79. Kim, *History of Korea*, pp. 348–9.

80. Ibid., p. 350.

81. Min, Pyong Gap, 'Korean "Comfort Women": The Intersection of Colonial Power, Gender, and Class', *Gender & Society*, Vol. 17, No. 3, Dec. 2003, pp. 940–1.

82. Uchida, Jun, 'Between Collaboration and Conflict: State and Society in Wartime Korea', in Masato Kimura and Tosh Minohara (eds), *Tumultuous Decade: Empire, Society, and Diplomacy in 1930s Japan*, Cambridge: Cambridge University Press, 2018, pp. 140–2.

83. 'Text of Hirohito's Radio Rescript', *New York Times*, 15 Aug. 1945, p. 3.

84. Rusk, Dean, as told to Richard Rusk, Papp, Daniel S. (ed.), *As I Saw It*, New York: W. W. Norton, 1990, pp. 123–4.

85. Cumings, *Korea's Place in the Sun*, pp. 188–9.

86. Johnston, Richard J. H., 'Koreans Angered by "Trusteeship"', *New York Times*, 31 Dec. 1945, p. 1.

87. Hwang, *History of Korea*, pp. 168–9.

88. Ibid.

89. Kim, *History of Korea*, pp. 392–6.

90. Hwang, *History of Korea*, pp. 170–2.

91. Kraus, Charles, 'Kim Gu on Reunification and War, 1948', NKIDP e-Dossier, No. 19, June 2015, https://www.wilsoncenter.org/publication/kim-gu-reunification-and-war-1948, accessed 28 Apr. 2021.

92. Jeju 4.3 Peace Foundation, 'Facts & Truth: Introduction', 2018, http://jeju43peace.org/historytruth/fact-truth, accessed 28 Apr. 2021.

1. INDEPENDENCE, WAR AND POVERTY, 1948–60

1. *Dong-A Ilbo* staff writers, '棄權없는選擧로 獨立政府樹立하자' (We will establish an independent government without giving up the right to vote), *Dong-A Ilbo*, 10 May 1948, p. 1.

2. Croissant, Aurel, 'Korea (Republic of Korea/South Korea)', in Dieter Nohlen, Florian Grotz and Christof Hartmann (eds), *Elections in Asia and the Pacific: A Data Handbook; Volume II; South East Asia, East Asia, and the South Pacific*, Oxford: Oxford University Press, 2001, p. 428.

3. Johnston, Richard J. H., 'South Korea Turns Out 85% Vote Despite Terrorism That Kills 38', *New York Times*, 11 May 1948, p. 1.

4. Cumings, *Korea's Place in the Sun*, pp. 211–12.

5. Stueck, William, *The Korean War: An International History*, Princeton: Princeton University Press, 1995, p. 33.

6. Ibid.

7. Croissant, *Elections in Asia and the Pacific*, p. 428.

8. Lew, Young Ick, *The Making of the First Korean President: Syngman Rhee's Quest for Independence, 1875–1948*, Honolulu: University of Hawai'i Press, 2014.

9. '今日萬代에빗날盛典 憲法公布式擧行' (The constitution announcement ceremony is held today), *Dong-A Ilbo*, 17 May 1948, p. 1.

10. Lew, *Making of the First Korean President*, p. 278.

11. Hyuk, Pak Ki, 'Outcome of the Land Reform in the Republic of Korea', *Journal of Farm Economics*, Vol. 38, No. 4, Nov. 1956, p. 1015.

12. Ibid.

13. Johnston, Richard J. H., 'North Korea Gets Full Puppet Rule', *New York Times*, 11 Sept. 1948, p. 4.

14. Hwang, *History of Korea*, p. 173.

15. Kim, Hun Joon, *The Massacres at Mt. Halla: Sixty Years of Truth Seeking in South Korea*, Ithaca: Cornell University Press, 2014, p. 34.

16. Jeju 4.3 Peace Foundation, 'The Nightmare of the Bukchon Massacre', 9 Dec. 2018, http://jeju43peace.org/the-nightmare-of-the-bukchon-massacre, accessed 29 Apr. 2021.

17. Stueck, *Korean War*, p. 106.

18. US Department of State, 'Review of the Position as of 1950: Address by the Secretary of State, January 12, 1950', *American Foreign Policy 1950–1955: Basic Documents; Volume II; Publication 6446; General Foreign Policy Series 117*, Washington, DC: US Government Printing Office, 1957, pp. 2310–28.

19. Knowles, Clayton, '2 Votes Block Korea Aid Bill; House Test a Blow to Truman', *New York Times*, 20 Jan. 1950, p. 1.

20. Kim, Dong Choon, 'Forgotten War, Forgotten Massacres: The Korean War (1950–1953) as Licensed Mass Killings', *Journal of Genocide Research*, Vol. 6, No. 4, 2004, pp. 533–5.

21. Johnston, Richard J. H., 'Killing of Kim Koo Is "Shock" to Rhee', *New York Times*, 28 June 1949, p. 1.

22. Stueck, *Korean War*, pp. 18–19.

23. United Nations Security Council Resolution 82, 'Resolution of 25 June 1950', S/RES/82/1950 [S/1501], 25 June 1950.

24. United Nations Security Council Resolution 83, 'Resolution of 27 June 1950', S/RES/83/1950 [S/1511], 27 June 1950.

25. Stueck, *Korean War*, pp. 19–20.

26. Cumings, *Korea's Place in the Sun*, p. 266.

27. Hwang, *History of Korea*, p. 178.

28. Ibid.

29. Cumings, *Korea's Place in the Sun*, p. 268–70.

30. Kim, *History of Korea*, p. 411.

31. Clodfelter, Michael, *A Statistical History of the Korean War: 1950–1953*, Bennington: Merriam Press, 1989, p. 11.

32. Stueck, *Korean War*, pp. 98–9.

33. Hwang, *History of Korea*, p. 179.

34. Barrett, George, 'Village Massacre Stirs South Korea', *New York Times*, 11 Apr. 1951, p. 4; Parrott, Lindesay, 'Korea Foe Accuses UN of "Massacre" in Prison Camp Riot', *New York Times*, 23 Feb. 1952, p. 1.

35. Croissant, *Elections in Asia and the Pacific*, p. 464.

36. Stueck, *Korean War*, pp. 289–90.

37. MacGregor, Greg, 'Fugitives Mingle with Populace of Pusan; POW Head Says He Lacks Pursuers', *New York Times*, 19 June 1953, p. 2.

38. 'President Is Firm; Pledges Mutual Defense Treaty and Continued Aid to South Korea', *New York Times*, 8 June 1953, p. 1.

39. Keefer, Edward C. (ed.), 'The President of the Republic of Korea (Rhee) to President Eisenhower', *American Foreign Policy 1952–1954, Korea, Volume XV, Part 1, Document 565*, Washington, DC: US Government Printing Office, 1984, pp. 1224–6.

40. Millett, Allan, 'Battle Casualties of the Korean War (1950–53)', *Encyclopaedia Britannica*, 4 May 1999 [revised 10 Sept. 2020], https://

www.britannica.com/event/Korean-War/additional-info#history, accessed 30 Apr. 2021.

41. Bank of Korea, *Economic Statistics Yearbook 1955*, Seoul: Bank of Korea, 1955, pp. 13, 110.

42. World Bank, *Republic of Korea: Four Decades of Equitable Growth*, Washington, DC: World Bank, 2004, p. 26.

43. Kim, Doo-Sub, 'Population Growth and Transition', in Doo-Sub Kim and Cheong-Seok Kim (eds), *The Population of Korea*, Daejeon: Korea National Statistical Office, 2004, p. 9.

44. Shin, Yong-Ha, 'Land Reform in Korea, 1950', *Bulletin of the Population and Development Studies Center*, Vol. 5, Sept. 1976, p. 14.

45. Han, Ri-hye, 'Graveyard Geomancy in Korea under Japanese Rule: Focusing on the 1930s', *Contemporary Japan*, Vol. 32, No. 1, 2020, p. 25.

46. Oh, Arissa H., *To Save the Children of Korea: The Cold War Origins of International Adoption*, Stanford: Stanford University Press, 2015, pp. 48–75.

47. Ibid.

48. Ibid.

49. Hong, Yong-Pyo, *State Security and Regime Security: President Syngman Rhee and the Insecurity Dilemma in South Korea 1953–60*, Basingstoke: Palgrave Macmillan, 2000, pp. 7–8.

50. Ibid., pp. 40–56.

51. Croissant, *Elections in Asia and the Pacific*, p. 464.

52. Ibid.

53. Kim, Mi-ju, 'Cho Bong-am Unjustly Executed: Supreme Court', *Korea JoongAng Daily*, 20 Jan. 2011.

54. US Department of State, 'Letter from the Ambassador in Korea (Dowling) to the Director of the Office of Northeast Asian Affairs (Hemmendinger)', *Foreign Relations of the United States, 1955–1957, Korea, Volume XXIII*, Washington, DC: US Government Printing Office, 1993, p. 303.

55. Croissant, *Elections in Asia and the Pacific*, p. 464.

56. USAID, 'Country Summary', 2021, https://explorer.usaid.gov/prepared/us_foreign_aid_country.csv, accessed 5 July 2021.

57. Kane, Tim, *Global U.S. Troop Deployment, 1950–2005*, Washington, DC: Heritage Foundation, 2006, p. 9.

58. Sorensen, Clark W., 'Success and Education in South Korea', *Comparative Education Review*, Vol. 38, No. 1, Feb. 1994, p. 16.

59. Society for the 2.28 Movement for Democracy, 'The 2.28 Movement for Democracy', 2021, http://www.228.or.kr/front/index.php?g_page=guide&m_page=guide02, accessed 5 July 2021.

60. Croissant, *Elections in Asia and the Pacific*, p. 464.

61. Han, Sungjoo, *The Failure of Democracy in South Korea*, Berkeley: University of California Press, 1974, p. 28.

62. Hong, Yong-Pyo, State Security and Regime Security, pp. 138–41.

63. Croissant, *Elections in Asia and the Pacific*, p. 477.

64. Ibid., p. 412.

65. Haggard, Stephan, *Pathways from the Periphery: The Politics of Growth in the Newly Industrializing Countries*, Ithaca: Cornell University Press, 1990, pp. 60, 72.

66. National Archives of Korea, '계획수립 이전 (1948–1962)' (Before planning (1948–1962)), 2021, https://theme.archives.go.kr/next/economicDevelopment/reconstruction.do, accessed 5 July 2021.

67. World Bank, 'Fertility Rate, Total (Births per Woman): Korea, Rep.', 2021, https://data.worldbank.org/indicator/SP.DYN.TFRT.IN?locations=KR, accessed 5 July 2021.

68. Haggard, *Pathways from the Periphery*, p. 60.

69. Han, Yong-Sup, 'The May Sixteenth Military Coup', in Byung-Kook Kim and Ezra Vogel (eds), *The Park Chung Hee Era: The Transformation of South Korea*, Cambridge: Harvard University Press, 2011, p. 41.

70. 'Coup in South Korea', *New York Times*, 17 May 1961, p. 36.

71. Kim and Kim, *History of Korean Christianity*, pp. 234–5.

72. Constitution of the Republic of Korea, 19 Oct. 1987.

2. THE PARK CHUNG-HEE ERA, 1961–79

1. Han, 'May Sixteenth Military Coup', p. 53.

2. Ibid., p. 50.

3. Lee, Chong-Sik, *Park Chung Hee: From Poverty to Power*, Seoul: KHU Press, 2012.

4. Kim, Hyung-A., 'State Building: The Military Junta's Path to Modernity through Administrative Reforms', in Kim and Vogel, *The Park Chung Hee Era*, p. 88.

5. Ibid., pp. 91–3.

6. *Korea Journal*, Vol. 1, No. 1, Sept. 1961, p. 54.

7. National Archives of Korea, '제1차 경제개발 5개년 계획 (1962–1966)' (First five-year economic development plan (1962–1966)), 2021, https://theme.archives.go.kr/next/economicDevelopment/primary. do, accessed 5 July 2021.

8. Kim, 'State Building', p.91, 98.

9. 'Summary and Revision of Recommendations of Task Force Report on Korea', 12 June 1961, https://www.jfklibrary.org/asset-viewer/ archives/JFKPOF/121/JFKPOF-121-004, accessed 5 July 2021.

10. Kim, 'State Building', pp. 86–7.

11. Croissant, *Elections in Asia and the Pacific*, pp. 465, 474.

12. 'Assembly Meets as Military Rule Ends in South Korea', *New York Times*, 18 Dec. 1963, p. 4.

13. Han, 'May Sixteenth Military Coup', pp. 51, 54.

14. Hwang, *History of Korea*, pp. 197–8.

15. Kim Young-sam, 김영삼 회고록: 민주주의를 위한 나의 투쟁 (Memoirs of Kim Young-sam: my struggle for democracy), vol. 1, 3rd edn, Seoul: Baeksan Seodang, 2015.

16. Kim, Dae-Jung, *Conscience in Action: The Autobiography of Kim Dae-jung*, trans. Jeon Seung-hee, London: Palgrave Macmillan, 2019, pp. 68–81.

17. Kim, Hyung-jin, 'Kim Jong-pil, Spymaster and Two-Time Prime Minister of South Korea, Dies at 92', *Washington Post*, 25 June 2018.

18. Hwang, *History of Korea*, pp. 198–9.

19. *New York Times* staff writers, 'Korean Protests against Regime Flare in 12 Cities', *New York Times*, 5 June 1964.

20. Kim, Sarah, 'Treaty that Struggled to Be Born Still Confounds', *Korea JoongAng Daily*, 21 June 2015.

21. United Nations Economic and Social Council, 'Report on the Mission to the Democratic People's Republic of Korea, the Republic of Korea and Japan on the Issue of Military Sexual Slavery in Wartime', 4 Jan. 1996, http://hrlibrary.umn.edu/commission/country52/53-add1.htm, accessed 5 July 2021.

22. Lee, Min Yong, 'The Vietnam War: South Korea's Search for National Security', in Kim and Vogel, *Park Chung Hee Era*, pp. 403–29.

23. Kwon, Hyuk-joo, 'Why Move Yi Sun-shin?', *Korea JoongAng Daily*, 23 Jan. 2019.

24. Croissant, *Elections in Asia and the Pacific*, pp. 465, 474.

25. *New York Times* staff writers 'North Korean Says Aim Was to Assassinate Park', *New York Times*, 23 Jan. 1968, p. 6.

26. Han, Y. C., 'The 1969 Constitutional Revision and Party Politics in South Korea', *Pacific Affairs*, Vol. 44, No. 2, Summer 1971, pp. 242, 246–7.

27. Croissant, *Elections in Asia and the Pacific*, p. 465.

28. Park, Chung-hee, *Major Speeches by Korea's Park Chung Hee*, Seoul: Samhwa Publishing, 1976.

29. Sakong, Il, *Korea in the World Economy*, Washington, DC: Institute for International Economics, 1993, p. 25.

30. World Bank, 'GDP Growth (Annual %): Korea, Rep.', 2021, https://data.worldbank.org/indicator/NY.GDP.MKTP.KD.ZG?locations=KR, accessed 6 July 2021.

31. Industrial Statistics Analysis System, '1차,2차,3차 기준' (Primary, secondary, tertiary sector), 2021, https://istans.or.kr/su/newSuTab.do?scode=S111, accessed 6 July 2021.

32. World Bank, 'Exports of Goods and Services (Current US$): Korea, Rep.', 2021, https://data.worldbank.org/indicator/NE.EXP.GNFS.CD?end=2019&locations=KR&start=1960, accessed 6 July 2021.

33. World Bank, *Korea: Current Economic Position and Prospects*, Washington, DC: World Bank, 1963.

34. Kim, Eun Mee, *Big Business, Strong State: Collusion and Conflict in South Korean Development, 1960–1990*, New York: SUNY Press, 1997, pp. 102–3.

35. Ibid., pp. 59, 153

36. Kim, Eun Mee, and Gil-Sung Park, 'The Chaebol', in Kim and Vogel, *Park Chung Hee Era*, pp. 267, 272.

37. Ibid., p. 266

38. Ibid., pp. 273–4.

39. National Archives of Korea, '제2차 경제개발 5개년 계획 (1967–1971)' (Second five-year economic development plan (1967–1971)), 2021, https://theme.archives.go.kr/next/economicDevelopment/secondary.do, accessed 5 July 2021.

40. *Dong-A Ilbo* staff writers, '九老 出産業工業團地준공' (Completion of Guro Export Industrial Complex), *Dong-A Ilbo*, 1 Apr. 1967, p. 1.

41. POSCO, 'History of POSCO', 2021, https://www.posco.co.kr/homepage/docs/eng6/jsp/company/posco/s91a1000012c.jsp, accessed 6 July 2021.

42. World Bank, 'School Enrollment (Secondary), Gross, Gender Parity Index (GPI): Korea, Rep.', 2021, https://data.worldbank.org/indicator/SE.ENR.SECO.FM.ZS?locations=KR, accessed 6 July 2021.

43. World Bank, 'School Enrollment (Tertiary), Gross, Gender Parity Index (GPI): Korea, Rep.', 2021, https://data.worldbank.org/indicator/SE.ENR.TERT.FM.ZS?locations=KR, accessed 6 July 2021.

44. KAIST, 'Founding Philosophy', 2021, https://www.kaist.ac.kr/en/html/kaist/011701.html, accessed 6 July 2021.

45. Lee, Jong-Chan, 'Health Care Reform in South Korea: Success or Failure?', *American Journal of Public Health*, Vol. 93, No. 1, Jan. 2003, p. 48.

46. Lee, Jeong-rok, and Lee Seung-ah, 'Seoul Metro Turns 40: The Subway's Past and Present', 15 Aug. 2014, https://www.korea.net/NewsFocus/Society/view?articleId=121100, accessed 6 July 2021.

47. USAID, 'Country Summary'.

48. Kim, Se Jin, 'South Korea's Involvement in Vietnam and Its Economic and Political Impact', *Asian Survey*, Vol. 10, No. 6, June 1970, pp. 519–23.

49. Kim, Hyun Sook, and Pyong Gap Min, 'The Post-1965 Korean Immigrants: Their Characteristics and Settlement Patterns', *Korea Journal of Population and Development*, Vol. 21, No. 2, Dec. 1992, pp. 121–43.

50. Immigration and Nationality Act of 1965, 3 Oct. 1965.

51. Kim and Min, 'Post-1965 Korean Immigrants', pp. 122–4.

52. Garz, Detlef, 'Going Away: Going Home! Coming Home? The Migration of Korean Nurses and Miners to Germany and Their Return in Retirement to Korea's German Village', *OMNES: The Journal of Multicultural Society*, Vol. 6, No. 1, 2015, pp. 161–83.

53. Jeon Tae-il Foundation, '아름다운 청년 전태일' (Jeon Tae-il, a beautiful young man), 2021, http://www.chuntaeil.org, accessed 7 July 2021.

54. Jeon Tae-il Foundation, '삶과 죽음' (Life and death), 2021, http://www.chuntaeil.org/c/1/2, accessed 7 July 2021.

55. Kim, Sang-bon, 'Remembering the Life of Jeon Tae-il and His Sacrifice 49 Years Ago', *Hankyoreh*, 13 Nov. 2019.

56. Cho, Nam Joo, *Kim Jiyoung, Born 1982*, trans. Jamie Chang, London: Scribner, 2020, p. 20.

57. Shin, Ki-young, 'The Politics of the Family Reform Movement in Contemporary Korea', *Journal of Korean Studies*, Vol. 11, No. 1, Fall 2006, pp. 93–125.

58. Cho, *Kim Jiyoung, Born 1982*, pp. 18–19.

59. Lee, Kyong-hee, 'Legacy of a Pioneer Feminist Thinker and Pioneer', *Korea Herald*, 15 Oct. 2020.

60. Trumbull, Robert, 'Seoul Unit Set to Bar Aid Abuse', *New York Times*, 5 May 1960, p. 5.

61. Scott Stokes, Henry, 'He Ran South Korea, Down to Last Detail', *New York Times*, 27 Oct. 1979, p. 1.

62. Kang, David C., *Crony Capitalism: Corruption and Development in South Korea and the Philippines*, Cambridge: Cambridge University Press, 2002.

63. Asian Development Bank, 'The *Saemael* Undong Movement in the Republic of Korea: Sharing Knowledge on Community-Driven Development', Mandaluyong City: Asian Development Bank, 2012.

64. Park, Chung-hee, '신년 메시지' (New Year message), 1 Jan. 1964.

65. Fischer, Hannah, *North Korean Provocative Actions 1950–2007*, Washington, DC: Congressional Research Service, 2007, pp. 4–6.

66. US Department of State, 'Banquet Honoring President Nixon, Shanghai, February 27', *Department of State Bulletin*, Vol. LXVI, No. 1697, 3 Jan. 1972, p. 432.

67. Office of the Historian of the US Department of State, 'Milestones: 1977–1980', 2021, https://history.state.gov/milestones/1977-1980/china-policy, accessed 7 July 2021.

68. July 4 South–North Joint Communiqué, 4 July 1972.

69. KBS World, 'First Inter-Korean Red Cross Talks in 1972', 2021, https://rki.kbs.co.kr/service/contents_view.htm?lang=e&menu_cate=history&id=&board_seq=275254&page=3&board_code=koreamoment, accessed 7 July 2021.

70. Fischer, 'North Korean Provocative Actions 1950–2007'.

71. Pacheco Pardo, Ramon, *North Korea–US Relations from Kim Jong Il to Kim Jong Un*, 2nd edn, London: Routledge, 2019, p. 23.

72. US Department of State, 'Letter From President Nixon to Korean President Park', *Foreign Relations of the United States, 1969–1976, Korea*, Volume XIX, Washington, DC: US Government Printing Office, 2009, pp. 153–5.

73. Kane, 'Global U.S. Troop Deployment', p. 9.

74. Croissant, *Elections in Asia and the Pacific*, p. 427.

75. Constitution of the Republic of Korea, 27 Dec. 1972.

76. Croissant, *Elections in Asia and the Pacific*, p. 413.

77. Kim, *Conscience in Action*, pp. 187–91.

78. *New York Times* staff writers, 'Warnings Said to Have Saved Korean', *New York Times*, 20 Aug. 1973, p. 3.

79. Zainichi Koreans are ethnic Koreans long-term residents of Japan who moved there during Korea's colonization or are descended from them.

80. Keon, Michael, *Korean Phoenix: A Nation from the Ashes*, Englewood Cliffs: Prentice-Hall International, p. 199.

81. Park, Chung-hee, quoted in Oberdorfer, Don, *The Two Koreas: A Contemporary History*, New York: Basic Books, 2001, p. 56.

82. '어제오전 人革黨관련 8명 死刑執行' (Eight people related to the People's Revolutionary Party were executed yesterday morning), *Dong-A Ilbo*, 10 Apr. 1975, p. 1.

83. Select Committee on Ethics of the United States Senate, 'Korean Influence Inquiry', Washington, DC: US Government Printing Office, 1978.

84. Yoon, Min-sik, 'Cho Yong-pil, King of Korean Pop Music', *Korea Herald*, 18 May 2018.

85. Song, Seung-hyun, 'Youn Yuh-jung's Storied 5-Decade Career Culminates in Oscar Win', *Korea Herald*, 16 Apr. 2021.

86. KMDb, 'Winter Woman (Gyeo-ul-yeoja)', 2006–18, https://www.kmdb.or.kr/eng/db/kor/detail/movie/K/03153, accessed 8 July 2021.

87. National Archives of Korea, '제3차 경제개발 5개년 계획 (1972–1976)' (Third five-year economic development plan (1972–1976)), 2021, https://theme.archives.go.kr/next/economicDevelopment/tertiary.do, accessed 5 July 2021; National Archives of Korea, '제4차 경제개발 5개년 계획 (1977–1981)' (Fourth five-year economic development plan (1977–1981)), 2021, https://theme.archives.go.kr/next/economicDevelopment/fourth.do, accessed 5 July 2021.

88. Tulk, Mitchell, 'The Hyundai Pony: Korea's First Home-Grown Car', 2021, https://drivetribe.com/p/the-hyundai-pony-koreas-first-home-RjWzQ35kTPCNUpAdCNAqJA?iid=QCTmD-YTRHKwDJ6Rw3Ow0w, accessed 8 July 2021.

89. Statistics Korea, '지역별 인구 및 인구밀도' (Population and popula-

tion density by region), 2021, https://www.index.go.kr/potal/stts/idxMain/selectPoSttsIdxSearch.do?idx_cd=1007&stts_cd=100701&freq=Y, accessed 8 July 2021.

90. Industrial Statistics Analysis System, '1차,2차,3차 기준' (Primary, secondary, tertiary sector).

91. Statistics Korea, '가구원수' (Number of household members), 2021, https://www.index.go.kr/unify/idx-info.do?idxCd=4229, accessed 8 July 2021.

92. Kim, Jee-hee, 'Shin Choon-ho, Founder of Ramyeon Giant Nongshim, Dies at 91', *Korea JoongAng Daily*, 28 Mar. 2021.

93. Kim and Min, 'Post-1965 Korean Immigrants', pp. 121–43.

94. Croissant, *Elections in Asia and the Pacific*, p. 428.

95. Lee, Jin-kyung, *Service Economies: Militarism, Sex Work, and Migrant Labor in South Korea*, Minneapolis: University of Minnesota Press, pp. 93–9.

96. KMDb, 'Yeong-Ja's Heydays (Yeongja-ui jeonseongsidae)', 2006–18, https://www.kmdb.or.kr/eng/db/kor/detail/movie/K/02874, accessed 8 July 2021.

97. KMDb, 'Heavenly Homecoming to Stars (Byeoldeul-ui gohyang)', 2006–18,https://www.kmdb.or.kr/eng/db/kor/detail/movie/K/02746, accessed 8 July 2021.

98. Hwang, Okon, 'Kim Min-ki and the Making of a Legend', in Hyunjoon Shin and Seung-Ah Lee (eds), *Made in Korea: Studies in Popular Music*, Abingdon: Routledge, 2017, pp. 134–5.

99. Hwang, *History of Korea*, pp. 206–7.

100. Kim and Kim, *History of Korean Christianity*, p. 157.

101. *Minjung* would translate as 'the people'. The minjung movement came to refer to the groups that fought for democracy from the late 1970s and throughout the 1980s: workers, students, intellectuals, women and ordinary citizens who felt unrepresented when not oppressed by South Korea's dictatorial regimes.

102. Lee, Chengpang, and Myungsahm Suh, 'State Building and Religion: Explaining the Diverged Path of Religious Change in Taiwan and

Korea, 1950–1980', *American Journal of Sociology*, Vol. 123, No. 2, Sept. 2017, pp. 491–6.

103. Chapman, William, 'President Park Killed in South Korea', *Washington Post*, 27 Oct. 1979; 'President Park Is Slain in Korea by Intelligence Chief, Seoul Says; Premier Takes Over, G.I.'s Alerted', *New York Times*, 27 Oct. 1979, p. 1.

104. Scott Stokes, Henry, 'Foe of Seoul Regime Asks Decision by U.S.', *New York Times*, 16 Sept. 1979, p. 17.

105. Reuters, 'Martial Law Is Set in South Korea City after Student Riot', *New York Times*, 18 Oct. 1979, p. 1.

106. Scott Stokes, Henry, 'Opposition Attacks Korea Vote Plan', *New York Times*, 11 Nov. 1979, p. 22.

107. Youn, Dong Shin, 'South Korean Women Labourers Protest Closing of YH Wig Manufacturing Company 1979', 5 Apr. 2015, https://nvdatabase.swarthmore.edu/content/south-korean-women-labourers-protest-closing-yh-wig-manufacturing-company-1979, accessed 12 July 2021.

108. Katsiaficas, George N., *Asia's Unknown Uprisings: South Korean Social Movements in the 20th Century*, Oakland: PM Press, pp. 152–5.

109. Breen, Michael, 'Inner Circle Collapses: Kim Jae-gyu and Cha Ji-cheol', *Korea Times*, 15 Feb. 2012.

110. Chun, Young-gi, and Jin-kyu Kang, 'The Inside Story of the Park Chung Hee Killing', *Korea JoongAng Daily*, 2 Nov. 2015.

111. '金載圭·金桂元사형' (Execution of Kim Jae-gyu and Kim Gye-won), *Dong-A Ilbo*, 20 Dec. 1979, p. 1.

112. Keesing's Worldwide, 'Assassination of President Park Chung Hee—Mr Choi Kyu Hah Elected President—Cabinet Formed by Mr Shin Hyon Hwack—Other Internal Developments, August 1979 to March 1980', *Keesing's Record of World Events*, Vol. 26, Apr. 1980, p. 30216.

113. 'President Park Is Slain in Korea by Intelligence Chief'.

114. Scott Stokes, Henry, 'South Korea Calls Presidential Vote', *New York Times*, 10 Nov. 1979, p. 1.

### 3. ON THE ROAD TO RICHES AND DEMOCRACY, 1980–87

1. Chon, Kum-song, *Chun Doo Hwan, Man of Destiny: A Biography of the President of the Republic of Korea*, trans. W. Y. Joh, Los Angeles: North American Press, 1982.

2. Scott Stokes, Henry, '7 Top Generals Are Held in Seoul Military Power Struggle; Military Power Struggle Is Seen', *New York Times*, 14 Dec. 1979.

3. Editors of *Encyclopaedia Britannica*, 'Chung Sung-Hwa', 2021, https://www.britannica.com/biography/Chung-Sung-Hwa, accessed 12 July 2021.

4. Suh, Dae-Sook, 'South Korea in 1981: The First Year of the Fifth Republic', *Asian Survey*, Vol. 22, No. 1, Jan. 1982, pp. 107–15.

5. Kim, *Conscience in Action*, p. 372.

6. Croissant, *Elections in Asia and the Pacific*, p. 413.

7. Ibid., p. 428.

8. Katsiafikas, *Asia's Unknown Uprisings*, pp. 155–8.

9. Shin, Gi-Wook, and Kyung Moon Hwang, *Contentious Kwangju: The May 18 Uprising in Korea's Past and Present*, Lanham: Rowman & Littlefield, pp. xiv–xx.

10. May 18 Memorial Foundation, 'History', 2016, http://eng.518.org/sub.php?PID=0201, accessed 12 July 2021.

11. Mosler, Hannes B., 'The Contested Political Remembrance of the Kwangju Uprising and Presidential Speeches in South Korea', *S/N Korean Humanities*, Vol. 6, No. 1, pp. 47–92.

12. Ibid.

13. Shin and Hwang, *Contentious Kwangju*, pp. xiii–xiv.

14. Mosler, 'Contested Political Remembrance of the Kwangju Uprising', p. 63.

15. Yonhap News Agency, 'Committee Launches Fact-Finding Mission over 1980 Pro-democracy Movement', 12 May 2020.

16. KMDb, 'A Taxi Driver (Taeg-si-un-jeon-sa)', 2006–18, https://www.kmdb.or.kr/eng/db/kor/detail/movie/K/16150, accessed 8 July 2021.

17. World Bank, 'GDP Growth (Annual %): Korea, Rep.'.

18. Suh, 'South Korea in 1981', p. 112.

19. Kwon, Hyeong-ki, *Changes by Competition: The Evolution of the South Korean Developmental State*, Oxford: Oxford University Press, 2021, pp. 90–1.

20. Ibid., pp. 95–6

21. Williamson, John, 'What Washington Means by Policy Reform', in John Williamson (ed.), *Latin American Adjustment: How Much Has Happened?*, Washington, DC: Institute for International Economics, 1989, pp. 7–20.

22. National Archives of Korea, '제5차 경제개발 5개년 계획 (1982–1986)' (Fifth five-year economic development plan (1982–1986)), 2021, https://theme.archives.go.kr/next/economicDevelopment/fifth.do, accessed 5 July 2021.

23. National Archives of Korea, '제6차 경제개발 5개년 계획 (1987–1991)' (Sixth five-year economic development plan (1987–1991)), 2021, https://theme.archives.go.kr/next/economicDevelopment/sixth.do, accessed 5 July 2021.

24. World Bank, 'School Enrollment (Primary), Gross, Gender Parity Index (GPI): Korea, Rep.', 2021, https://data.worldbank.org/indicator/SE.ENR.PRIM.FM.ZS?locations=KR, accessed 6 July 2021.

25. World Bank, 'School Enrollment (Secondary), Gross, Gender Parity Index (GPI): Korea, Rep.', 2021, https://data.worldbank.org/indicator/SE.ENR.SECO.FM.ZS?locations=KR, accessed 6 July 2021.

26. World Bank, 'School Enrollment (Tertiary), Gross, Gender Parity Index (GPI): Korea, Rep.', 2021, https://data.worldbank.org/indicator/SE.ENR.TERT.FM.ZS?locations=KR, accessed 6 July 2021.

27. Lee, 'Health Care Reform in South Korea', p. 64.

28. Kwon, *Changes by Competition*, p. 92.

29. Lars, Bruno, and Stig Tenold, 'The Basis for South Korea's Ascent in the Shipbuilding Industry, 1970–1990', *Mariner's Mirror*, Vol. 97, No. 3, 2011, pp. 201–17.

30. Stern, Milton, 'To Excel in America: Hyundai's First Car Sold in the

United States', Jan. 2020,   https://www.hemmings.com/stories/article/to-excel-in-america, accessed 12 July 2021.

31.  Kim, 'Shin Choon-ho, Founder of Ramyeon Giant Nongshim, Dies at 91'.

32.  Industrial Statistics Analysis System, '1차,2차,3차 기준' (Primary, secondary, tertiary sector).

33.  Boyer, William W., and Byong Man Ahn, *Rural Development in South Korea: A Sociopolitical Analysis*, Newark: University of Delaware Press, 1991, p. 53.

34.  Ibid., pp. 51–2

35.  Korea Labor Institute, '2018_V_Industrial Relations', 22 Nov. 2018, https://www.kli.re.kr/kli_eng/selectBbsNttView.do?key=381&bbsNo=35&nttNo=134320&searchY=&searchCtgry=&searchDplcCtgry=&searchCnd=all&searchKrwd=&pageIndex=1&integrDeptCode, accessed 12 July 2021.

36.  Economic Planning Board, '1985 Population and Housing Census Report', Seoul, 1987, pp. 72–6.

37.  World Bank, 'Fertility Rate, Total (Births per Woman): Korea, Rep.'.

38.  Industrial Statistics Analysis System, '1차,2차,3차 기준' (Primary, secondary, tertiary sector).

39.  KMDb, 'Deep Blue Night (Gipgo puleun bam)', 2006–18, https://www.kmdb.or.kr/eng/db/kor/detail/movie/K/03851, accessed 8 July 2021.

40.  KMDb, 'Whale Hunting ("Goraesanyang")', 2006–18, https://www.kmdb.or.kr/eng/db/kor/detail/movie/K/03778, accessed 8 July 2021.

41.  Gillett, Chris, 'Understanding the Phenomenon That Is K-Pop', *South China Morning Post*, 14 Nov. 2018.

42.  Den Boer, Andrea, and Valerie Hudson, 'Patrilineality, Son Preference, and Sex Selection in South Korea and Vietnam', *Population and Development Review*, Vol. 43, No. 1, Mar. 2017, p. 119.

43.  Statistics Korea, '국내 입양아 수 및 입양 비율' (Number of adoptees in Korea and adoption rate), 2021, http://index.go.kr/potal/main/EachDtlPageDetail.do?idx_cd=2708, accessed 8 July 2021.

44. Kong, Sae Kwon, and Minja Kim Choe, 'Labor Force Participation of Married Women in Contemporary Korea', *Journal of Population and Health Studies*, Vol. 9, No. 2, Dec. 1989, p. 124.

45. Suh, Doowon, and Inn Hea Park, 'Framing Dynamics of South Korean Women's Movements, 1970s–90s: Global Influences, State Responses, and Interorganizational Networks', *Journal of Korean Studies*, Vol. 19, No. 2, Fall 2014, p. 339.

46. UNESCO, 'The Archives of the KBS Special Live Broadcast "Finding Dispersed Families"', 2014, http://www.unesco.org/new/fileadmin/MULTIMEDIA/HQ/CI/CI/pdf/mow/nomination_forms/korea_dispersed_persons_eng.pdf, accessed 12 July 2021.

47. Lohr, Steve, 'War-Scattered Korean Kin Find Their Kin at Last', *New York Times*, 18 Aug. 1983, p. 2.

48. UNESCO, 'The Archives of the KBS Special Live Broadcast "Finding Dispersed Families"'.

49. Park, Kyung Ae, and Sung-Chull Lee, 'Changes and Prospects in Inter-Korean Relations', *Asian Survey*, Vol. 32, No. 5, May 1992, p. 432.

50. Chapman, William, 'North Korean Leader's Son Blamed for Rangoon Bombing', *Washington Post*, 3 Dec. 1983; Oberdorfer, Don, and *Washington Post* staff writer, 'Blast Kills Top Aides to South Korean President', *Washington Post*, 10 Oct. 1983.

51. Selth, Andrew, 'The Rangoon Bombing: A Historical Footnote', 16 May 2012, https://archive.lowyinstitute.org/the-interpreter/rangoon-bombing-historical-footnote, accessed 12 July 2021.

52. Feaver, Douglas B., David Hoffman and *Washington Post* staff writers, 'Plane's Tragic Odyssey Mysterious', *Washington Post*, 4 Sep. 1983.

53. KBS World, 'N. Korea's Flood Relief Aid for S. Korea in 1984', 22 Mar. 2018, http://world.kbs.co.kr/service/contents_view.htm?lang=e&menu_cate=history&id=&board_seq=275253, accessed 12 July 2021.

54. Kim, C. I. Eugene, 'South Korea in 1985: An Eventful Year amidst Uncertainty', *Asian Survey*, Vol. 26, No. 1, Jan. 1986, p. 72.

55. BBC, 'Nine Charts Which Tell You All You Need to Know about North Korea', 26 Sept. 2017.

56. Haberman, Clyde, '5 Dead, 36 Hurt in an Explosion at Seoul Airport', *New York Times*, 15 Sep. 1986, p. 1.

57. Associated Press, 'Woman Says She Put Bomb on a Korean Jet, Killing 115', *New York Times*, 15 Jan. 1988, p. 8.

58. Kim, E. Tammy, 'Korea's Tireless Patriot Revolutionary', *New York Review*, 17 Dec. 2020.

59. Scott Stokes, Henry, 'Anti-U.S. Sentiment Is Seen in Korea', *New York Times*, 28 Mar. 1982, p. 3.

60. Burgess, John, 'Kim Dae Jung Stays Home after Fracas at Airport', *Washington Post*, 9 Feb. 1985.

61. Croissant, *Elections in Asia and the Pacific*, p. 428.

62. Koh, B. C., 'The 1985 Parliamentary Election in South Korea', *Asian Survey*, Vol. 25, No. 9, Sept. 1985, p. 896.

63. '57,561 People Reeducated in Social Purification Drive', *Korea Herald*, 9 Jan. 1981; Stokes, Henry Scott, 'Seoul Said to Hold 15,000 in Camps without Trial', *New York Times*, 20 Sept. 1981, p. 5.

64. Kim, Tong-Hyun, and Foster Klug, 'S. Korea Covered Up Mass Abuse, Killings of "Vagrants"', Associated Press, 20 Apr. 2016.

65. Lim, C. W., 'South Korea to Build Dam against "Water Offensive"', Associated Press, 27 Nov. 1986.

66. Hiatt, Fred, 'Death of Student Triggers Renewed Clashes in Seoul', *Washington Post*, 6 July 1987.

67. Lee, Namhee, *The Making of Minjung: Democracy and the Politics of Representation in South Korea*, Ithaca: Cornell University Press, 2007, pp. 301–2.

68. Haberman, Clyde, 'President of South Korea Orders a Halt to Debate on Constitution', *New York Times*, 13 Apr. 1987, p. 1.

69. Ibid.

70. *JoongAng Ilbo* staff writers, '김영삼 위원장내일상오 회견' (Chairman Kim Young-sam, tomorrow's morning meeting), *JoongAng Ilbo*, 13 Apr. 1987.

71. Special Reporting Team, '30 Years On, Son's Murder Still Haunts Family', *Korea JoongAng Daily*, 12 Jan. 2017.

72. Korea Labor Institute, '2018_V_Industrial Relations', 22 Nov. 2018, https://www.kli.re.kr/kli_eng/selectBbsNttView.do?key=381&bbsNo=35&nttNo=134320&searchY=&searchCtgry=&searchDplcCtgry=&searchCnd=all&searchKrwd=&pageIndex=1&integrDeptCode, accessed 12 July 2021.

73. Oberdorfer, Don, 'U.S. Intensifies Pressure on Chun', *Washington Post*, 27 June 1987.

74. Samaranch, Juan-Antonio, Roh, Tae-woo and Chun, Doo-hwan, 'Meeting between President Chun Doo Hwan and President Samaranch', 25 Apr. 1986, https://digitalarchive.wilsoncenter.org/document/113918, accessed 13 July 2021.

75. Haberman, Clyde, 'Fury and Turmoil: Days that Shook Korea', *New York Times*, 6 July 1987, p. 1.

76. MBC News, '[6.29 선언]직선제 개정관련 특별선언발표' ([June 29 Declaration] announcement of a special declaration related to the amendment of the direct election), 29 June 1987.

77. Ibid.

78. KBS News, '<이한열 열사 사망사건> 고 이한열군 유해 고향에 영면' (The death of martyr Lee Han-yeol: The remains of the late Lee Han-yeol are buried in his hometown), 9 July 1987.

79. Croissant, *Elections in Asia and the Pacific*, p. 427.

80. Constitution of the Republic of Korea, 29 Oct. 1987.

81. Croissant, *Elections in Asia and the Pacific*, pp. 467, 470.

82. Mundy, Simon, and Song Jung-a, 'Lee Kun-hee, Samsung Family Patriarch, 1942–2020', *Financial Times*, 25 Oct. 2020; Yonhap News Agency, 'Samsung Chief Lee, Staunch Force behind S. Korea's Rise to Tech Powerhouse, Dies', 25 Oct. 2020.

4. FREEDOM AND CRISIS, 1988–97

1. Roh, Tae-woo, '보통사람들의 위대한 시대 제13대 대통령 취임사' (A great era for the ordinary people: inaugural address of the thirteenth president), 25 Feb. 1988.

2. Hiatt, Fred, 'Roh Grants Partial Amnesty to Political Prisoners', *Washington Post*, 27 Feb. 1988.

3. Haberman, Clyde, 'Koreans Install a New President', *New York Times*, 25 Feb. 1988, p. 6.

4. Kang, WooJin, 'Conservative Democratisation', in JeongHun Han, Ramon Pacheco Pardo and Yongho Cho (eds), *The Oxford Handbook of South Korean Politics*, Oxford: Oxford University Press, 2023, Ch. 6.

5. Haberman, 'Koreans Install a New President'.

6. Kang, 'Conservative Democratisation'.

7. Korea Labor Institute, '2018_V_Industrial Relations', 22 Nov. 2018, https://www.kli.re.kr/kli_eng/selectBbsNttView.do?key=381&bbsN o=35&nttNo=134320&searchY=&searchCtgry=&searchDplcCtgry =&searchCnd=all&searchKrwd=&pageIndex=1&integrDeptCode, accessed 13 July 2021.

8. Ibid.

9. Associated Press, 'S. Korea's Chief Justice Resigns as Judges Urge Independent Courts', *Los Angeles Times*, 18 June 1988.

10. Ahn, Chung-si, 'Democratization and Political Reform in South Korea: Development, Culture, Leadership and Institutional Change', *Asian Journal of Political Science*, Vol. 1, No. 2, 1993, pp. 93–109.

11. Kim, Hunjoon, 'Seeking Truth after 50 Years: The National Committee for Investigation of the Truth about the Jeju 4.3 Events', *International Journal of Transitional Justice*, Vol. 3, No. 3, Nov. 2009, p. 414.

12. Croissant, *Elections in Asia and the Pacific*, p. 428.

13. *New York Times* staff writers, '2 Parties in Seoul Agree to a Merger with Ruling Group', *New York Times*, 23 Jan. 1990, p. 1.

14. Ibid.

15. Olympics, 'Seoul 1988: Opening Ceremony | Seoul Replays', 9 June 2020, https://www.youtube.com/watch?v=KeWSC7iCnpM, accessed 13 July 2021.

16. Joo, Yu-Min, Yooil Bae and Eva Kassens-Noor, *Mega-Events and*

*Mega-Ambitions: South Korea's Rise and the Strategic Use of the Big Four Events*, London: Palgrave Macmillan, 2017, p. 36.

17. Olympics, 'Seoul 1988: Opening Ceremony'.

18. Joo, Bae and Kassens-Noor, *Mega-Events and Mega-Ambitions*, p. 28.

19. Ibid., p. 38.

20. Pacheco Pardo, Ramon, 'South Korea's Strategic Reset under Roh Tae-woo: *Nordpolitik*', in Andrew Ehrhardt and Nicholas Kaderbhai (eds), *Historical Case Studies for the Integrated Review*, Part I, London: King's College London, 2020, p. 11.

21. Chung, Tae Dong, 'Korea's *Nordpolitik*: Achievements & Prospects', *Asian Perspective*, Vol. 15, No. 2, Fall–Winter 1991, p. 152.

22. Lee, Manwoo, *The Odyssey of Korean Democracy: Korean Politics, 1987–1990*, New York: Praeger, 1990, p. 108.

23. Cha, Victor, *The Impossible State: North Korea, Past and Future*, New York: Vintage, 2013, p. 118.

24. United Nations, 'Member States', 2021, https://www.un.org/en/about-us/member-states, accessed 13 July 2021.

25. Agreement on Reconciliation, Non-Aggression and Exchanges and Cooperation between the South and the North, 13 Dec. 1991.

26. Joint Declaration on the Denuclearization of the Korean Peninsula, 20 Jan. 1992.

27. Rosenbaum, David E., 'U.S. to Pull A-Bombs from South Korea', *New York Times*, 20 Oct. 1991, p. 3.

28. Sanger, David E., 'Death of a Leader; Kim Il Sung, Enigmatic "Great Leader" of North Korea for 5 Decades Dies', *New York Times*, 10 July 1994, p. 13.

29. Crossette, Barbara, 'Korean Famine Toll: More than 2 Million', *New York Times*, 20 Aug. 1999, p. 6.

30. Satterwhite, David H., 'North Korea in 1997: New Opportunities in a Time of Crisis', *Asian Survey*, Vol. 38, No. 1, Jan. 1998, pp. 16–20.

31. Croissant, *Elections in Asia and the Pacific*, p. 466.

32. Shin, Gi-Wook, *Ethnic Nationalism in Korea: Genealogy, Politics, and Legacy*, Stanford: Stanford University Press, 2006, pp. 185–7.

33. Kim, Kyong Ju, *The Development of Modern South Korea: State Formation, Capitalist Development and National Identity*, Abingdon: Routledge, 2006, pp. 155–8.

34. Hoffman, Diane M., 'Culture, Self, and "URI": Anti-Americanism in Contemporary South Korea', *Journal of Northeast Asian Studies*, Vol. 12, No. 2, 1993, pp. 3–18.

35. Park, Chae Bin, and Nam-Hoon Cho, 'Consequences of Son Preference on a Low-Fertility Society', *Population and Development Review*, Vol. 91, No. 1, Mar. 1995, pp. 59–84.

36. Den Boer and Hudson, 'Patrilineality, Son Preference, and Sex Selection', pp. 126, 142.

37. Suh and Park, 'Framing Dynamics of South Korean Women's Movements, 1970s–90s', pp. 342–7.

38. Chung, Woojin, and Monica Das Gupta, *Why Is Son Preference Declining in South Korea? The Role of Development and Public Policy, and Implications for China and India*, Washington, DC: World Bank, p. 5.

39. Ibid.

40. Lewis, Linda S., 'Female Employment and Elite Occupations in Korea', *Korean Studies*, Vol. 21, 1997, p. 54.

41. Koh, B. C., 'South Korea in 1995: Tremors of Transition', *Asian Survey*, Vol. 36, No. 1, Jan. 1996, pp. 56–7.

42. Jordan, Mary, 'President's Son Jailed in S. Korea', *Washington Post*, 18 May 1987.

43. Bong, Youngshik D., 'The Gay Rights Movement in Democratizing Korea', *Korean Studies*, Vol. 32, 2008, pp. 86–103.

44. Kim, Suk-Young, *K-Pop Live: Fans, Idols, and Multimedia Performance*, Stanford: Stanford University Press, 2018.

45. Kim, Jiyoon, 'National Identity under Transformation: New Challenges to South Korea', in Gilbert Rozman (ed.), *Asia's Alliance Triangle: US–Japan–South Korea Relations at a Tumultuous Time*, London: Palgrave Macmillan, 2015, pp. 208–11.

46. Cho, Myhie, *Entrepreneurial Seoulite: Culture and Subjectivity in Hongdae, Seoul*, Ann Arbor: University of Michigan Press, 2019.

47. *Joong-Ang Ilbo* staff writers, '전두환씨 내일증언' (Chun Doo-hwan's testimony tomorrow), *Joong-Ang Ilbo*, 30 Dec. 1989.

48. Tamyalew, Arsema, *A Review of the Effectiveness of the Anti-corruption and Civil Rights Commission of the Republic of Korea*, Washington, DC: World Bank, 2014, p. 48.

49. Editors of *Encyclopaedia Britannica*, 'Chung Sung-Hwa'.

50. Pollack, Andrew, 'New Korean Leader Agrees to Pardon of 2 Ex-Dictators', *New York Times*, 21 Dec. 1997, p. 10.

51. Federation of American Scientists, 'National Intelligence Service', 18 July 1999, https://fas.org/irp/world/rok/nis.htm, accessed 13 July 2021.

52. World Bank, 'GDP growth (Annual %): Korea, Rep.'.

53. US Department of the Treasury, 'Report to the Congress on International Economic and Exchange Rate Policies', Washington, DC: US Government Printing Office, 1992, pp. 21–2.

54. National Archives of Korea, '제7차 및 신경제 경제개발 5개년 계획 (1992–1997)' (Seventh and new five-year economic development plan (1992–1997)), 2021, https://theme.archives.go.kr/next/economicDevelopment/newEconomy.do, accessed 5 July 2021.

55. Ministry of Economy and Finance, 'History', 1 Aug. 2018, https://english.moef.go.kr/co/selectAboutMosf.do?boardCd=C0005, accessed 13 July 2021.

56. Graham, Edward M., *Reforming Korea's Industrial Conglomerates*, Washington, DC: Peterson Institute for International Economics, 2003, p. 91.

57. Kim, 'Seeking Truth after 50 Years', pp. 275–6.

58. Mundy and Song, 'Lee Kun-hee'; Yonhap News Agency, 'Samsung Chief Lee'.

59. Jin, Dal Yong, Kyong Yoon and Wonjung Min, *Transnational Hallyu: The Globalization of Korean Digital and Popular Culture*, Lanham: Rowman & Littlefield, 2021, p. 31.

60. KMDb, 'Swiri (Swili)', 2006–18, https://www.kmdb.or.kr/eng/db/kor/detail/movie/K/04983, accessed 8 July 2021.

61. World Bank, 'GDP Growth (Annual %): Korea, Rep.'.

62. Statistics Korea, '취업자 수/실업률 추이' (Number of employed/unemployment trend rate), 2021, https://www.index.go.kr/potal/stts/idxMain/selectPoSttsIdxSearch.do?idx_cd=1063&stts_cd=106301&freq=Y, accessed 8 July 2021.

63. Kang, Seoghoon, 'Globalization and Income Inequality in Korea: An Overview', Dec. 2001, p. 31, https://www.oecd.org/dev/2698445.pdf, accessed 13 July 2021.

64. Kim, Young-sam, 'OECD 가입 축하 리셉션 연설(세계화시책 더욱 강력히 추진)' (Reception speech celebrating joining the OECD (stronger promotion of globalization policy)), 12 Dec. 1996.

65. KBS News, '공식활동 개시' (Start of official activities), 12 Dec. 1996.

66. World Bank, *The East Asian Miracle: Economic Growth and Public Policy*, Oxford: Oxford University Press, 1993.

67. Park, Se-il, *Managing Education Reform: Lessons from the Korean Experience; 1995–1997*, Sejong: Korea Development Institute, 2000.

68. World Bank, 'School Enrollment (Tertiary), Gross, Gender Parity Index (GPI): Korea, Rep.', 2021, https://data.worldbank.org/indicator/SE.ENR.TERT.FM.ZS?locations=KR, accessed 6 July 2021.

69. Seth, Michael J., *Education Fever: Society, Politics, and the Pursuit of Schooling in South Korea*, Honolulu: University of Hawai'i Press, 2002, p. 232.

70. Ibid., p. 256.

71. Ibid., pp. 186–7.

72. Ibid., p. 187.

73. Framework Act on Informatization Promotion, 4 Aug. 1995.

74. Schuman, Michael, 'Korea's Big Cellular Gamble Appears to Be Paying Off', *Wall Street Journal*, 30 Sept. 1997.

75. 'Letter of Intent of the Government of Korea', 3 Dec. 1997, https://www.imf.org/external/np/loi/120397.htm, accessed 13 July 2021.

76. International Monetary Fund, 'IMF Stand-By Arrangement: Summary

of the Economic Program', 5 Dec. 1997, https://www.imf.org/external/np/oth/korea.htm, accessed 13 July 2021.

77. Pollack, Andrew, 'Crisis in South Korea: The Bailout; Package of Loans Worth $55 Billion Is Set for Korea', *New York Times*, 4 Dec. 1997, p. 1.

78. International Monetary Fund, 'Crisis, Restructuring, and Recovery in Korea: Remarks by Michael Camdessus', 2 Dec. 1999, https://www.imf.org/en/News/Articles/2015/09/28/04/53/sp120299, accessed 13 July 2021.

79. Haggard, Stephan, and Jongryn Mo, 'The Political Economy of the Korean Financial Crisis', *Review of International Political Economy*, Vol. 7, No. 2, 2000, pp. 197–218.

80. Ibid.

81. Reuters, 'Hanbo Steel Founder Given 15 Years in Korean Scandal', *New York Times*, 2 June 1997, p. 2.

82. Economist Intelligence Unit, *Country Report: South Korea, North Korea*, London: Economist Intelligence Unit, 1997.

83. Lauridsen, Laurids S., 'The Financial Crisis in Thailand: Causes, Conduct and Consequences?', *World Development*, Vol. 26, No. 8, Aug. 1998, pp. 1575–91.

84. International Monetary Fund, 'Camdessus Welcomes Korea's Request for IMF Assistance', 21 Nov. 1997, https://www.imf.org/en/News/Articles/2015/09/29/18/03/nb9725, accessed 13 July 2021.

5. THE LIBERAL DECADE, 1998–2007

1. Croissant, *Elections in Asia and the Pacific*, pp. 466, 474.

2. Effron, Sonni, and David Holley, 'Opposition Leader Wins Presidential Race in S. Korea', *Los Angeles Times*, 19 Dec. 1997.

3. Kang, Won-Taek, and Hoon Jaung, 'The 1997 Presidential Election in South Korea', *Electoral Studies*, Vol. 18, No. 4, Dec. 1999, p. 606.

4. World Bank, 'GDP Growth (Annual %): Korea, Rep.'.

5. OECD, 'Unemployment Rate', 2021, https://data.oecd.org/unemp/unemployment-rate.htm, accessed 13 July 2021.

6.  World Bank, 'GDP Growth (Annual %): Korea, Rep.'.

7.  OECD, 'Unemployment Rate'.

8.  OECD, 'OECD Economic Surveys: Korea 2001', Paris, OECD, 2001, pp. 152–3.

9.  Fackler, Martin, 'South Korea Makes a Quick Economic Recovery', *New York Times*, 6 Jan. 2011.

10. For data about the KOSPI composite index and the value of listed companies, see Korea Exchange, 2015, https://www.krx.co.kr/main/main.jsp, accessed 13 July 2021.

11. Korea Fair Trade Commission, 'Annual Report 1998', Seoul: Korea Fair Trade Commission, 1998.

12. Kim, *Conscience in Action*, pp. 480–91.

13. Seok, Kyong-Hwa, 'Hyundai to Take Over Kia Motors', Associated Press, 19 Oct. 1998.

14. Strieber, Andrew, 'Hyundai-Kia Now the Fifth Largest Automaker in the World', *MotorTrend*, 2 July 2008.

15. OECD, 'Incidence of Permanent Employment', 2021, https://stats.oecd.org/Index.aspx?DataSetCode=TEMP_I, accessed 13 July.

16. OECD, 'Part-time Employment Rate', 2021, https://data.oecd.org/emp/part-time-employment-rate.htm, accessed 13 July 2021.

17. OECD, 'Youth Unemployment Rate', 2021, https://data.oecd.org/unemp/youth-unemployment-rate.htm, accessed 13 July 2021.

18. Klingler-Vidra, Robyn, and Ramon Pacheco Pardo, 'Beyond the Chaebol? The Social Purpose of Entrepreneurship in South Korea', *Asian Studies Review*, Vol. 43, No. 4, 2019, p. 645.

19. Lee, Jae Kyu, Choonmo Ahn and Kihoon Sung, 'IT Korea: Past, Present and Future', in Soumitra Dutta and Irene Mia (eds), *The Global Information Technology Report: Mobility in a Networked World*, Geneva: INSEAD and World Economic Forum, 2009, p. 126.

20. Naver, 'Company', 2021, https://www.navercorp.com/en/naver/company, accessed 13 July 2021.

21. Daum Kakao, 'Mobile Life Platform', Nov. 2014, pp. 4–5, https://

www.kakaocorp.com/upload_resources/ir/event/ir_event_20141121114858.pdf, accessed 13 July 2021.

22. Celltrion, 'History', 2021, https://www.celltrionhealthcare.com/en-us/aboutus/history, accessed 13 July 2021.

23. National Human Rights Commission of Korea, 'Purpose', 2021, https://www.humanrights.go.kr/site/homepage/menu/viewMenu?menuid=002001001001, accessed 13 July 2021.

24. Kim, Dae-jung, 'Is Culture Destiny? The Myth of Asia's Anti-democratic Values', *Foreign Affairs*, Vol. 73, No. 6, Nov./Dec. 1994, pp. 189–94.

25. National Human Rights Commission of Korea, 'Statistics', 2021, https://www.humanrights.go.kr/site/program/link/statisticsEng?menuid=002003005, accessed 13 July 2021.

26. National Human Rights Commission of Korea, 'History', 2021, https://www.humanrights.go.kr/site/homepage/menu/viewMenu?menuid=002001001002, accessed 13 July 2021.

27. Bae, Sangmin, 'South Korea's De Facto Abolition of the Death Penalty', *Pacific Affairs*, Vol. 82, No. 3, Fall 2009, p. 421.

28. National Intelligence Service Korea Act, 4 Oct. 2006.

29. Larkin, John, 'Cleaning House', *Washington Post*, 9 June 2003.

30. Kwon, Jong-bum, 'Exorcizing the Ghosts of Kwangju: Policing Protest in the Post-Authoritarian Era', in Gi-Wook Shin and Paul Y. Chang (eds), *South Korean Social Movements: From Democracy to Civil Society*, Abingdon: Routledge, 2011, pp. 63–5.

31. Tamyalew, 'Review of the Effectiveness of the Anti-corruption and Civil Rights Commission of the Republic of Korea', p. 6.

32. Ibid., p. 49.

33. Ibid., p. 51.

34. Ibid., pp. 14, 53.

35. Koreanet, 'The Reunion Awaited Half a Century (2000)', 17 Apr. 2018, https://www.youtube.com/watch?v=TFaeLdD2fd4, accessed 13 July 2021.

36. Ibid.

37. Kim, *Conscience in Action*.

38. Koreanet, 'Reunion Awaited Half a Century (2000)'.

39. Kim, *Conscience in Action*.

40. Cha, Victor D., 'The Rationale for "Enhanced" Engagement of North Korea: After the Perry Policy Review', *Asian Survey*, Vol. 39, No. 6, Nov.–Dec. 1999, pp. 848, 857.

41. 'Inter-Korean Summit', KBS World Radio, 2020.

42. South–North Joint Declaration, 15 June 2000.

43. Nobel Prize, 'The Nobel Peace Prize 2000: Kim Dae-jung', 2021, https://www.nobelprize.org/prizes/peace/2000/summary, accessed 14 July 2021.

44. Ha, Yoong-Chol, 'South Korea in 2000: A Summit and the Search for New Institutional Identity', *Asian Survey*, Vol. 41, No. 1, Jan.–Feb. 2001, pp. 30–1.

45. Associated Press, 'Two Koreas, One Flag in Ceremonies', ESPN, 15 Sept. 2000.

46. Foley, James A., *Korea's Divided Families: Fifty Years of Separation*, London: Routledge Curzon, 2003, pp. 120–37.

47. Pacheco Pardo, *North Korea–US Relations from Kim Jong Il to Kim Jong Un*.

48. Lee, Soyoung, with Ahn Daehoe, Chin-Sung Chang and Lee Soomi, *Diamond Mountains: Travel and Nostalgia in Korean Art*, New York: Metropolitan Museum, 2018, p. 117.

49. Kim, Suk Hi, and Eul-Chul Lim, 'The Kaesong Inter-Korean Industrial Complex: Perspectives and Prospects', *North Korean Review*, Vol. 5, No. 2, Fall 2009, p. 83.

50. Lee, Jong-Heon, 'Analysis: Hyundai Facing Payments Scandal', UPI, 27 Feb. 2003.

51. BBC, 'Korean Dream Lives On', 22 June 2002.

52. ESPN, 'Match Commentary', 2002, https://tv5.espn.com/football/commentary?gameId=48866, accessed 13 July 2002.

53. Incheon Airport, 'History', 2021, https://www.airport.kr/ai_cnt/en/story/history.do, accessed 14 July 2021.

54. Kim, 'National Identity under Transformation', pp. 203–17.

55. Campbell, Emma, *South Korea's New Nationalism: The End of 'One Korea'?*, Boulder: First Forum Press, 2016, pp. 2–3.

56. Seoul Solution, 'Bukchon Conservation Project (2001–2004)', 2014, https://seoulsolution.kr/en/content/urban-regeneration-historic-neighborhood-bukchon, accessed 14 July 2021.

57. Lee, Charles, 'U.S. Army Apologizes for Korean Toxic Dump', UPI, 24 July 2000.

58. Kirk, Don, 'Road Accident Galvanizes the Country: Deaths in Korea Ignite Anti-American Passion', *New York Times*, 31 July 2002.

59. Kirk, Don, 'Bush Apologizes to Koreans for Killing of 2 Girls by G.I.'s', *New York Times*, 28 Nov. 2002, p. 12.

60. *Dong-A Ilbo* staff writers, 'Growing Anger of Koreans over Acquittal of US Soldiers Who Killed School Girls', *Dong-A Ilbo*, 2 Dec. 2002.

61. Associated Press, 'South Korea DQ'd; Officials Promised Protest', ESPN, 20 Feb. 2002.

62. Demick, Barbara, '50,000 in South Korea Protest U.S. Policies', *Los Angeles Times*, 14 June 2003.

63. Lee, Dong Sun, 'Democratization and the US–South Korean Alliance', *Journal of East Asian Studies*, Vol. 7, No. 3, Sept.–Dec. 2007, p. 479.

64. CNN, 'Countries Move to Ban U.S. Beef', 24 Dec. 2003.

65. Jin, Yoon and Min, *Transnational Hallyu*, p. 25.

66. Shim, Doobo, 'Hybridity and the Rise of Korean Popular Culture in Asia', *Media, Culture & Society*, Vol. 28, No. 1, 2006, p. 31.

67. Kim, *K-Pop Live*, p. 220.

68. Shim, 'Hybridity and the Rise of Korean Popular Culture in Asia', p. 29.

69. Short, Stephen, 'Girl, Interrupted', *Time*, 4 Mar. 2002.

70. Shim, 'Hybridity and the Rise of Korean Popular Culture in Asia', p. 34.

71. Chun, Su-jin, 'A "Korean Wave" in Japan', *Korea JoongAng Daily*, 24 June 2004.

72. Kim, *K-Pop Live*.

73. Shim, 'Hybridity and the Rise of Korean Popular Culture in Asia', p. 28.

74. Jin, Yoon and Min, *Transnational Hallyu*, p. 32.

75. Seo, Il-ho, '가수 비/ 춤판의 "짱" 스크린에 서다' (Singer Rain/"Number One" on the dance floor starts his screen career), *Weekly Chosun*, 26 Dec. 2002.

76. Jin, Yoon and Min, *Transnational Hallyu*, pp. 31–2.

77. Shim, 'Hybridity and the Rise of Korean Popular Culture in Asia', pp. 34–5.

78. Kim, HeeMin, *Korean Democracy in Transition: A Rational Blueprint for Developing Societies*, Lexington: University Press of Kentucky, 2011, p. 88.

79. Ibid., p. 89.

80. Shin, Eui Hang, 'Presidential Elections, Internet Politics, and Citizens' Organizations in South Korea', *Development and Society*, Vol. 34, No. 1, June 2005, p. 25.

81. Ibid.

82. Demick, Barbara, 'South Korea Proposes a Capital Change', *Los Angeles Times*, 9 July 2004.

83. Salmon, Andrew, 'Korea Court Rejects Plan for Capital Relocation', *New York Times*, 22 Oct. 2004.

84. Yang, Jae-jin, *The Political Economy of the Small Welfare State in South Korea*, Cambridge: Cambridge University Press, 2017, pp. 125–53.

85. OECD, 'Average Annual Hours Actually Worked per Worker', 2021, https://stats.oecd.org/index.aspx?DataSetCode=ANHRS, accessed 13 July 2021.

86. Framework Act on Clearing up Past Incidents for Truth and Reconciliation, 31 May 2005.

87. Truth and Reconciliation Commission of the Republic of Korea, 'Truth and Reconciliation: Activities of the Past Three Years', 2009.

88. Republic of Korea–Chile Free Trade Agreement, 15 Feb. 2003.

89. *Dong-A Ilbo* staff writers, 'Union Calls Halt to 4-Day Rail Strike', *Dong-A Ilbo*, 6 Mar. 2006.

90. Yonhap News Agency, 'S Korean Man Attempts Self-immolation against FTA with US', 1 Apr. 2007.

91. Choe, Sang-Hun, 'South Korea's Governing Party Suffers a Blow in Local Elections', *New York Times*, 1 June 2006.

92. Onishi, Norimitsu, 'Conservative Wins Vote in South Korea', *New York Times*, 20 Dec. 2007.

93. Korean Statistical Information Service, 'General Divorce Rates of Husband and Wife for Provinces', 2021, https://kosis.kr/eng/statisticsList/statisticsListIndex.do?menuId=M_01_01&vwcd=MT_ETITLE&parmTabId=M_01_01#SelectStatsBoxDiv, accessed 14 July 2021.

94. World Bank, 'Fertility Rate, Total (Births per Woman): Korea, Rep.'.

95. Korean Statistical Information Service, 'Mean Age at First Marriage of Bridegroom and Bride for Provinces', 2021, https://kosis.kr/statHtml/statHtml.do?orgId=101&tblId=DT_1B83A05&vw_cd=MT_ETITLE&list_id=&scrId=&seqNo=&language=en&obj_var_id=&itm_id=&conn_path=E3&path=%252Feng%252Fsearch%252Fsearch01_List.jsp, accessed 14 July 2021.

96. Lee, Ji-young, and Jae-un Limb, 'Single Parents Changing Korean Society', *Korea JoongAng Daily*, 26 Jan. 2006.

97. Cho, Nam-Joo, *Kim Ji-young, Born 1982: A Novel*, trans. Jamie Chang, London: Scribner, 2020, p. 85.

98. Ibid.

99. OECD, 'Incidence of Permanent Employment'.

100. Choi, Eleanor Jawon, and Jisoo Hwang, 'Transition of Son Preference: Evidence from South Korea', *Demography*, Vol. 57, 2020, p. 627.

101. Ministry of Gender Equality and Family, 'History', 2015, http://www.mogef.go.kr/eng/am/eng_am_f005.do, accessed 14 July 2021.

102. Shin, Ki-young, 'The Politics of the Family Law Reform Movement in Contemporary Korea', *Journal of Korean Studies*, Vol. 11, No. 1, Fall 2006, pp. 93–4.

103. Smith, Simon, James Choi, Michael Danagher, Michael Reiterer,

Philip Turner, Frode Solberg and Harry Harris, '20 Years of the Seoul Queer Culture Festival', *Korea Times*, 4 June 2019.

104. Gluck, Caroline, 'Gay Actor Stuns S Korea', BBC, 1 Nov. 2000.

105. Shim, Sun-ah, 'Landmark Supreme Court Ruling Allows Legal Change of Sex', *Hankyoreh*, 22 June 2006.

106. World Values Service, 'Time Series Data (1981–2020)', 2021, https://www.worldvaluessurvey.org/WVSOnline.jsp, accessed 14 July 2021.

107. OECD, 'Recruiting Immigrant Workers: Korea 2019', Paris: OECD, 2019, pp. 43–66.

108. Ibid.

109. Ibid.

110. World Values Service, 'Time Series Data (1981–2020)'.

## 6. GLOBAL SOUTH KOREA, 2008–22

1. Lee, Myung-bak, *The Uncharted Path: An Autobiography*, Naperville: Sourcebooks, 2011.

2. Choe, Sang-Hun, 'Beef Furor Provokes a Turnover in Seoul', *New York Times*, 21 June 2008.

3. World Bank, 'GDP Growth (Annual %): Korea, Rep.'.

4. Park Yong-geun, '"7% 성장, 4만불 소득, 7위 경제대국"' ('7% growth, $40,000 income, 7th largest economy'), *Chosun Biz*, 20 Aug. 2007.

5. Kim, Jae-kyoung, 'Is Tax Cut Hanging the Underprivileged to Dry?', *Korea Times*, 3 Nov. 2010.

6. Yonhap News Agency, 'Presidential Contenders Gear Up to Strengthen Public Support Ahead of Chuseok', 17 Sept. 2012.

7. Yonhap News Agency, 'Park Geun-hye Wins Presidential Election', 20 Dec. 2012.

8. Ramstad, Evan, 'How Did Park Win? A Breakdown', *Wall Street Journal*, 20 Dec. 2012.

9. Kasulis, Kelly, 'Inside Ilbe: How South Korea's Angry Young Men Formed a Powerful New Alt-Right Movement', Mic, 19 Sept. 2017.

10. Cho, Chung-un, 'Queen of Isolation: Park Geun-hye's "Frozen" Image', *Korea Herald*, 18 Feb. 2014.

11. Limb, Jae-un, 'Gov't Move to Sejong Now Complete', Korea.net, 24 Dec. 2014.

12. Lee, Joo-hee, 'Park Maintains Over 60 Percent Approval', *Korea Herald*, 1 Aug. 2013.

13. Korean Cultural Centre UK, 'Hallyu (Korean Wave)', 2021, https://kccuk.org.uk/en/about-korea/culture-and-arts/hallyu-korean-wave, accessed 14 July 2021.

14. Jin, Yoon and Min, *Transnational Hallyu*, pp. 70–1.

15. *Dong-A Ilbo* staff writers, 'Korean Wave in Iran', *Dong-A Ilbo*, 30 Apr. 2016.

16. Korean Cultural Centre UK, 'Hallyu (Korean Wave)'.

17. Cook, Ryan, 'KCON 2014 Doubles Attendance for Second Year; Features Performances from Girls' Generation and G-Dragon', *Music Times*, 15 Aug. 2014.

18. Jung, SooKeung, and Hongmei Li, 'Global Production, Circulation, and Consumption of Gangnam Style', *International Journal of Communication*, Vol. 8, 2014, pp. 2790–810.

19. G20, 'About the G20', 2021, https://www.g20.org/about-the-g20.html, accessed 14 July 2021.

20. G20 Seoul Summit Leaders' Declaration, 12 Nov. 2010.

21. Global Green Growth Institute, 'About GGGI', 2021, https://gggi.org/about, accessed 14 July 2021.

22. International Olympic Committee, '2018 Host City Election', 2021, https://olympics.com/ioc/2018-host-city-election, accessed 14 July 2021.

23. United Nations, 'UN Office for Sustainable Development', 2021, https://unosd.un.org, accessed 14 July 2021.

24. Seoul Communiqué, 2012 Seoul Nuclear Security Summit, 27 Mar. 2012.

25. Editors of *Encyclopaedia Britannica*, 'Kim Yuna', 2021, https://www.britannica.com/biography/Kim-Yu-Na, accessed 14 July 2021.

26. Jason, Kim, Dong-hwan Kim and Seek Kim, 'Even among the All-

time Greats, Kim Yu-na Skates Apart', *Korea JoongAng Daily*, 1 Mar. 2010.

27. BBC, '"Fake Photo" Reviews Kim Rumours', 12 Nov. 2008.

28. CSIS, 'North Korean Missile Launches & Nuclear Tests: 1984–Present', 20 Apr. 2017, https://missilethreat.csis.org/north-korea-missile-launches-1984-present, accessed 14 July 2021.

29. Yonhap News Agency, 'Chronology of Events Related to Sinking of S. Korean Naval Ship', 20 May 2010.

30. BBC, 'North Korean Artillery Hits South Korean Island', 23 Nov. 2010.

31. BBC, 'North Korea's Kim Jong-un Named Marshal', 18 July 2012.

32. Lee, Hanhee, 'Inevitable Reform? The Politico-Economic Choices Facing North Korea under Kim Jong-Un's Rule', *North Korean Review*, Vol. 11, No. 1, Spring 2015, pp. 84–5.

33. CSIS, 'North Korean Missile Launches & Nuclear Tests'.

34. KCNA, 'Traitor Jang Song Thaek Executed', 13 Dec. 2013.

35. North Korean Human Rights Act, 3 Mar. 2016.

36. Pacheco Pardo, *North Korea–US Relations from Kim Jong Il to Kim Jong Un*.

37. Kim, Jiyoon, Karl Friedhoff, Kang Chungku and Lee Euicheol, *South Korean Attitudes toward North Korea and Reunification*, Seoul: Asan Institute for Policy Studies, 2014.

38. Klingler-Vidra, Robyn, and Ramon Pacheco Pardo, 'Legitimate Social Purpose and South Korea's Support for Entrepreneurial Finance since the Asian Financial Crisis', *New Political Economy*, Vol. 25, No. 3, 2020, pp. 337–53.

39. Boston Consulting Group, National Association of Manufacturers and Manufacturing Institute, 'International Innovation Index', 2009.

40. Lee, Myung-bak, 'Inaugural Speech of President Lee Myung-back: Together We Shall Open, a Road to Advancement', 25 Feb. 2008.

41. Chung, Y. S., and H. S. Kim, 'Observations of Massive Air-Pollution Transport and Associated Air Quality in the Yellow Sea Region', *Air Quality, Atmosphere & Health*, Vol. 1, 2008, p. 69.

42. OECD, 'PISA 2009 Assessment Framework: Key Competencies in Reading, Mathematics and Science', Paris: OECD, 2009; OECD, 'PISA 2012 Frameworks: Mathematics, Problem Solving and Financial Literacy', Paris: OECD, 2012.

43. OECD, 'Understanding the Drivers of Trust in Government Institutions in Korea', Paris: OECD, 2018, p. 48.

44. Duffy, Bobby, and Kully Kaur-Ballagan, *Inequalities around the Globe: What the World Sees as Most Serious*, London: King's College London, 2021.

45. Schleicher, Andreas, 'PISA 2018: Insights and Interpretations', Paris: OECD, 2019.

46. Free Trade Agreement between the European Union and Its Member States, of the One Part, and the Republic of Korea, of the Other Part, 6 Oct. 2010; US–Korea Free Trade Agreement, 30 June 2007.

47. Pacheco Pardo, Ramon, and Robyn Klingler-Vidra, 'The Entrepreneurial Developmental State: What Is the Perceived Impact of South Korea's Creative Economy Action Plan on Entrepreneurial Activity?', *Asian Studies Review*, Vol. 43, No. 2, 2019, pp. 313–31.

48. Klingler-Vidra and Pacheco Pardo, 'Legitimate Social Purpose and South Korea's Support for Entrepreneurial Finance', pp. 337–53.

49. Ibid.

50. Google Asia Pacific Blog, 'Coming Soon: Campus Seoul!', 27 Aug. 2014, https://asia.googleblog.com/2014/08/coming-soon-campus-seoul.html, accessed 14 July 2021.

51. Pacheco Pardo and Klingler-Vidra, 'Entrepreneurial Developmental State', pp. 313–31.

52. Dayton, Leigh, 'How South Korea Made Itself a Global Innovation Leader', *Nature*, 27 May 2020.

53. Jamrisko, Michelle, Wei Lu and Alexandra Tanzi, 'South Korea Leads World in Innovation as U.S. Exits Top Ten', Bloomberg, 3 Feb. 2021.

54. Ock, Hyun-ju, 'More than 2 Million Take to Streets Calling for Park's Resignation', *Korea Herald*, 3 Dec. 2016.

55. Delury, John, 'The Candlelight Revolution', *Dissent*, Vol. 64, No. 2, Spring 2017, pp. 98–101.

56. Cho, Chung-un, 'Political Tension Rises over NIS Probe', *Korea Herald*, 27 Oct. 2013.

57. Nam, Eun-ju, 'After Choi Sun-sil Scandal, Blacklisted Movies Coming into the Light', *Hankyoreh*, 18 Dec. 2016.

58. Park, Madison, 'What Went Wrong on Sewol', CNN, 15 May 2014.

59. Choe, Sang-Hun, 'An Overloaded Ferry Flipped and Drowned Hundreds of Schoolchildren: Could It Happen Again?', *New York Times*, 10 June 2019; Park, 'What Went Wrong on Sewol?', CNN.

60. Ser, Myo-ja, 'Seven Hour Mystery about Park, Sewol Solved', *Korea JoongAng Daily*, 28 Mar. 2018.

61. World Health Organization, 'MERS Outbreak in the Republic of Korea, 2015', 2021, https://www.who.int/westernpacific/emergencies/2015-mers-outbreak, accessed 16 July 2021.

62. Lee, Kyu-Myong, and Kyujin Jung, 'Factors Influencing the Response to Infectious Diseases: Focusing on the Case of SARS and MERS in South Korea', *International Journal of Environmental Research and Public Health*, Vol. 16, No. 8, 2019, pp. 1–19.

63. Kim, Victoria, 'Zombies Are Everywhere in South Korea, Feeding on Fears and Anxieties', *Los Angeles Times*, 23 Feb. 2021.

64. Kil, Sonia, 'Korean Box Office Flat in 2016 Despite Local Hits', *Variety*, 2 Jan. 2017.

65. Park, 'It's Time for Justice'.

66. Ibid.

67. Campbell, Charlie, 'Moon Jae-in Elected South Korea's New President by Landslide', *Time*, 9 May 2017.

68. Moon, Jae-in, 문재인의 운명 (Fate of Moon Jae-in), 1st edn, Seoul: Gagyo, 2011.

69. Park, S. Nathan, 'South Korea Is a Liberal Country Now', *Foreign Policy*, 16 Apr. 2020.

70. Park, S. Nathan, 'It's Time for Justice, Not Healing', *Foreign Policy*, 20 Jan. 2021.

71. Chase-Lubitz, Jesse, 'South Korean Spy Agency Admits to Meddling in 2012 Election', *Foreign Policy*, 4 Aug. 2017.

72. Jeong, Eun-Young, 'Samsung Heir Lee Jae-yong Convicted of Bribery, Gets Five Years in Jail', *Wall Street Journal*, 25 Aug. 2017.

73. Choe, Sang-Hun, 'Former South Korean Spy Chief Sentenced for Trying to Sway Election', *New York Times*, 30 Aug. 2017.

74. Choe, Sang-Hun, 'Former South Korean President Gets 15 Years in Prison for Corruption', *New York Times*, 5 Oct. 2018.

75. Jeong, Eun-Young, 'South Korea's Former President Park Geun-hye Is Jailed for 24 Years', *Wall Street Journal*, 6 Apr. 2018.

76. Yoon, Dasl, 'South Korea's Disgraced Former President Park Geun-hye Is Pardoned', *Wall Street Journal*, 24 Dec. 2021.

77. Choe, 'Former South Korean President Gets 15 Years in Prison for Corruption'.

78. Kim, Yeong-Soon, *A Balanced Understanding of the South Korean Welfare State: Development and Underdevelopment*, Seoul: East Asia Foundation, July 2021, pp. 2, 4.

79. Duffy and Kaur-Ballagan, 'Inequalities around the Globe'.

80. World Economic Forum, 'Social Mobility Index, 2021', http://reports.weforum.org/social-mobility-report-2020/social-mobility-rankings, accessed 19 July 2021.

81. Yonhap News Agency, 'Labor, Management Struggle to Narrow Gaps over Next Year's Minimum Wage', 17 June 2021.

82. OECD, 'Minimum Relative to Average Wages of Full-Time Workers', 2021, https://stats.oecd.org/Index.aspx?DataSetCode=MIN2AVE, accessed 13 July 2021.

83. OECD, 'Hours Worked', 2021, https://data.oecd.org/emp/hours-worked.htm, accessed 13 July 2021.

84. OECD, 'Government at a Glance 2017', Paris: OECD, 2017, p. 91.

85. OECD, 'Income Inequality', 2021, https://data.oecd.org/inequality/income-inequality.htm, accessed 13 July 2021.

86. OECD, 'Unemployment Rate'.

87. OECD, 'Incidence of Permanent Employment'.

88. Klingler-Vidra and Pacheco Pardo, 'Legitimate Social Purpose and South Korea's Support for Entrepreneurial Finance', pp. 337–53.

89. Pacheco Pardo, Ramon, Tongfi Kim, Linde Desmaele, Maximilian Ernst, Paula Cantero Dieguez and Riccardo Villa, *Moon Jae-In's Policy towards Multilateral Institutions: Continuity and Change in South Korea's Global Strategy*, Brussels: Institute for European Studies and KF-VUB Korea Chair, 2019, p. 21.

90. The PyeongChang Organizing Committee for the Winter Olympic Games decided to capitalize the 'c' for the official name of the Games to make the name of the city more distinct from Pyongyang, the capital of North Korea.

91. Pacheco Pardo, *North Korea–US Relations from Kim Jong Il to Kim Jong Un*.

92. Ibid.

93. Park, 'South Korea Is a Liberal Country Now'.

94. Yun, Ho-woo, 'X세대였던 40대, "일편단심 민주당"', (Generation X in their 40s, 'one-sided towards the Democratic Party'), *Kyunghyang Shinmun*, 24 Oct. 2020.

95. Park, S. Nathan, 'Anti-Balloon Launching Laws Are No Threat to South Korean Democracy', *Foreign Policy*, 31 Dec. 2020.

96. Min, Kyoung-sun, 'Corruption', in Han, Pacheco Pardo and Cho, *Oxford Handbook of South Korean Politics*, chapter 31.

97. Duffy and Kaur-Ballagan, 'Inequalities around the Globe'.

98. KBS World, 'Half of S. Korea's Population Resides in Seoul Metro Area as of 2019', 28 Aug. 2020.

99. Jung, Damin, 'Anti-discrimination Law Back in Table at National Assembly', *Korea Times*, 3 July 2020.

100. Moon, Jae-in, 'Remarks by President Moon Jae-in Regarding Republic of Korea's Declaration of 2050 Carbon Neutrality', 10 Dec. 2020.

101. Gallo, William, and Lee Juhyun, 'In South Korea, Universal Basic Income Is Having a Pandemic Moment', VOA, 9 Mar. 2021.

102. BBC, 'Global Citizenship a Growing Sentiment among Citizens of Emerging Economies: Global Poll', 27 Apr. 2016.

103. Kim, 'National Identity under Transformation', pp. 208–11.

104. Park, So-young, '국민 10명 중 9명 차별금지법 제정에 찬성' (Nine out of ten people in favour of the Anti-Discrimination Act), *Hankook Ilbo*, 15 June 2020.

105. OECD, 'Gender Wage Gap', 2021, https://data.oecd.org/earnwage/gender-wage-gap.htm, accessed 13 July 2021; OECD, 'LFS by Sex and Age', 2021, https://stats.oecd.org/Index.aspx?DataSetCode=lfs_sexage_i_r, accessed 13 July 2021.

106. Kim, Bo-eun, 'Random Murder Triggers Angry Response from Women', *Korea Times*, 19 May 2016.

107. Song, Jung-a, and Edward White, 'Seoul Mayor Found Dead after Media Publish Sexual Harassment Claims', *Financial Times*, 10 July 2020.

108. Yonhap News Agency, 'Prosecution Indicts Former Busan Mayor for Sexual Assault', 28 Jan. 2021.

109. Cho, *Kim Jiyoung, Born 1982*.

110. Kim, Hiyeoon, 'Six Poems by Choi Young-mi', *Azalea: Journal of Korean Literature & Culture*, Vol. 14, 2021, pp. 205–6.

111. Lee, Youjin, 'The Prosecutor Who Exploded #MeToo in Korea: The JTBC Interview with Seo Ji-hyun', *April Magazine*, 6 Feb. 2018.

112. Lee, Sun-Min, and Min-ji Jin, 'Art World Joins the Chorus of #MeToo', *Korea JoongAng Daily*, 7 Feb. 2018.

113. Yonhap News Agency, 'Ex-prosecutor in "Me Too" Case Gets 2 Years in Jail', 23 Jan. 2019.

114. World Bank, 'Fertility Rate, Total (Births per Woman): Korea, Rep.'.

115. Yonhap News Agency, 'S. Korea's Total Population to Fall for First Time This Year: Agency', 9 Dec. 2021.

116. Song, Ju-Eun, Jeong-Ah Ahn, Sun-Kyoung Lee and Eun Ha Roh, 'Factors Related to Low Birth Rate among Married Women in Korea', *PLoS One*, Vol. 13, No. 3, 2018.

117. Kim, Seung-yeon, 'More Fathers Opt for Parental Leave amid Changing Culture, Strong Policy Drive', Yonhap News Agency, 24 Feb. 2021.

118. Botelho, Greg, and K. J. Kwon, 'Court Rules: Adultery No Longer a Crime in South Korea', CNN, 27 Feb. 2015.

119. Song, Jung-a, 'South Korean Court Rules Abortion Ban "Unconstitutional"', *Financial Times*, 11 Apr. 2019.

120. Jung, Damin, 'Seoul Mayoral Candidate's Remarks on LGBTQ Bring Controversy', *Korea Times*, 21 Feb. 2021.

121. Poushter, Jacob, and Nicholas Kent, 'The Global Divide on Homosexuality Persists', 25 June 2020, https://www.pewresearch.org/global/2020/06/25/global-divide-on-homosexuality-persists, accessed 16 July 2021.

122. World Values Service, 'Time Series Data (1981–2020)'.

123. Ko, Jun-tae, 'What Seoul Mayor Candidates Have to Say on LGBTQ Festival', *Korea Herald*, 23 Feb. 2021.

124. Cha, Sangmi, and Josh Smith, 'Death of South Korea's First Transgender Soldier Spurs Calls for Change', Reuters, 4 Mar. 2021.

125. Korean Statistical Information Service, '국적(지역) 및 연령별 등록외국인 현황' (Status of registered foreigners by nationality (region) and age), 2021, https://kosis.kr/statHtml/statHtml.do?orgId=111&tblId=DT_1B040A8&conn_path=I2, accessed 14 July 2021.

126. Statistics Korea, '국제결혼 현황' (International marriage status), 2021, http://www.index.go.kr/potal/main/EachDtlPageDetail.do?idx_cd=2430, accessed 8 July 2021.

127. Korean Statistical Information Service, '국적(지역) 및 연령별 등록외국인 현황' (Status of registered foreigners by nationality (region) and age).

128. Ministry of Unification, 'Policy on North Korean Defectors', 2021, https://www.unikorea.go.kr/eng_unikorea/relations/statistics/defectors, accessed 16 July 2021.

129. Kim, Hyung-Jin, 'North–South Korean Couples Trying to Bridge 75-Year Division', Associated Press, 9 Sept. 2020.

130. Stangarone, Troy, 'Young Koreans Are Winning Their Generational War', *Foreign Policy*, 9 May 2017.

131. Heo, Jeong-Won, and Seo Ji-Eun, 'Singe Household Registrations Hit a High of 40.1%', *Korea JoongAng Daily*, 6 Oct. 2021.

132. Poushter and Kent, 'Global Divide on Homosexuality Persists'.

133. Pew Research Center, 'The Age Gap in Religion around the World', 13 June 2018, https://www.pewforum.org/2018/06/13/the-age-gap-in-religion-around-the-world/, accessed 16 July 2021.

134. Park, Madison, and Paula Hancocks, 'Korean Air Executive Jailed over "Nut Rage" Incident', CNN, 12 Feb. 2015.

135. Duffy and Kaur-Ballagan, 'Inequalities around the Globe'.

136. Hwang, Minsoo. 연애, 결혼, 출산 을 포기 한 '삼포 세대' (*The 'Sampo Generation' that gave up dating, marriage and childbirth*), Incheon: Sangwon, 2011.

137. Sohn, Julie, 'TBS' "Kim OuJoon's News Factory" Ranked No. 1 Radio Show in Seoul', TBS, 11 May 2020.

138. Kim, Ji-hyun, 'Why Are South Korea's Young Men Turning against Moon Jae-in and His Ruling Party?', *South China Morning Post*, 30 Apr. 2021.

139. Kwon, Jake, 'South Korea's Young Men Are Fighting against Feminism', CNN, 24 Sept. 2019.

140. Cha, Sangmi, 'South Korea Roiled by Property Scandal amid Soaring Prices', Reuters, 9 Mar. 2021.

141. Shin, Hyonhee, 'South Korea Ruling Party Suffers Defeat in Mayoral Elections', Reuters, 8 Apr. 2021.

142. Hiatt, Brian, 'The Triumph of BTS', *Rolling Stone*, 13 May 2021.

143. Lynch, Joe, 'BTS Beam in "Dynamite" from South Korea at 2021 Grammy Awards: Watch Full Performance', *Billboard*, 22 Apr. 2021.

144. Yoon, So-yeon, 'Bloomberg Names Blackpink "Biggest Band in the World"', *Korea JoongAng Daily*, 11 Nov. 2020.

145. Yonhap News Agency, 'Number of Global "Hallyu" Fans Crosses 100 Million Mark', 15 Jan. 2021.

146. Liu, Marian, 'The Branding Genius of K-pop Band BTS', *Washington Post*, 30 Jan. 2020.

147. Williams, Jazmin, 'There's Plans for a Stadium to Be Built in South

Korea to Accommodate High Demand for BTS Concerts: The Power Is Unreal!', Honey Pop, 11 Aug. 2020.

148. Chow, Andrew R., '*Parasite*'s Best Picture Oscar Is Historic: Is This the Beginning of a New Era in Film?', *Time*, 9 Feb. 2020.

149. Berkman, Seth, 'Korean TV's Unlikely Star: Subway Sandwiches', *New York Times*, 14 Mar. 2021; Nguyen, Sue, 'Korean Cosmetic Industry: Complete Overview of the K-Beauty Market', Seoulz, 8 Mar. 2021.

150. Middleton, Richard, 'MBC's South Korean Format "The Masked Singer" Reaches 50 Country Milestone', *Television Business International*, 13 Jan. 2020.

151. Song, 'Youn Yuh-jung's Storied 5-Decade Career Culminates in Oscar Win'.

152. Yonhap News Agency, '"Squid Game" Becomes Most-Watched Netflix Show with Record 1.65 bln Hours', 15 Jan. 2021.

153. Park, T. K., and Youngdae Kim, 'How BTS's Embrace of Korean Tradition Helped Them Blow Up', Vulture, 25 Sept. 2018.

154. Lee, David D., 'The Unreal World of Korean Webtoons', Vice, 24 Mar. 2021.

155. Hopfner, Jonathan, 'A Look at Seoul's Flourishing Hanok Culture', *DestinAsian*, 4 Sept. 2019.

156. Yoon, Hahna, 'A Centuries-Old Korean Style Gets an Update', *New York Times*, 19 Oct. 2020.

157. Park, Ju-min, 'Trot Is Hot: It's Not Just K-pop in South Korea', Reuters, 13 Nov. 2020.

158. Choe, Sang-Hun, 'Kimchi Making at Home Was Going Out of Style: Rural Towns to the Rescue', *New York Times*, 21 Nov. 2020.

159. *Korea JoongAng Daily* staff writers, 'Statue of King Sejong Is Unveiled', *Korea JoongAng Daily*, 9 Oct. 2009.

160. Evans, Stephen, 'Naval Epic Takes South Korea by Storm', BBC, 3 Oct. 2014.

161. Turak, Natasha, 'The Coolest Tech Innovations You'll See at South Korea's 2018 Winter Olympics', CNBC, 8 Feb. 2018.

162. Jamrisko, Lu and Tanzi, 'South Korea Leads World in Innovation as U.S. Exits Top Ten'.

163. Mundy and Song, 'Lee Kun-hee'; 'Samsung Chief Lee'.

164. Pacheco Pardo, Ramon, Mauricio Avendano Pabon, Xuechen Chen, Bo-jiun Jing, Jeong-ho Lee, Joshua Ting, Takuya Matsuda and Kaho Yu, *Preventing the Next Pandemic: Lessons from East Asia*, London: King's College London, 2020, pp. 17–19.

165. Cheong Wa Dae, 'President Visits Plant for Making Syringes to Inject Vaccine', 19 Feb. 2021.

166. Cha, Sangmi, 'How South Korea Turbocharged Specialty Syringe Production for COVID-19 Vaccines', Reuters, 22 Apr. 2021.

167. Reporters Without Borders, '2021 World Press Freedom Index', 2021, https://rsf.org/en/ranking, accessed 16 July 2021.

168. Koh, Ewe, 'The Wholesome Appeal of Watching People Study on YouTube', Vice, 16 Feb. 2021.

169. Jie, Ye-eun, 'Rise of Retail Investors Pushes Stocks, Mitigates "Korea Discount": Experts', *Korea Herald*, 14 Jan. 2021.

170. Lee, David D., 'As Their "American Dream" Sours, Koreans in the US Eye a Return Home', *South China Morning Post*, 22 Nov. 2020.

171. *Korea Herald* staff writers, 'Korean Language Learning Booming on Back of Hallyu: Report', *Korea Herald*, 7 Feb. 2021.

172. McGuire, Liam, 'Marvel's South Korean Hero Is One of the Strongest Ever', Screen Rant, 30 June 2021.

173. Robinson, James, 'Hyundai Pony EV Concept Shows Off Retro Style', Car, 16 Apr. 2021.

174. Yonhap News Agency, 'Moon's G-7 Presence Highlights S. Korea's Bigger Role on Global Stage', 13 June 2021.

175. Vigdor, Neil, 'BTS Took Center Stage at the U.N. Over One Million Fans Watched Live', *New York Times*, 22 Sep. 2021.

176. Yonhap News Agency, 'BLACKPINK Calls for Global Actions to Tackle Climate Change', 3 Nov. 2021.

177. Song, Jung-a, 'Samsung to Build $17bn Chip Plant in Texas', *Financial Times*, 24 Nov. 2021.

178. Ji, Da-gyum, 'S. Korea's President, Top Diplomat Attend Global Summits Excluding China', *Korea Herald*, 10 Dec. 2021.

EPILOGUE

1. Economist Intelligence Unit, 'Democracy Index 2020: In Sickness and in Health?', 2021, https://www.eiu.com/n/campaigns/democracy-index-2020, accessed 20 Dec. 2021; OECD Better Life Index, 'Civic Engagement', 2021, https://www.oecdbetterlifeindex.org/topics/civic-engagement, accessed 20 Dec. 2021.

2. International Monetary Fund, 'World Economic Outlook Database', 2021, https://www.imf.org/en/Publications/WEO/weo-database/2021/April, accessed 19 July 2021.

3. Global Firepower, '2021 Military Strength Ranking', 2021, https://www.globalfirepower.com/countries-listing.php, accessed 19 July 2021.

4. Brand Finance, 'Global Soft Power Index 2021', London: Brand Finance, 2021, p. 4.

5. McGann, James G., '2020 Global Go To Think Tank Index Report', *TTCSP Global Go To Think Tank Index Reports*, Vol. 18, 2021, p. 55.

6. Ministry of Foreign Affairs of the Republic of Korea, 'Korea's Accession to the OECD Development Assistance Committee (DAC) Approved', 27 Nov. 2009, https://www.mofa.go.kr/eng/brd/m_5676/view.do?seq=307957&srchFr=&amp%3BsrchTo=&amp%3BsrchWord=Outcome&amp%3BsrchTp=0&amp%3Bmulti_itm_seq=0&amp%3Bitm_seq_1=0&amp%3Bitm_seq_2=0&amp%3Bcompany_cd=&amp%3Bcompany_nm=, accessed 19 July 2021.

7. OECD, 'Digital Governance Index: 2019 Results', Paris: OECD, 2020, p. 3.

8. Global Entrepreneurship Monitor, 'GEM 2020/2021 Global Report', London: Global Entrepreneurship Research Association, 2021, p. 79.

# INDEX

# INDEX

# INDEX

# INDEX

# INDEX

# INDEX

# INDEX

# INDEX

# INDEX

# INDEX

# INDEX

# INDEX

# INDEX

textiles industry, 44, 50
Thailand, 140, 184, 203
Thirteenth Festival of Youth and
    Students (1989), 120
thirty-eighth parallel, 23, 24, 25,
    26, 31, 34
386 generation, 104–5, 123, 127,
    142, 155, 163–7, 176, 197,
    204–5, 206
Three Kims, 52, 85, 103, 109,
    114, 122, 164
Three Kingdoms, 2–3
*Tongnip Sinmun*, 14–15
torture, 19, 49, 71, 103, 106, 113
toy industry, 53, 74, 89
Toyotomi Hideyoshi, 11
*Train to Busan* (2016 film), 192,
    210
transgender people, 202–3
travel, 94, 135
Treaty of Portsmouth (1905), 16
*Tripitaka Koreana*, 6
*trot*, 211
Truman, Harry, 31
Trump, Donald, 196
Truth and Reconciliation
    Commission, 165–6
Tsushima Island, 11
TVXQ, 162
12.12 Military Insurrection
    (1979), 84
Twice, 209

Uibyeong, 16
Uijeongbu, 8, 12

Ulsan, South Korea, 74, 91
unemployment, 133, 142, 144–5,
    195
unequal treaties, 13–14
Ungnyeo, 1
Unified Silla (668–935), 3–4, 5
Union of College Lesbians and
    Gays, 126
United Kingdom, 214
United Nations
    Climate Change Conference
    (2021), 215
    Convention against Corruption
    (2003), 148
    Global Green Growth Institute,
    180
    K-Pop stars at, 208, 215
    Koreas, accession of (1991),
    120–21
    Korean elections (1948), 24,
    25, 26
    Korean War (1950–53), 32, 33,
    34, 35, 36
    Japanese war crimes, views on,
    54
    Office for Sustainable
    Development, 180
    PRC accession (1971), 68
    San Francisco Conference
    (1945), 27
    West Sea islands, control of, 69
United States, xiv, 29, 218
    anti-communism, 23, 30, 31,
    54, 62, 69–70

# INDEX

# INDEX

# INDEX

315